AF552579

RISE OF INDIAN NATIONALISM AND MODERATE POLITICS

Encyclopaedic History of India Series

RISE OF INDIAN NATIONALISM AND MODERATE POLITICS

Dr. Mahesh Vikram Singh
Professor, Deptt. of History
Mahatma Gandhi Kashi Vidyapeeth
Varanasi (UP)

Dr. Brij Bhushan Shrivastava
Head of Deptt., Ancient History, Archeology & Culture
SMMTPG College, Ballia (UP)

CENTRUM PRESS
NEW DELHI-110002 (INDIA)

CENTRUM PRESS
H.O.: 4360/4, Ansari Road, Daryaganj,
New Delhi-110002 (India)
Tel: 23278000, 23261597, 23255577, 23286875
B.O.: No. 1015, Ist Main Road, BSK IIIrd Stage,
IIIrd Phase, IIIrd Block, Bangalore-560085 (INDIA)
Tel: 080-41723429
Email: centrumpress@gmail.com
Visit us at: www.centrumpress.com

Rise of Indian Nationalism and Moderate Politics

First Edition, 2011

ISBN 978-93-80836-87-4

PRINTED IN INDIA

Printed at Mehra Offset Press, Delhi

प्रो. विपिन चंद्रा
अध्यक्ष
Prof. Bipan Chandra
Chairman

नेशनल बुक ट्रस्ट, इंडिया
नेहरू भवन
5 इंस्टीट्यूशनल एरिया, फेज़-II, वसंत कुंज, नई दिल्ली-110 070
फोन/ Phone: 011-26121880 फैक्स/ Fax: 011-26121883

NATIONAL BOOK TRUST, INDIA
Nehru Bhawan
5 Institutional Area, Phase II, Vasant Kunj, New Delhi-110 070
ई-मेल / E-mail: chairman@nbtindia.org.in
वेबसाइट / Website: www.nbtindia.org.in

FOREWORD

The term 'history' is derived from the Greek word 'historia' that means knowledge acquired through investigation. Obviously, this knowledge can be correct if the method of investigation is objective and not vitiated by any kind of bias. In other words, if the study of human past is comprehensive and obtained through scientific inquiry, it can provide perspective on the present day problems and help one plan for the future.

A true historian has to identify the sources that can be most useful in a given context. Documents, coins, archaeology, anthropology, geography, travel accounts, oral traditions, mythology and so on can be useful but they can be used only after their veracity is tested and they are critically examined. They should be checked and counter-checked.

Over the centuries, one finds the study and writing of history vitiated by biases. There are numerous instances in which historical data have been distorted to support or oppose certain preconceived ideas and purposes. Strictly speaking such history is just like fiction to accord with preconceived notions and serve some ulterior purposes.

The study of the past has never been static. Conclusions go on changing because of the discovery of new materials and tools of investigation. To give a concrete example, the carbon 14 or radiocarbon dating test has revolutionized the study of civilizations and settlements, especially of prehistoric times, for which written documents, coins, etc. are seldom available. This method has enabled historians to determine more accurately than before the time period of a particular civilization or settlement. This method was discovered only 70 years ago by American scientists.

In our country, excavations brought to light the Indus Valley Civilization and its various features, hitherto unknown. Similarly, no complete text of Kautilya's Arthashastra was available before it was discovered by Shamasastry, the chief of the Mysore Government Oriental Library in the first decade of the last century. Likewise, people's knowledge of the history of the Buddhist period got extended after excavations at Sarnath and the ruins of the Asokan period at Patna. In the future, if the Harappan inscriptions are deciphered, our knowledge of the Indus Valley Civilization will increase enormously. All these instances underline the fact that our knowledge of history is never static and its frontiers go on extending.

In the light of what has been said above the encyclopedic history is going to be of great help to students interested in Indian history. It is comprehensive and as far as possible free from biases. It includes the latest materials, and objective conclusions.

Prof . Bipan Chandra
Professor Emeritus, JNU
Chairman, National Book Trust, India

Contents

Preface

The people of India have had a continuous civilization since 2500 B.C., when the inhabitants of the Indus River valley developed an urban culture based on commerce and sustained by agricultural trade. This civilization declined around 1500 B.C., probably due to ecological changes. During the second millennium B.C., pastoral, Aryan-speaking tribes migrated from the northwest into the subcontinent. As they settled in the middle Ganges River valley, they adapted to antecedent cultures.

The political map of ancient and medieval India was made up of myriad kingdoms with fluctuating boundaries. In the 4th and 5th centuries A.D., northern India was unified under the Gupta Dynasty. During this period, known as India's Golden Age, Hindu culture and political administration reached new heights. Islam spread across the Indian subcontinent over a period of 500 years. In the 10th and 11th centuries, Turks and Afghans invaded India and established sultanates in Delhi. In the early 16th century, descendants of Genghis Khan swept across the Khyber Pass and established the Mughal (Mogul) Dynasty, which lasted for 200 years. From the 11th to the 15th centuries, southern India was dominated by Hindu Chola and Vijayanagar Dynasties. During this time, the two systems—the prevailing Hindu and Muslim—mingled, leaving lasting cultural influences on each other.

The first British outpost in South Asia was established in 1619 at Surat on the northwestern coast. Later in the century, the East India Company opened permanent trading stations at Madras, Bombay, and Calcutta, each under the protection of native rulers. The British expanded their influence from these footholds until, by the 1850s, they controlled most of present-day India, Pakistan, and Bangladesh. In 1857, a rebellion in north India led by mutinous Indian soldiers caused the British Parliament to transfer all political power from the East India Company to the Crown. Great Britain began administering most of India directly while controlling the rest through treaties with local rulers.

In the late 1800s, the first steps were taken toward self-government in British India with the appointment of Indian councillors to advise the British viceroy and the establishment of provincial councils with Indian members; the British subsequently widened participation in legislative councils. Beginning in 1920, Indian leader Mohandas K. Gandhi transformed the Indian National Congress political party into a mass movement to campaign against British colonial rule.

—*Authors*

1

Rise of Indian Nationalism

The first spurts of nationalistic sentiment that rose amongst Congress members were when the desire to be represented in the bodies of government, to have a say, a vote in the lawmaking and issues of administration of India. Congressmen saw themselves as loyalists, but wanted an active role in governing their own country, albeit as part of the Empire. This trend was personified by Dadabhai Naoroji, who went as far as contesting, successfully, an election to the British House of Commons, becoming its first Indian member.

Bal Gangadhar Tilak was the first Indian nationalist to embrace *Swaraj* as the destiny of the nation. Tilak deeply opposed the British education system that ignored and defamed India's culture, history and values. He resented the denial of freedom of expression for nationalists, and the lack of any voice or role for ordinary Indians in the affairs of their nation. For these reasons, he considered Swaraj as the natural and only solution. His popular sentence "Swaraj is my birthright, and I shall have it" became the source of inspiration for Indians.

In 1907, the Congress was split into two. Tilak advocated what was deemed as *extremism*. He wanted a direct assault by the people upon the British Raj, and the abandonment of all things British. He was backed by rising public leaders like Bipin Chandra Pal and Lala Lajpat Rai, who held the same point of view. Under them, India's three great states-Maharashtra, Bengal and Punjab shaped the demand of the people and India's nationalism. Gokhale criticized Tilak for encouraging acts of violence and disorder. But the Congress of 1906 did not have public membership, and thus Tilak and his supporters were forced to leave the party.

But with Tilak's arrest, all hopes for an Indian offensive were stalled. The Congress lost credit with the people, A Muslim deputation met with the Viceroy, Minto (1905–10), seeking concessions from the impending constitutional reforms, including special considerations in government service and electorates. The British recognised some of Muslim League's petitions by increasing the number ,of elective offices reserved for Muslims in the Government of India Act 1909. The Muslim League insisted on its separateness from the Hindu-dominated Congress, as the voice of a "nation within a nation."

Dadabhai Naoroji

Dadabhai Naoroji (4 September 1825 – 30 June 1917), known as the "Grand Old Man of India", was a Parsi intellectual, educator, cotton trader, and an early Indian political leader. His book *Poverty and Un-British Rule in India* brought attention to the draining of India's wealth into Britain. He was a Member of Parliament (MP) in the British House of Commons between 1892 and 1895, and the first Asian to be a British M He is also credited with the founding of the Indian National Congress, along with A.O. Hume and Dinshaw Edulji Wacha.

Early Years

Naoroji was the son of Maneckbai and Naoroji Palanji Dordi, born into a poor family of Parsi-Zoroastrian priests in Navsari in Southern Gujarat. His father died when he was four, leaving his illiterate mother to raise him. Naoroji was educated at Elphinstone College, Mumbai. At the early age of 25, he was appointed leading Professor at the Elphinstone Institution in 1850, becoming the first Indian to hold such an academic position. Being an Athornan (ordained priest), Naoroji founded the Rahnumae Mazdayasne Sabha (Guides on the Mazdayasne Path) on 1 August 1851 to restore the Zoroastrian religion to its original purity and simplicity. In 1854, he also founded a fortnightly publication, the *Rast Goftar* (or The Truth Teller), to clarify Zoroastrian concepts. By 1855 he was Professor of Mathematics and Natural philosophy in Mumbai. He travelled to London in 1855 to become a partner in Cama & Co, opening a Liverpool location for the first Indian company to be established in Britain. Within three years, he had resigned on ethical grounds. In 1859 he established his own cotton trading company, Naoroji & Co. Later he became professor of Gujarati at University College London.

In 1867 Naoroji helped establish the East India Association, one of the predecessor organizations of the Indian National Congress. In 1874 he became Prime Minister of Baroda and was a member of the Legislative Council of Mumbai (then Bombay) (1885-88). He also founded the Indian National Association from Calcutta a few years before the founding of the Indian National Congress in Mumbai, with the same objectives and practices. The two groups later merged into the INC, and Naoroji was elected President of the Congress in 1886.

Naoroji moved to Britain once again and continued his political involvement. Elected for the Liberal Party in Finsbury Central at the 1892 general election, he was the first British Indian MP. He refused to take the oath on the Bible as he was not a Christian, but was allowed to take the oath of office in the name of God on his copy of *Khordeh Avesta*. In Parliament he spoke on Irish Home Rule and the condition of the Indian people. In his political campaign and duties as an MP, he was assisted by Muhammed Ali Jinnah, the future Muslim nationalist and founder of Pakistan. In 1906, Naoroji was again elected president of the Indian National Congress. Naoroji was a staunch moderate within the Congress, during the phase when opinion in the party was split between the moderates and extremists.

Naoroji was a mentor to both Gopal Krishna Gokhale and Mohandas Karamchand Gandhi. Naoroji was the paternal uncle of famous industrialist J. R. D. Tata. He was married to Gulbai from the age of eleven. He died in Mumbai on 30 June 1917, at age 92. Dadabhai Naoroji written a book named poverty and unbritish rule in India

Bal Gangadhar Tilak

Bal Gangadhar Tilak 23 July 1856(1856-07-23)–1 August 1920 (aged 64), was an Indian nationalist, teacher, social reformer and independence fighter who was the first popular leader of the Indian Independence Movement. The British colonial authorities infamously and derogatorily called the great leader as "Father of the Indian unrest". He was also conferred upon the honorary title of Lokmanya, which literally means "Accepted by the people (as their leader)". Tilak was one of the first and strongest advocates of "Swaraj" (self-rule) in Indian consciousness. His famous quote, *"Swaraj is my birthright, and I shall have it !"* is well-remembered in India even today.

Early Life

Tilak was born in *Madhali Alee* (Middle Lane) in Ratnagiri, Maharashtra, into a middle class Chitpavan Brahmin family. His father was a famous schoolteacher and a scholar of Sanskrit. He died when Tilak was sixteen. His brilliance rubbed off on young Tilak, who graduated from Deccan College, Pune in 1877. Tilak was among one of the first generation of Indians to receive a college education.

Tilak was expected, as was the tradition then, to actively participate in public affairs. He believed that "Religion and practical life are not different. To take to Samnyasa (renunciation) is not to abandon life. The real spirit is to make the country your family instead of working only for your own. The step beyond is to serve humanity and the next step is to serve God." This dedication to humanity would be a fundamental element in the Indian Nationalist movement.

After graduating, Tilak began teaching mathematics in a private school in Pune. Later due to some philosophical differences with the colleagues in the New School, he decided to withdraw from that activity. In that time frame he became a journalist. He was a strong critic of the Western education system, feeling it demeaned the Indian students and disrespected India's heritage. He organized the Deccan Education Society with a few of his college friends, including Gopal Ganesh Agarkar, Mahadev Ballal Namjoshi and Vishnu Krishna Chiplunkar whose goal was to improve the quality of education for India's youth. The Deccan Education Society was set up to create a new system that taught young Indians nationalist ideas through an emphasis on Indian culture. Tilak began a mass movement towards independence that was camouflaged by an emphasis on a religious and cultural revival. He taught Mathematics at Fergusson College.

Political Career

Journalism

Tilak co-founded two newspapers with Gopal Ganesh Agarkar, Vishnushastri Chiplunakar and other colleagues: Kesari, which means "Lion" in Sanskrit and was a Marathi newspaper, and 'The Maratha', an English newspaper in 1881. In just two years 'Kesari' attracted more readers than any other language newspaper in India. The editorials were generally about the people's sufferings under the British. These newspapers called upon every Indian to fight for his or her rights. Tilak used to say to his colleagues: "You are not writing for the university students. Imagine you are talking to a villager. Be sure of your facts. Let your words be clear as daylight."

Tilak strongly criticized the government for its brutality in suppressing free expression, especially in face of protests against the division of Bengal in 1905, and for denigrating India's culture, its people and heritage. He demanded that the British immediately give Indians the right to self-government.

Indian National Congress

Tilak joined the Indian National Congress in the 1890. He opposed its moderate attitude, especially towards the fight for self government.

In 1891 Tilak opposed the Age of Consent bill. The act raised the age at which a girl could get married from 10 to 12. The Congress and other liberals supported it, but Tilak was set against it, terming it an interference with Hinduism. However, he personally opposed child marriage, and his own daughters married at 16.

Plague epidemic spread from Mumbai to Pune in late 1896, and by January 1897, it reached epidemic proportions. In order to suppress the epidemic and prevent its spread, it was decided to take drastic action, accordingly a Special Plague Committee, with jurisdiction over Pune city, its suburbs and Pune cantonment was appointed under the Chairmanship of W. C. Rand, I. C. S, Assistant Collector of Pune by way of a government order dated 8 March 1897. On 12 March 1897, 893 officers and men both British and native, under command of a Major Paget of the Durham Light Infantry were placed on plague duty. By the end of May the epidemic had ebbed and the military action was gradually ended. In his report on the administration of the Pune plague, Rand wrote, "*It is a matter of great satisfaction to the members of the Plague Committee that no credible complaint that the modesty of a woman had been intentionally insulted was made either to themselves or to the officers under whom the troops worked"*. He also writes that closest watch was kept on the troops employed on plague duty and utmost consideration was shown for the customs and traditions of the people. Indian sources however report that Rand used tyrannical methods and harassed the people.

An account based on local Indian sources writes that the appointment of military officers introduced an element of severity and coercion in the house searches, the high handedness of the government provoked the people of Pune and some soldiers were beaten in re-establish locality.

It quotes Kelkar on the conduct of British soldiers, "Either, through ignorance or impudence, they would mock, indulge in monkey tricks, talk foolishly, intimidate, touch innocent people, shove them, enter any place without justification, pocket valuable items, etc.."

Tilak took up the people's cause by publishing inflammatory articles in his paper *Kesari*, quoting the Hindu scripture, the Bhagavad Gita, to say that no blame could be attached to anyone who killed an oppressor without any thought of reward.

Following this, on 22 June, Rand and another British officer Lt. Ayerst were shot and killed by the Chapekar brothers and their other associates. Tilak was charged with incitement to murder and sentenced to 18 months' imprisonment. When he emerged from prison, he was revered as a martyr and a national hero and adopted a new slogan, "Swaraj (Self-Rule) is my birth right and I will have it."

Following the partition of Bengal in 1905, which was a strategy set out by Lord Curzon to weaken the nationalist movement, Tilak encouraged a boycott, regarded as the Swadeshi movement.

Tilak opposed the moderate views of Gopal Krishna Gokhale, and was supported by fellow Indian nationalists Bipin Chandra Pal in Bengal and Lala Lajpat Rai in Punjab.

They were referred to as the Lal-Bal-Pal triumvirate. In 1907, the annual session of the Congress Party was held at Surat (Gujarat). Trouble broke out between the moderate and the extremist factions of the party over the selection of the new president of the Congress. The party split into the "Jahal matavadi" ("Hot Faction," or extremists), led by Tilak, Pal and Lajpat Rai, and the "Maval matavadi" ("Soft Faction," or moderates).

Arrest

On 30 April 1908 two Bengali youths, Prafulla Chaki and Kudiram Bose, threw a bomb on a carriage at Muzzafurpur in order to kill a District Judge Douglass Kenford but erroneously killed some women travelling in it. While Chaki committed suicide when caught, Bose was tried and hanged. Tilak in his paper Kesari defended the revolutionaries and called for immediate Swaraj or Self-rule. The Government swiftly arrested him for sedition. He asked a young Muhammad Ali Jinnah to represent him. But the British judge convicted him and he was imprisoned from 1908 to 1914 in the Mandalay Prison, Burma. While imprisoned, he continued to read and write, further developing his ideas on the Indian Nationalist movement.

Much has been said of his trial of 1908, it being the most historic trial. His last words on the verdict of the Jury were such: *"In spite of the verdict of the Jury, I maintain that I am innocent. There are higher powers that rule the destiny of men and nations and it may be the will of providence that the cause which I represent may prosper more by my suffering than my remaining free"*. These words now can be seen imprinted on the wall of Room. No. 46 at Bombay High Court.

Life After prison

Tilak had mellowed after his release in June 1914. When World war I started in August, Tilak, cabled the King-Emperor in Britain of his support and turned his oratory to find new recruits for war efforts. He welcomed The Indian Councils Act, popularly known as Minto-Morley Reforms which had been passed by British parliament in May 1909 terming it as 'a marked increase of confidence between the Rulers and the Ruled'. Acts of violence actually retarded than hastened the pace of political reforms, he felt. He was eager for reconciliation with Congress and had abandoned his demand for direct action and settled for agitations 'strictly by constitutional means'-a line advocated his rival Gopal Krishna Gokhale since beginning

All India Home Rule League

Later, Tilak re-united with his fellow nationalists and re-joined the Indian National Congress in 1916. He also helped found the All India Home Rule League in 1916-18 with Joseph Baptista,

Annie Besant, G. S. Khaparde and Muhammad Ali Jinnah. After years of trying to reunite the moderate and radical factions, he gave up and focused on the Home Rule League, which sought self-rule. Tilak travelled from village to village trying to conjure up support from farmers and locals to join the movement towards self-rule. Tilak was impressed by the Russian Revolution, and expressed his admiration for Lenin.

Tilak, who started his political life as a Maratha protagonist, during his later part of life progressed into a prominent nationalist after his close association with Indian nationalists following the partition of Bengal. When asked in Calcutta whether he envisioned a Maratha type of government for Free India, Tilak replied that the Maratha dominated Governments of 17th and 18th centuries were outmoded in 20th century and he wanted a genuine federal system for Free India where every religion and race were equal partners. He added that only such a form of Government would be able to safeguard India's freedom. He was the first Congress leader to suggest that Hindi written in the Devanagari script, should be accepted as the sole national language of India.

Social Contribution

In 1894, Tilak transformed household worshipping of Ganesha into Sarvajanik Ganeshotsav and he also made Shiva jayanthi as a social festival. It is touted to be an effective demonstration of festival procession. Gopal Ganesh Agarkar was the first editor of Kesari, a prominent Marathi weekly in his days which was started by Lokmanya Tilak in 1880-81. Gopal Ganesh Agarkar subsequently left Kesari out of ideological differences with Bal Gangadhar Tilak concerning the primacy of political reforms versus social reforms, and Gopal Ganesh Agarkar started his own periodical Sudharak.

Later Years and Legacy

After Tilak's death on August 1, 1920, on the first day of Gandhi's first non-cooperation campaign, Gandhi paid his respects at his cremation in Mumbai, along with 20,000,000 people. Gandhi called Tilak "The Maker of Modern India". The court which convicted Tilak bears a plaque that says, "The actions of Tilak has been justified as the right of every individual to fight for his country. Those two convictions have gone into oblivion — oblivion reserved by history for all unworthy deeds".

Books

In 1903, he wrote the book The Arctic Home in the Vedas. In it he argued that the Vedas could only have been composed in the Arctics, and the Aryan bards brought them south after the onset of the last Ice age. He proposed the radically new way to determine the exact time of Vedas. Up to that time, antiquity of Vedas was mostly decided by the form of the language used in it. He tried to calculate the time of Vedas by using the position of different Nakshatras. Positions of Nakshtras were described in different Vedas. Knowing the motion of Nakshtras and there positions (at the time of Vedas and current) we can calculate the time of Vedas. Sri Tilak found that the vedas were written around 4500 B.C., when the Vernal equinox was in the constellation of Mega or Orion during the period of the Vedic hymns, and that it had receded to the constellation of the Kittikas, or the Pleiades (about 2500 B.C.) in the days of the Brahmanas. This was his basic idea. This idea was criticized by some scholars, praised by some others. But originality and charm of this new way of looking towards this problem was largely accepted.

Tilak also authored 'Shrimadbhagwadgeetarahasya'- the analysis of 'Karmayoga' in the Bhagavadgita, which is known to be gist of the Vedas and the Upanishads.

Rise of Indian Nationalism

Indians did not generally feel content about British rule in India. Indians lacked equal job opportunities. They were not allowed to advance to high positions in government service or to become officers in the army. In 1885, a number of

Indian lawyers and professionals formed the Indian National Congress. Members of the organization belonged to various religions and came from all parts of India. Congress members debated political and economic reforms, the future of India, and ways for Indians to achieve equal status with the British.

Some Muslims believed the Indian National Congress was a Hindu organization aiming for Hindu rule. In 1906, several Muslim leaders, encouraged by the British, formed the All-India Muslim League.

Members of the organization sought to give the Muslims a voice in political affairs. However, most Muslims continued to support the Indian National Congress. In 1905, the British divided the state of Bengal into separate Hindu and Muslim sections. Indians protested this action with a boycott of British goods and a series of bombings and shootings. In an effort to stop the violence, the British introduced the Morley-Minto Reforms of 1909. These reforms enlarged the viceroy's executive council to include an Indian. They also allowed Indians to elect representatives to the provincial legislative councils. In 1911, the British reunited Bengal.

When World War I broke out in 1914, Britain declared that India was also at war with Germany. Indian troops fought in many parts of the world. In return for support, the British promised more reforms and agreed to let Indians have a greater role in political affairs. Nevertheless, protests against the British continued.

In March 1919, the British passed the Rowlatt Acts to try to control protests in India. The acts attempted to restrict the political liberties and rights of Indians, including the right to trial by jury. But demonstrations against the government increased in response to the acts. On April 13, 1919, thousands of Indians assembled in an enclosed area in Amritsar. Troops entered the meeting place and blocked the entrance. The British commander then ordered the soldiers to open fire on the unarmed crowd. The shots killed about 400 people and wounded about 1,200. This event, called the Amritsar Massacre, proved to be a turning point. From then on, Indians demanded complete independence from British rule. The British promised more reforms, but at the same time, they tried to crush the independence movement.

The Montage-Chelmsford Reforms were passed in late 1919 and went into full effect in 1921. The reforms increased the powers of the provincial legislative councils, where Indians were most active. The central legislative council was replaced by a legislature with most of its members elected. However, the viceroy and the governors still had the right to veto any bill. The Indians did not believe the reforms gave them enough power.

By 1920, Mohandas K. Gandhi had become a leader in the Indian independence movement and in the Indian National Congress, which had become the most important Indian political organization. Gandhi persuaded the Congress to adopt his program of nonviolent disobedience, also known as nonviolent noncooperation. Gandhi's program asked Indians to boycott British goods, to refuse to pay taxes, and to stop using British schools, courts, and government services. As a result, some Indians gave up well-paying jobs that required them to cooperate with the British. Gandhi changed the Indian National Congress from a small party of educated men to a mass party with millions of followers.

Bipin Chandra Pal

Bipin Chandra Pal (November 7, 1858-May 20, 1932) was an Indian nationalist. He was among the triumvirate of Lal Bal Pal.

Early Life and Background

Bipin Chandra Pal was born in Poil Village, Habiganj District, Bangladesh, in a wealthy Hindu Vaishnava family. His father was Ramchandra Pal, a Persian scholar and small landowner. His son was Niranjan pal, one of the founders of Bombay Talkies. B.C. Pal is known as the 'Father Of Revolutionary Thoughts' in India.

Career

Bipin Chandra Pal was a teacher, journalist, orator, writer and librarian, he was famous as one of the triumvirate of three militant patriots of the Congresses-the "Pal" of *Lal Bal Pal*. The trio were responsible for initiating the first popular upsurge against British colonial policy in the 1905 partition of Bengal, before the advent of Gandhi into Indian politics. Pal was also the founder of the nationalistic journal *Bande Mataram*.

Even though he understood the positive aspects of Empire as a 'great idea', the 'Federal-idea is greater'.. In both public and private life he was radical. He married a widow (he had to sever ties to his family for this). At the time of B. G. Tilak's ("Bal") arrest and government repression in 1907, he left for England, where he was briefly associated with the radical India House and founded the *Swaraj* journal. However, political repercussions the wake of Curson Wyllie's assassination in 1909 by Madanlal Dhingra lead to the collapse of this publication, driving Pal to penury and mental collapse in London. In the aftermath of totally moved away from his 'extremist' phase and even nationalism, as he contemplated an association of free nations as the great federal-idea. His plea for a transcendence to a broader entity than nation derived from the notion of the sociability of human beings, which he thought would create a common bond between nations. He was among the first to criticize Gandhi or the 'Gandhi cult' since it 'sought to replace the present government by no government or by the priestly autocracy of the Mahatma.' His criticism of Gandhi was persistent beginning with Gandhi's arrival in India and open in 1921 session of the Indian National Congress he delivered in his presidential speech a severe criticism of Gandhi's ideas as based on magic rather than logic, addressing Gandhi: 'You wanted magic.

I tried to give you logic. But logic is in bad odour when the popular mind is excited. You wanted mantaram, I am not a Rishi and cannot give Mantaram...I have never spoken a half-truth when I know the truth...I have never tried to lead people in faith blind-folded', for his 'priestly, pontifical tendencies', his alliance with pan-Islamism during the Khilafat movement, which led to Pal's eclipse from political life from 1922 till his death in 1932 under conditions of abject poverty. Comparing Gandhi with Leo Tolstoy during the year he died, Pal noted that Tolstoy 'was an honest philosophical anarchist' while Gandhi remained in his eyes as 'a papal autocrat' Firm and ethically grounded, not only did he perceive the 'Congress Babel' in terms of its shortsightedness in late 1920s or, Congress as an instance of repudiating debt's folly, composed of a generation 'that knows no Joseph', Pal's critical comments should be located in context, since nobody can jump out of his skin of time. An estimation of Bipin Chandra Pal's entire corpus and the depth of his published writing cannot produce a fair idea or provide due justice if that is produced with the benefit of post-independence hindsight. Though there are many articles and books written about him from India and Europe, most of which is not hagiographical, his 'pen played not an inconsiderable part in the political and social ferments that have stirred the waters of Indian life', as the Earl of Ronaldshay wrote in 1925, what Nehru said in a speech during Pal's birth centenary in 1958 surmises 'a great man who functioned on a high level on both religious and political planes' opens a gate for enquiring this high-minded yet anomalous persona.

The trio had advocated *extremist* means to get their message across to the British, like boycotting British manufactured goods, burning Western clothes made in the mills of Manchester and strikes and lockouts of British owned businesses and industrial concerns.

He came under the influence of eminent Bengali leaders, not as a hero-worshipper or somebody looking for a guru for guidance, of his time such as Keshab Chandra Sen and Sibnath Shastri, as his family were in Brahmo Samaj. He was imprisoned for six months on the grounds of his refusal to give evidence against Sri Aurobindo in the *Bande Mataram* sedition case. He died on May 20, 1932.

Rise of Indian Nationalism

In India, the decades after the First War for Independence (1857) were a period of growing political awareness, manifestation of public opinion, and emergence of leadership at national and provincial levels. Gloomy economic uncertainties created by British colonial rule and the limited opportunities that awaited for the increasing number of western-educated graduates began to dominate the rhetoric of leaders who had begun to think of themselves as a nation despite differences along the lines of region, religion, language, and caste.

Dadabhai Naoroji formed East India Association in 1867, and Surendranath Banerjee founded Indian National Association in 1876. Indian National Congress is formed in 1885 in a meeting in Bombay attended by seventy-three Indian delegates. The delegates were mostly members of the upwardly mobile and successful Western-educated provincial elites, engaged in professions such as law, teaching, and journalism. They had acquired political experience from regional competition in the professions and from their aspirations in securing nomination to various positions in legislative councils, universities, and special commissions.

The Congress had no well-defined ideology or necessary resources to be a political organization at the beginning. It functioned more as a debating society that met annually to express its loyalty to the British Raj and passed numerous resolutions on less controversial issues such as civil rights or opportunities in government etc. These resolutions were submitted to the viceroy's government and, sometimes to the British Parliament without any positive results. With a membership consists only of urban elites the Congress voiced their interests even though it claims to represent India.

Indian National Congress failed to attract Muslims to the organization. Although the Congress made efforts to enlist the

Muslim community in its struggle for Indian independence, most of the Muslims remained reluctant to join the Party.

Islamic rule was established across northern India between the 7th and the 14th centuries. The Muslim Mughal Empire ruled most of India from Delhi from the early 16th century until its power was broken by the British in the 19th century. This left a disempowered and discontented Muslim minority, afraid of being swamped by the Hindu majority. Muslims represented about 23% of the population of British India, and constituted the majority of the population in several regions.

By 1900, the Indian National Congress had emerged as an all-India political organization, Muslims began to realize their inadequate education and under representation in government service. Muslim leaders saw that their community had fallen behind the Hindus. Attacks by Hindu reformers against religious conversion, cow killing, and the preservation of Urdu in Arabic script deepened their fears of minority status and denial of their rights if the Congress alone were to represent the people of India. For many Muslims, loyalty to the British crown seemed preferable to cooperation with Congress leaders. Sir Sayyid Ahmad launched a movement for Muslim regeneration that culminated in the founding in 1875 of the Muhammadan Anglo-Oriental College (renamed Aligarh Muslim University in 1921) at Aligarh, United Provinces (now Uttar Pradesh). Its objective was to educate wealthy students by emphasizing the compatibility of Islam with modern Western knowledge. The diversity among India's Muslims, however, made it impossible to bring about uniform cultural and intellectual regeneration. A turning point came in 1900 when the British administration in the United Provinces acceded to Hindu demands and made Hindi as the official language. This seemed to aggravate Muslim fears that the Hindu majority would seek to suppress Muslim culture and religion in an independent India. A British official, Sir Percival Griffiths, wrote of "the Muslim belief that their interest must be regarded as completely separate from those of the Hindus, and that no fusion of the two communities was possible."

All India Muslim League founded at Dhaka in 1906 on the occasion of the annual All India Muhammadan Educational Conference in Shahbagh, Dhaka. The meeting was hosted by Nawab Salimullah Khan and was attended by three thousand delegates.

The resolution was moved by Nawab Salimullah says "The musalmans are only a fifth in number as compared with the total population of the country, and it is manifest that if at any remote period the British government ceases to exist in India, then the rule of India would pass into the hands of that community which is nearly four times as large as ourselves ...our life, our property, our honour, and our faith will all be in great danger, when even now that a powerful British administration is protecting its subjects, we the Musalmans have to face most serious difficulties in safe-guarding our in terests from the grasping hands of our neig

Rise of Indian Nationalism

Indians did not generally feel content about British rule in India. Indians lacked equal job opportunities. They were not allowed to advance to high positions in government service or to become officers in the army. In 1885, a number of Indian lawyers and professionals formed the Indian National Congress. Members of the organization belonged to various religions and came from all parts of India. Congress members debated political and economic reforms, the future of India, and ways for Indians to achieve equal status with the British.

Some Muslims believed the Indian National Congress was a Hindu organization aiming for Hindu rule. In 1906, several Muslim leaders, encouraged by the British, formed the All-India Muslim League.

Members of the organization sought to give the Muslims a voice in political affairs. However, most Muslims continued to support the Indian National Congress.

In 1905, the British divided the state of Bengal into separate Hindu and Muslim sections. Indians protested this action with a boycott of British goods and a series of bombings and shootings. In an effort to stop the violence, the British introduced the Morley-Minto Reforms of 1909. These reforms enlarged the viceroy's executive council to include an Indian. They also allowed Indians to elect representatives to the provincial legislative councils. In 1911, the British reunited Bengal.

When World War I broke out in 1914, Britain declared that India was also at war with Germany. Indian troops fought in many parts of the world. In return for support, the British promised more reforms and agreed to let Indians have a greater role in political affairs. Nevertheless, protests against the British continued.

In March 1919, the British passed the Rowlatt Acts to try to control protests in India. The acts attempted to restrict the political liberties and rights of Indians, including the right to trial by jury. But demonstrations against the government increased in response to the acts. On April 13, 1919, thousands of Indians assembled in an enclosed area in Amritsar. Troops entered the meeting place and blocked the entrance. The British commander then ordered the soldiers to open fire on the unarmed crowd. The shots killed about 400 people and wounded about 1,200. This event, called the Amritsar Massacre, proved to be a turning point. From then on, Indians demanded complete independence from British rule. The British promised more reforms, but at the same time, they tried to crush the independence movement.

The Montage-Chelmsford Reforms were passed in late 1919 and went into full effect in 1921. The reforms increased the powers of the provincial legislative councils, where Indians were most active. The central legislative council was replaced by a legislature with most of its members elected. However, the viceroy and the governors still had the right to veto any bill. The Indians did not believe the reforrns gave them enough power.

By 1920, Mohandas K. Gandhi had become a leader in the Indian independence movement and in the Indian National Congress, which had become the most important Indian political organization. Gandhi persuaded the Congress to adopt his program of nonviolent disobedience, also known as nonviolent noncooperation. Gandhi's program asked Indians to boycott British goods, to refuse to pay taxes, and to stop using British schools, courts, and government services. As a result, some Indians gave up well-paying jobs that required them to cooperate with the British. Gandhi changed the Indian National Congress from a small party of educated men to a mass party with millions of followers.

Lala Lajpat Rai

Lala Lajpat Rai was an Indian author and politician who is chiefly remembered as a leader in the Indian fight for freedom from the British Raj. He was popularly known as *Punjab Kesari* (The Lion of Punjab). He was also the founder of Punjab National Bank and Lakshmi Insurance Company.

Early Life

(Born in Jagraon, on 28 January, India in 1865 in a Hindu Vysya Family, Lajpat Rai created a career of *reforming Indian policy through politics and writing*. (When studying law in Lahore, he continued to practice Hinduism. He became a large believer in the idea that Hinduism, above nationality, was the pivotal point upon which an Indian lifestyle must be based.) Hinduism, he believed, led to practices of peace to humanity, and the idea that when nationalist ideas were added to this peaceful belief system, a non-secular nation could be formed. His involvement with Hindu Mahasabhaite leaders gathered criticism from the Bharat Sabha as the Mahasabhas were anti-secularism, which did not conform with the system laid out by the Indian National Congress. This focus on Hindu practices in the subcontinent would ultimately lead him to the continuation of peaceful movements to create successful demonstrations for Indian independence.

Political Life

As the need for partition and independence took an important turn for the possible, Lajpat Rai's involvement became imperative to the Indian Independence Movement. His actions in anti-imperialist movements led to numerous arrests. He became an important member of the Arya Samaj. This political group was full of British-educated Indians who believed that Hinduism had a specific and direct impact on what it meant to be Indian.

The group also took the ideas of a merged western and eastern world and promoted the view that the subcontinent had benefited from its coagulation. The involvement of the Arya Samaj in constitutional reform supported the freedom movement which took hold of the Indian population. Lajpat Rai led political rallies which taught how the history of the subcontinent had always been heading to the philosophical idea that it would become an independent nation.

(Lajpat Rai presided over the first session of the All India Trade Union Congress in 1920. In 1923, he became a member of the Imperial Legislative Assembly. He also went to Geneva to attend the eighth International Labour Conference in 1926 as a representative of Indian labour. He had an opportunity to watch the labour movement in the USA and England where he was required to prolong his stay for political reasons.)

In addition to espousing his philosophical principles, Lajpat Rai engaged heavily in direct action and protest against British rule. (He led the Punjab protests against the Amritsar Massacre (1919), the Non-Cooperation Movement (1919-1922), and the "Simon go back" demonstrations against the Simon Commission (1928)). He was repeatedly arrested. He disagreed, however, with Mohandas Gandhi's suspension of the movement due to the Chauri Chaura incident. (He formed the *Congress Independence Party*, which was particularly pro-Hindu in voice and pollices.

He was not only a good orator but also a prolific and versatile writer. His journal *Arya Gazette* concentrated mainly on subjects related to the Arya Samaj. *Bande Mataram* and *People*, contained his inspiring speeches to end oppression by the foreign rulers. He founded the Servants of the People Society, which worked for the freedom movement as well as for social reform in the country. He also wrote an autobiography in English titled *The Story of My Life*.

Simon Commission Protests

In 1928, Lajpat Rai led a procession with Pandit Madan Mohan Malaviya to demonstrate against the Simon Commission. During this procession, Rai became the target of a lathi charge (a form of crowd control in which the police use heavy staves or 'lathis' in Hindi) led by British police. He was severely injured in the charge. Nevertheless, at a meeting held the same evening, he spoke with great vigour. His words at this meeting, *"Every blow aimed at me is a nail in the coffin of British imperialism"*, have become historic. Though he recovered from the fever and pain within three days, his health had received a permanent setback and on November 17, 1928, he died of his injuries. His death led to great disturbances in the country and it inspired national struggle for freedom.

Author

(Lajpat Rai's journey to the United States during World War I helped him to gather knowledge of how an independent nation formulates a nationalist identity.

This is where he gathered information about how foreign nations, specifically Britain's imperialist hold on India, had negative affects on the people, the lifestyles, and the ability to generate bonds with other nations. He wrote articles that persuaded foreign nations to side with the subcontinent's struggle for independence.

By accepting that westernized ideals were positive to the creation of nationalities, he gained support for breaking from Britain. In Europeanization and the Ancient Culture of India, Lajpat Rai wrote that nationalization of India was imperative to spread western ideology to the rest of the world.

Since the westernization of India had successfully been adapted while continuing traditions remained a large part of the culture, he believed that India no longer needed an overbearing imperialist government.

He wrote that: "at first sight it seems absurd to give one name to all Indian civilization. But a close examination for facts and data amply proves the unity of Indian civilization, at least for the present geological period." These ideas were passed to foreign countries in order to show that despite cultural differences from the western world, India's society had become a sustainable, functional nation which deserved its own nationality as opposed to being over seen by an alien western country.

(Writings by Lajpat Rai include *Josiah Wedgewood-The Man And His Work, The United States of America: A Hindu's impressions and a study, History of the Arya Samaj, Swaraj and social change, England's Debt to India: A historical narrative of Britain's fiscal policy in India, The Problems Of National Education In India* and *Unhappy India: Being a reply to Katherine Mayo's "Mother India"*, published in 1928.) (*Mother India* was a polemical account of India's self rule by American historian Katherine Mayo.)

Inspiration and Memorial

The Lala Lajpat Rai Memorial Trust was formed in 1959 on the eve of his Centenary Birth Celebration, to promote education. The trust was founded by a group of Punjabi philanthropists (including R.P Gupta and B.M Grover) who have settled and prospered in the Indian State of Maharashtra.

A statue of Lajpat Rai stands at the central square in Shimla, India. Lajpat Nagar and Lajpat Nagar Central Market in New Delhi, Lala Lajpat Rai Hall of Residence at Indian Institutes of Technology (IIT) in Kharagpur and Lala Lajpat Rai Institute of Engineering and Technology, Moga are named in his honour. Also many institutes, Schools and Library in his hometown of Jagraon, district Ludhiana are named after him.

Lal Bal Pal

Lal Bal Pal were the Swadeshi triumvirate who advocated the Swadeshi movement involving the boycott of all imported items and the use of Indian-made goods in 1907.

The last years of the nineteenth century, saw a radical sensibility emerge among some Indian Intellectuals. This position burst onto the national all-India scene in 1905 with the Swadeshi movement-the term is usually rendered as "self reliance" or "self sufficiency".

Lal-Bal-Pal, mobilized Indians across the country against the Bengal partition, and the demonstrations, strikes and boycotts of English goods that began in Bengal soon spread to other regions in a broader protest against the Raj.

Gopal Krishna Gokhale

Gopal Krishna Gokhale, CIE (May 9, 1866-February 19, 1915) was one of the founding social and political leaders during the Indian Independence Movement against the British Empire in India. Gokhale was a senior leader of the Indian National Congress and founder of the Servants of India Society. Through the Society as well as the Congress and other legislative bodies he served in, Gokhale promoted not only or even primarily independence from the British Empire but also social reform. To achieve his goals, Gokhale followed two overarching principles: avoidance of violence and reform within existing government institutions.

Background and Education

Gopal Krishna Gokhale was born May 9, 1866 in Kotaluk, Maharashtra, a state on the western coast of India that was then part of the Bombay Presidency. Although they were Chitpavan Brahmin, Gokhale's family was relatively poor. Even so, they ensured that Gokhale received an English education, which would place Gokhale in a position to obtain employment as a clerk or minor official in the British Raj. Being one of the first generations of Indians to receive a university education, Gokhale graduated from Elphinstone College in 1884. Gokhale's education tremendously influenced the course of his future career – in addition to learning English, he was exposed to western political thought and became a great admirer of theorists such as John Stuart Mill and Edmund Burke. Although he would come to criticize unhesitatingly many aspects of the English colonial regime, the respect for English political theory and institutions that Gokhale acquired in his college years would remain with him for the rest of his life.

Indian National Congress and Rivalry with Bal Gangadhar Tilak

Gokhale became a member of the Indian National Congress in 1889, as a protege of social reformer Mahadev Govind Ranade. Along with other contemporary leaders like Bal Gangadhar Tilak, Dadabhai Naoroji, Bipin Chandra Pal, Lala Lajpat Rai and Annie Besant, Gokhale fought for decades to obtain greater political representation and power over public affairs for common Indians. He was moderate in his views and attitudes, and sought to petition the British authorities by cultivating a process of dialogue and discussion which would yield greater British respect for Indian rights. Gokhale had visited Ireland and had arranged for an Irish nationalist, Alfred Webb, to serve as President of the Indian National Congress in 1894. The following year, Gokhale became the Congress's joint secretary along with Tilak. In many ways, Tilak and Gokhale's early careers paralleled – both were Chitpavan Brahmin (though unlike Gokhale, Tilak was wealthy), both attended Elphinstone College, both became mathematics professors, and both were important members of the Deccan Education Society. When both became active in the Congress, however, the divergence of their views concerning how best to improve the lives of Indians became increasingly apparent.

Gokhale's first major confrontation with Tilak centred around one of his pet projects, the Age of Consent Bill introduced by the British Imperial Government, in 1891-2. Gokhale and his fellow liberal reformers, wishing to purge what they saw as superstitions and abuses from their native Hinduism, wished through the Consent Bill to curb child marriage abuses.

Though the Bill was not extreme, only raising the age of consent from ten to twelve, Tilak took issue with it; he did not object per se to the idea of moving towards the elimination of child marriage, but rather to the idea of British interference with Hindu tradition. For Tilak, such reform movements were not to be sought after under imperial rule when they would be enforced by the British, but rather after independence was achieved when Indians would enforce it on themselves. Despite Tilak's opposition, however, Gokhale and the reformers won the day and the bill became law in the Bombay Presidency.

In 1905, Gokhale became president of the Indian National Congress. Gokhale used his now considerable influence to undermine his longtime rival, Tilak, refusing to support Tilak as candidate for president of the Congress in 1906. By now, Congress was split: Gokhale and Tilak were the respective leaders of the moderates and the "extremists" (the latter now known by the more politically correct term, 'aggressive nationalists') in the Congress. Tilak was an advocate of civil agitation and direct revolution to overthrow the British Empire, whereas Gokhale was a moderate reformist. As a result, the Congress Party split into two wings and was largely robbed of its effectiveness for a decade. The two sides would later patch up in 1916 after Gokhale died.

Servants of India Society

In 1905, when Gokhale was elected president of the Indian National Congress and was at the height of his political power, he founded the Servants of India Society to specifically further one of the causes dearest to his heart: the expansion of Indian education. For Gokhale, true political change in India would only be possible when a new generation of Indians became educated as to their civil and patriotic duty to their country and to each other. Believing existing educational institutions and the Indian Civil Service did not do enough to provide Indians with opportunities to gain this political education, Gokhale hoped the Servants of India Society would fill this need. In his preamble to the SIS's constitution, Gokhale wrote that "The Servants of India Society will train men prepared to devote their lives to the cause of country in a religious spirit, and will seek to promote, by all constitutional means, the national interests of the Indian people." The Society took up the cause of promoting Indian education in earnest, and among its many projects organized mobile libraries, founded schools, and provided night classes for factory workers. Although the Society lost much of its vigor following Gokhale's death, it still exists to this day, though its membership is small.

Involvement with British Imperial Government

Gokhale, though an earlier leader of the Indian nationalist movement, was not primarily concerned with independence but rather with social reform; he believed such reform would be best achieved by working within existing British government institutions, a position which earned him the enmity of more aggressive nationalists such as Tilak. Undeterred by such opposition, Gokhale would work directly with the British throughout his political career in order to further his reform goals.

In 1899, Gokhale was elected to the Bombay Legislative Council. He was elected to the Council of India of Governor-General of India on 22 May 1903 as non-officiating member represeting Bombay Province. He later served to Imperial Legislative Council after its expansion in 1909. He there obtained a reputation as extremely knowledgeable and contributed significantly to the annual budget debates. Gokhale developed so great a reputation among the British that he was invited to London to meet with secretary of state Lord John Morley, with whom he established a rapport. Gokhale would help during visit to shape the Morley-Minto Reforms introduced in1909. Gokhale was appointed a CIE (Companion of the Order of the Indian Empire) in the 1904 New Year's Honours List, a formal recognition by the Empire of his service.

Mentor to Both Jinnah and Gandhi

Gokhale was famously a mentor to Mahatma Gandhi in his formative years. In 1912, Gokhale visited South Africa at Gandhi's invitation. As a young barrister, Gandhi returned from his struggles against the Empire in South Africa and received personal guidance from Gokhale, including a knowledge and understanding of India and the issues confronting common Indians. By 1920, Gandhi emerged as the leader of the Indian Independence Movement. In his autobiography, Gandhi calls Gokhale his mentor and guide. Gandhi also recognised Gokhale as an admirable leader and master politician, describing him as 'pure as crystal, gentle as a lamb, brave as a lion and chivalrous to a fault and the most perfect man in the political field'. Despite his deep respect for Gokhale, however, Gandhi would reject Gokhale's faith in western institutions as a means of achieving political reform and ultimately chose not to become a member of Gokhale's Servants of India Society. Gokhale was also the role model and mentor of Mohammed Ali Jinnah, the future founder of Pakistan, who in 1912, aspired to become the "Muslim Gokhale". Gokhale famously praised Jinnah as an "ambassador of Hindu-Muslim Unity."

Gokhale Institute

The Gokhale Institute of Politics and Economics (GIPE), commonly known as Gokhale Institute, is one of the oldest research and training institutes in Economics in India. It is located on BMCC Road in the Deccan Gymkhana area of Pune, Maharashtra. The Institute was founded with an endowment offered to the Servants of India Society by Shri R R Kale. The Servants of India Society are the trustees of the Institute.

Death

Gokhale continued to be politically active through the last years of his life. This included extensive travelling abroad: in addition to his 1908 trip to England, he also visited South Africa in 1912, where his protege Gandhi was working to improve conditions for the Indian minority living there. Meanwhile, he continued to be involved in the Servants of India Society, the Congress, and the Legislative Council while constantly advocating the advancement of Indian education. All these stresses took their toll, however, and Gokhale died in Feb 19 1915 at forty-nine years of age.

Impact on Indian Nationalist Movement

Gokhale's impact on the course of the Indian nationalist movement was considerable. Through his close relationship with the highest levels of British imperial government, Gokhale forced India's colonial masters to recognize the capabilities of a new generation of educated Indians and to include them more than ever before in the governing process. Gokhale's firm belief in the need for a spiritualization of politics, social amelioration and universal education deeply inspired the next great man on the Indian political stage, Mohandas K. Gandhi; his ultimate faith in western political institutions and classical liberalism, though rejected by Gandhi, would come to ultimate fruition in the Westminster model of government adopted by an independent India in 1950.

Born in Kothluk, a village in Maharashtra, on May 9, 1866, Gopal Krishna Gokhale was raised in the home of his maternal grandfather. This village was not too far from Tamhanmala, the native town of his father, Krishna Rao, a farmer by occupation who w as forced to work as a clerk due to the poor soil of the region. His mother, Valubai, also known as Satyabhama, was a simple woman who instilled in her children the values of religion, devotion to one's family, and caring for one's fellow man.

Supported by his elder brother and sister-in-law, Gokhale managed an education at Rajaram High School in Kothapur. Due to his respect for his brother and a recognition of the compassion with which he was treated, Gokhale learned the value of self-sacrifice to avoid asking for more material support. At times he went without meals and studied by the light of street lamps to save his elder brother as much money as possible. A hard-working student, he moved on to college and graduated from Elphinstone College, Bombay in 1884 at the age of 18, earning a scholarship of Rs. 20 per month in his final year. His education influenced Gokhale's life in many ways. Primarily, his understanding of the English language allowed him to express himself without hesitation and with utmost clarity. Also, his appreciation and knowledge of history instilled in him a respect for liberty, democracy, and the parliamentary system. After graduation, he moved on to teaching, and took a position as an Assistant Master in the New English School in Pune. Among many achievements which testify to his talent and passion for teaching, perhaps the greatest of them all was a compilation, a book of arithmetic in collaboration with a colleague, N. J. Bapat, which became a widely used and widely translated textbook across the country. Gokhale moved on to become a founding member of Fergusson College in Pune in 1885, with colleagues in the highly honoured Deccan Education Society. He pledged twenty years of his life to this college, as a teacher and board member. So apt was he at teaching subjects of any variety, that he was known as the "Professor to Order."

The year 1886 saw the entry of Gopal Krishna Gokhale into public life. At only 20 years of age, he delivered a public address concerning "India under the British Rule" and was applauded for his expression and command of the English language. Gokhale soon moved on to managing public affairs. While contributing articles to the English weekly Mahratta, he was seduced by the idea of using education as a means to awaken patriotism among the people of India. Just as this idea was enveloping Gokhale was promoted to Secretary of the Deccan Education Society. Once in the limelight, there was no looking back. After being given charge of the Bombay Provincial Conference in 1893, he was elected to the Senate of the Bombay University. In time, Gokhale came to devote all his spare time to the causes of the common man: famine, plague relief measures, local self-government, land reform, and communal harmony. As a member of the Pune Municipality, twice elected its president, Gokhale continued to strive to solve the problems of the poor, and those who came to him with grievances concerning water supply, drainage, etc. were pleased with the practical manner in which he dealt with the problem. Gokhale also published a daily newspaper entitled Jnanaprakash, which allowed him to voice his reformist views on politics and society.

In 1905, he founded the Servants of India Society, which trained people to be selfless workers so they could work for the common good of the people. So strong was the desire to make a difference, that these kindred spirits vowed a simple life of dedication to these causes. Among the many things the organization did, there were the commendable services of helping victims of floods and famines, and taking the time to educate women in society, so that they too may have a voice. Many people influenced Gokhale and gave him the strength and discipline to bring his ideas to the realm of reality, but none more than Mahadev Govind Ranade, to whom he was apprenticed in 1887. Ranade trained him for 15 years in all spheres of public life, and taught him sincerity, devotion to public service, and tolerance. These qualities, which Ranade helped instill in Gokhale, are those qualities which helped make Gokhale the man he is known today.

Gokhale visited England and voiced his concerns relating to the unfair treatment of the Indian people by the British government. In one span of 49 days, he spoke in front of 47 different audiences, captivating every one of them. Before long, he was touted as the most effective pleader for India's cause. While Gokhale pleaded for gradual reform to ultimately attain Swaraj, or self-government, in India, some of his contemporaries, comprising a radical element, wished to use force as a means of persuasion. Gokhale maintained his moderate political views and worked out some reforms for the betterment of India. He was instrumental in the formation of the Minto-Morley Reforms of 1909, which eventually became law. Unfortunately, the Reforms Act became law in 1909 and it was disappointing to see that the people were not given a proper democratic system despite Gokhale's efforts. The communal harmony he had longed for was shattered when he realized that the Muslim community was steadfast in considering itself as a separate unit. On the bright side, however, Gokhale's efforts were clearly not in vain. Indians now had access to seats of the highest authority within the government, and their voices were more audible in matters of public interest. The years of hard work and devotion of Gopal Krishna Gokhale did much for the country of India, but sadly also took their toll on the health of this great leader. Excessive exertion and the resulting exhaustion only aggravated his diabetes and cardiac asthma. The end came peacefully, however, on February 19, 1915. Pointing his finger toward heaven and then folding his hands respectfully, Gopal Krishna Gokhale made his final statement to an audience, a fond farewell.

Mahadev Govind Ranade

Justice Mahadev Govind Ranade (16 January 1842–16 January 1901) was a distinguished scholar, great social reformer, and an author from India. He was a founding member of the Indian National Congress and owned several designations as member of the Bombay legislative council, member of the finance committee at the centre, and the judge of Bombay High Court..

Ranade was born in a small town in Nasik district named Niphad. Ranade began studies at the Elphinstone College in Mumbai, at the age of fourteen. He belonged to Bombay University, one of the three new British universities, and was part of the first batches for both the B.A. (1862) and the LL.B. (Government Law School, 1866) where he graduated at the top of his class. Great scholar and founder of BORI Mr.. Bhandarkar was his classmate.

He was appointed Presidency magistrate, fourth judge of the Bombay Small Causes Court in 1871, first-class sub-judge at Pune in 1873, judge of the Poona Small Causes Court in 1884, and finally to the Bombay High Court in 1893. From 1885 until he joined the High Court, he belonged to the Bombay legislative council. He was a well known public figure, who's personality as a calm and patient optimist would influence his attitude towards dealings with Britain, as well as with reform in India. During his life he helped establish the Poona Sarvajanik Sabha, the Prarthana Samaj, and would edit a Bombay Anglo-Marathi daily paper, the Induprakask, founding all on his ideology of social and religious reform. In 1897, Ranade served on a committee charged with the task of enumerating imperial and provincial expenditure and making recommendations for financial retrenchment. This service won him the decoration of Companion of the Order of the Indian Empire. Ranade also served as a special judge under the Deccan Agriculturists' Relief Act from 1887.

In addition, Ranade held the offices of syndic and dean in arts at Bombay University, where he displayed much organizing power and great intimacy with the needs of the student class. Himself a thorough Marathi scholar, he encouraged the translation of standard English works, and tried, with some success, to introduce vernacular languages into the university curriculum. He published books on Indian economics and on Maratha history. He stated the requirement of heavy industries such as Steel as necessity for economic progress. He believed in Western education as a vital element to the foundation of an Indian nation. He felt that by understanding the mutual problems of India and Britain, both reform and independence could be achieved to the benefit of all. He insisted that an independent India could only be stable after such reforms were made. Reform of Indian culture and use of an adaptation of Western culture, in Ranade's view, would bring about "common interest... and fusion of thoughts" amongst all men." With his friends Dr. Atmaram Pandurang, Bal Mangesh Wagle and Vaman Abaji Modak, Ranade founded the Prarthana Samaj, a Hindu movement inspired by the Brahmo Samaj, espousing principles of enlightened theism based on the ancient Vedas. Prarthan samaj was started by Keshav Chandra Sen, a staunch Brahma Samajist, with the objective of carrying out religious reforms in Maharashtra. Ranade founded the Poona Sarvajanik Sabha and later was one of the originators of the Indian National Congress. He has been portrayed as an early adversary of the politics of Bal Gangadhar Tilak and a mentor to Gopal Krishna Gokhale. The 1911 *Encyclopedia Britannica* stated that the Poona Sarvajanik Sabha "frequently helped the government with sound advice". Not everyone agreed. In a letter to Henry Fawcett, Florence Nightingale wrote: "The Poona Sarvajanik Sabha (National Association) [...] again pretends to represent the people and merely represents the money lenders, officials, and a few effete Mahratta landlords."

In 1943, B. R. Ambedkar praised Ranade and rated him favourably against Gandhi and Jinnah: "Ranade never received the honours of apotheosis as these great men of India today are destined to receive. How could he? He did not come with a message hot from Senai. He performed no miracles and promised no speedy deliverance and splendour. He was not a genius and he had no superhuman qualities. But there are compensations. If Ranade did not show splendour and dominance, he brought us no catastrophe. If he had no superhuman qualities to use in the service of India, India was saved from ruin by its abuse. If he was not a genius, he did not display that perverse super-subtlety of intellect, and a temper of mind which is fundamentally dishonest and which has sown the seeds of distrust and which has made settlement so difficult of achievement.

There is nothing exuberant and extravagant in Ranade. He refused to reap cheap notoriety by playing the part of an extremist. He refused to mislead people by playing upon and exploiting the patriotic sentiments of the people. He refused to be a party to methods which are crude, which have volume but no effect, and which are neither fool-proof nor knave-proof, and which break the back even of the most earnest and sincere servants of the country and disable them from further effort. In short, Ranade was like the wise Captain who knows that his duty is not to play with his ship clever and masterful tricks, just for effect and show in the midst of the ocean, but to take it safely to its appointed port. In short, Ranade was not a forged bank note and in worshipping him we have no feeling of kneeling before anything that is false."

Ranade was a founder of the Social Conference movement, which he supported till his death, directing his social reform efforts against child marriage, the shaving of widows' heads, the heavy cost of marriages and other social functions, and the caste restrictions on travelling abroad, and he strenuously advocated widow remarriage and female education. Ranade attempted to work with the structure of weakened traditions, reforming, but not destroying the social atmosphere that was India's heritage. Ranade valued India's history, having had a great interest in Shivaji and the Bhakti movement, but he also recognized the influence that British rule over India had on its development. Ranade encouraged the acceptance of change, believing traditional social structures, like the caste system, should accommodate change, thereby preserving India's ancient heritage. An overall sense of national regeneration was what Ranade desired.

Though Ranade criticised superstitions and blind faith, he was conservative in his own life. He chose to took *prayaschitta* (religious penance) in case of *Panch-houd Mission Case* rather than taking a strong side of his opinions. Ranade belonged to an orthodox Chitpavan Brahman family. He was born in Niphad and spent much of his childhood in Kolhapur where his father was a minister. Upon the death of his first wife, his reform-minded friends expected him to marry (and thereby rescue) a widow. However, he adhered to his family's wishes and married a child bride, Ramabai Ranade, whom he subsequently provided with an education. After his death, she continued his social and educational reform work. He had no children. Ramabai Ranade in her memoirs has stated that when one equally prominent Pune personality Vishnupant Pandit married a widow, Ranade entertained him and a few guests at his home. This was not liked by his orthodox father who decided to leave Ranade's home in Pune and go to Kolhapur. It was only after he (i.e Mahadev G. Ranade) told the father that he would resign from his government job that the father relented and cancelled his plans to go to Kolhapur. Ranade decided never to do any such thing in future.

The Main Stage in Indian Nationalism

In 1885 the 'Indian National Congress' was established. This organization was the main voice of Indian nationalism since its creation and up to India's independence in 1947. The Indian National Congress was not the first political organization of Indian orientation founded in British India. Other organizations preceded it.

In 1867 justice M. G. Ranade established in Bombay an organization based on the ideas of the 'Brahmo Samaj' with an aim of social and religious reforms in India. In 1876 Surendranath Benarjee established in Calcutta an organization with an aim to demand rights for Indians. Dadabhai Naoroji, who was the first Indian elected for the British parliament, established in Bombay some institutions with an aim of academic and social reforms in India. These three men along with other leaders were the founders of the Indian National Congress. Another organization established in India before the Indian National Congress was the 'Arya Samaj'. Some of the second-generation leaders in the Indian National Congress were inspired from the ideas of this organization.

In 1885 the 'Indian National Congress' was established. This organization, which was the main voice of the Indian nationalism under British rule, was established with British permission. The real purpose of the British in establishing this organization was to continue ruling India with the help of liberal and pro-British Indians. The British who at first aimed at annexing all of Indian kingdoms through the agreements the 'East India Company' had with local rulers changed their policy after the 'Mutiny' of 1857. The British Crown took back the charter from the 'East India Company' and ruled India directly through a viceroy. They stopped annexing Indian kingdoms and involved more Indians in their rule over India. They permitted the establishing of the 'Indian National Congress', an organization where Indians could express their opinions. The Englishman who endeavored for this cause was Allen Hume. In its first stages the 'Indian National Congress' was not supportive of independent India and most of its leaders were considered liberals and pro-British. But within a short period of time a militant nationalist opposition was established within the Congress who demanded an independent India. This militant group tried to dispose of the liberal leadership of the Congress.

In the last decade of the 19th century the salient leader of the Congress was Gopal Krishna Gokhale, a liberal and disciple of Ranade (one of the founders of the Congress). The militant Left group within the Congress tried to dispose of Gokhale as the leader of the Congress. The leader of this militant group was Bal Gangadhar Tilak. Two of his main associates were Lala Lajpat Rai and Bipin Chandra Pal. This trio was called in short Lal-Bal-Pal. These three men originated from three different parts of India. Rai was from Punjab in North India, Tilak was from Maharashtra in West India and Pal from Bengal in East India. Some Indians especially Hindus found an analogy between this trio and the trio of Hinduism, Brahma, Vishnu and Shiva. This militant group was strong supporter of Hindu nationalism. They spiced their nationalist philosophy with Hindu Gods and Goddesses. They were mainly inspired by the philosophies of Arya Samaj and Rama Krishna movement, which considered the Indian culture as the most humanistic and spiritual culture in the world.

Bal Gandadhar Tilak is considered by many to be the first Indian leader who moved the Indian independence cause from the closed rooms of the intellectuals to the ordinary people of India.

He succeeded in causing major uprisings against the British and was titled by the western press in 1907 as the 'father of Indian uprising'. Tilak and his associates were considered by the British as the main cause for the violence against them and therefore they arrested and deported them. This left the Congress under the control of the Liberals. Gokhale remained the leader of the Congress until his death in 1915. Before his death he managed to be the political guru of someone who more than anyone else is identified with Indian independence, Mahatma Gandhi. After Gokhale's death, Tilak, who returned from his deportation, became the leader the Indian nationalism. He managed to bridge between the extremes and liberals in the Congress and also succeeded in signing a cooperation agreement with another nationalist organization in British India, Muslim League.

During World War I, the British promised to the Indians independence if they supported the British during the war. After the war the British did not keep their promise, instead they offered Indians more political rights. In 1919 the first Indian Parliament was established, but the turning point of that year in India's independence movement was the Jallianwala Bagh massacre which occurred in Amritsar. In this event a British general arrived with his soldiers to Jallianwala Bagh, an open garden in Amritsar, and ordered his soldiers to shoot at the Indians who were having a peaceful political rally in the garden. In this massacre at least 800 Indians died. After this event, even liberal Indians, like Mahatma Gandhi, started demanding independence for India from the British. Mohandas Karamchand Gandhi (1869-1948) was reverently known as Mahatma Gandhi. He was called by the people 'Mahatma' which means great soul. He arrived in India from South Africa in 1915. Gandhi became the leader of the Indian National Congress after Tilak's death in 1920. Gandhi's philosophy of struggle against the British was nonviolent non-cooperation. He demanded from the Indians to restrain even if the British forces physically attacked them. He advised Indians to boycott anything British including British made garments, British universities, British courts and to refuse to follow British laws. He sometimes resorted to hunger strike. Gandhi succeeded in sweeping the Indian people after him like no other Indian leader before him.

Not all Indians admired Gandhi and his ideas. Even when he was the leader of Indian National Congress there were members of the Congress who did not accept his ideas. His opponents who had other ideas about India even established movements within the Indian National Congress. The Indian National Congress was always a roof organization and it included in it many factions. Besides the Indian National Congress, other political organizations and parties were established who fought for Indian's right for self-definition. Among these were communist and socialist parties and Hindu nationalist organizations, Hindu Mahasabha and Rashtriya Swayamsevak Sangh. Some of the Congress rivals even claimed that some businessmen were supporting the national struggle organized by the Congress in exchange for financial gain. For example Mahatma Gandhi's call to boycott British textile caused Indians to buy Indian made textile. The Congress party's financial supporters owned these textile mills.

Along with organizations, some individual persons also contributed to the establishment of the Indian identity. People like Chandrashekhar Azad and Bhagat Singh, who became martyrs while fighting the British forces, also strengthened Indian identity among the people of the sub-continent. Other people who helped strengthened the Indian identity were intellectuals like authors and poets. These intellectuals were mostly from the Bengal region in east India and their works were mostly in Bengali language. But they were recognized worldwide as Indian authors and poets and their works also had Indian nationalistic messages. One such famous Bengali intellectual was Rabindranath Tagore who won the Nobel Prize for literature in 1919 and was then the first Indian to win this prestigious prize. Mahatma Gandhi who became the leader of the Indian National Congress in 1920 did not always lead the Congress. Sometimes he was arrested and was therefore completely disconnected from nationalist movement.

At other times he severed from nationalist movement for other causes. In the early 1930s he resigned from the Congress leadership because of criticism from other Congress leaders. One of Gandhi's rivals within the Congress was Subhas Chandra Bose who won the Congress leadership in 1939 but resigned because he did not get Gandhi's political support. Subhas Chandra Bose was wanted by the British but escaped to Germany. In 1943 he arrived in Japan and with Japanese help established in Singapore 'Free India' government and the Indian National Army whose soldiers were Indians who lived in East Asia and also Indian defectors from the British army. And so he gave the Indians a feeling that they to were capable of creating their own army by themselves. During the Second World War this army penetrated east India and attacked British posts. But this army did not have major successes because of logistics reasons.

Another rival of Gandhi who had a lot of respect in India was Vinayek Savarkar. Savarkar supported violent acts against the British. Many of his supporters claim that the main reason the British left India wasn't the struggle organized by the Indian National Congress but the violent terrorist acts organized by people like Savarkar. Many of his supporters claim that his role in India's freedom struggle has not been given the right respect because of his anti-Gandhi slogans and because the assassin of Mahatma Gandhi was his close associate.

In 1939 the Second World War began which lasted until 1945. The British requested support from the Indian leadership. The Congress leaders demanded that against their support for the British, the British in return would give them independence. While at the same time the Muslim League gave clear supportive statements towards the British. The Congress did not only clearly not supported the British, they even started a new non-cooperative stage in their struggle for independence. This stage is called in Indian history as 'Quit India' movement. In this movement the Indians again used the technique of nonviolent non-cooperation. Because of this movement all of the Congress leadership got arrested and remained behind bars until the end of the war. During the 'Quit India' movement Muslim League leaders advised the Muslims in India not to take part in this movement. Many believe that because of the Congress leaders and Muslim League leaders stand during the war the British became more supportive of the Muslim stands compared to the Congress stands.

In 1945 the war was over. The Allied forces, of which the British were part of, won in this war. In that year elections occurred in England. The Labour Party claimed it was time to end the British Empire. In these elections the Labour Party won and it became clear that the British would leave India. At this stage different communities in India began demanding from the British to establish in India a state or states according to their political philosophies. And so the final road towards the creation of India began.

2

The Foundation of the Indian National Congress

Legacy of National Movement with Reference to Development, Rights and Participation

The developmental aspirations of the people of India unfolded themselves through the various stages of the freedom movement. The violent resistance of the Indian people to the British rule in 1857 and the subsequent tribal upsurges were defensive movements against foreign rule. They were almost totally political. But the peasant struggles that occurred since the late nineteenth century had a clear economic perspective. They were against the oppressive land revenue system that came along with foreign rule even though the peasants were not always aware of the colonial mechanism and they often turned their wrath on the intermediate landowners like the zamindars and mouzadars. After the consolidation of the British rule in 1858, new organisations and movements of the people came to the fore choosing 'constitutionalist' strategies. Landlords formed their own organisations to demand reduction of Government revenue claims.

Simultaneously nationalist leaders like Dadabhai Naoroji, M.G. Ranade and R.C. Dutt started critiquing the colonial economic exploitation. They argued that the main reason of poverty in India was the colonial exploitation. The end of colonial rule was necessary for the alleviation poverty in India.

Foundation of The Indian National Congress

In 1885 the educated elite formed the Indian National Congress as an umbrella organisation of all sections of the Indian people beginning with the demand for adequate representation of the Indians in the senior Government services and the legislative bodies created by the Indian Councils Act of 1861. Indeed, initially they did not take up the cause of the workers and peasants considering them as 'local issues.' But individual nationalists were engaged in 'philanthropic works' among the workers and the peasants.

The Indian National Congress was founded with a modest constitutionalist outlook and chose the strategy of petitions and persuasion rather than pressure and agitation. The earliest plea that it made to the Government was for the facilitation of the Indians' access to the Indian civil service which indeed was an elitist demand. On the other hand, the organisation declined to take up the issue of the condition of plantation and industrial labour which appeared to it to be 'local' issues even though philanthropists and labour leaders were given platform. In 1893 the Congress demanded the uniform introduction of permanent settlement of land to save the landholders from harassment by the Government.

As early as 1895 Dr. Annie Besant, founder of the Indian Home Rule League and a leader of the Indian National Congress, drafted a Constitution of India Bill envisaging a Constitution that guaranteed to every citizen freedom of expression, inviolability of one's house, right to property, equality before the law and in regard to admission to public offices, right to present claims, petition and complaints and the right to personal property. At a special session at Bombay in 1918 on the Montague-Chelmsford Report, the Congress demanded that the new Government of India Act contain a declaration of the rights of the Indians containing, among other things, equality before the law, protection in respect of liberty, life and property, freedom of speech and press and right of association.

In 1925 a sub-committee set up by the All-Parties Conference chaired by M.K. Gandhi prepared a Commonwealth of India Bill that demanded self-government for Indians from the village upwards – the village, the taluka, the district, the province and India. It also demanded the rights to liberty, security of dwelling and property, freedom of conscience and to profess and practise religion, freedom to express opinion, to assemble peacefully and without arms and to form associations or unions, free elementary education, use of roads, public places, courts of justice and the like, equality before the law irrespective of nationality and freedom of the sexes.

The Motilal Nehru Committee Report of 1928 incorporated all these demands and added the right of all citizens to the writ of *habeas corpus'* protection in respect of punishment under *ex post facto laws*, non-discrimination against any person on grounds of race, religion or creed in the matter of public employment, office of power or honour and in the exercise of any trade or calling, equal access of all citizens to public road, public wells and places of public resort, freedom of combination and association for the maintenance and improvement of labour and economic conditions and the right to keep arms in accordance with regulations. It will be seen that, although the above demands had certain economic implications, the demands were essentially political and elitist. It was not until the appearance in the scene of Gandhi that the socioeconomic problems of the common people came to focus. Gandhi brought the common people into national politics. He had to reflect their aspirations.

Congress & The Freedom Movement

Birth of the Congress

The 1857 revolt was suppressed. The British Empire in India was saved. Queen Victoria was proclaimed Empress of India and the new policy was ushered in. It was even more reactionary and in the long run proved very harmful. The native princes were now to be used as British tools and propped as bulwark against forces of resistance and progress. Government was no longer to encourage social reform. The benign rule was thus to carefully preserve decaying aristocracies, superstition and warring dogmas and cults. These were to provide the pattern for British imperialism with its foundations laid deep in the religious differences, caste and untouchabilitly and the feudal states and the aristocracy.

Economic and Political Discontent

The policy of economic exploitation, however, became even worse though more subtle. Mass unrest was the inevitable result of the ever growing poverty and helplessness of the peasantry. The common people, Hindus and Muslims, struggled against the terrible oppression, wherever they could and with whatever weapons they could muster. There was a new English educated class which was used to run the Government machinery. I was great admirer of everything Western which lent its support to the Government.

The belief of the educated classes in the English tradition of liberal thought and institutions received setbacks as a result of various Government measures. The Freedom of the press, introduced earlier by Metcalfe, was soon done away with. The vernacular Press was gagged in 1878 and the Bengali *Amrita Bazar Patrika* had to change overnight into an English garb.·The Arms Act was passed in 1879. This disillusionment advanced further when the *Illbert* Bill to abolish "Judicial discrimination, based on racial distinction" had to be virtually dropped on account of fierce opposition by the European community and the Civil Service. The Europeans did not hesitate to threaten the Viceroy, Lord Ripon, with violence if the Bill was passed. Indians learned the lesson at this time. In 1853 the first Cotton Mill was established in Bombay. The number of mills rose to 156 by 1880. This was an alarming progress and under pressure of Lancashire, all duties on cotton imports into India were removed in 1882.

Social Renaissance

It was not merely the economic exploitation and the sense of political subjection that gave birth to the Congress. For fifty years and more before the birth of the Congress, the leaven of national rejuvenation had been at work. In fact national life was in a state of ferment as early as in the times of *Rammohan Roy,* who could in a way be regarded as the prophet of Indian Nationalism and the father of modern India. He had a wide vision and a broad outlook. While it is true that the socio-religious condition of his day was the subject of his special attention in his reformist activities, he had nevertheless a keen sense of the grave political wrongs by which his country was afflicted at that time and made a strenuous effort to seek an early redress of those wrongs. Rammohan Roy was born in 1776 and passed away at Bristol in 1833. His name is associated with two great reforms in India, namely, the abolition of Sati and the introduction of Western learning in the country. In the closing period of his life he chose to visit England and his passion for liberty was so great that when he reached the Cape of Good Hope he insisted on his being carried to a French vessel where he saw the flag of liberty flying, so that he might be able to do homage to that flag, and when he saw the flag he shouted, "Glory, Glory, Glory to the Flag." Although he had gone to England primarily as the ambassador of the Mughal Emperor to plead his cause in London, yet he took the opportunity to place some of the pressing Indian grievances before a Committee of the House of Commons. He submitted three papers, on the Revenue system of India, the Judicial system of India, and the Material condition of India. He was honoured by the East India Company with a public dinner. When in 1832 the Charter Act was before Parliament he vowed that if the Bill was not passed he would give up his residence in the British dominion and reside in America.

The Universities were established in 1858 and the High Courts and the Legislative Councils in India between 1861 and 1863. Just before the "mutiny", the "Widow Re-marriage Act" was passed as also the Act relating to conversion into Christianity. In the sixties of the nineteenth century, an intimate contact was established with Western learning -and literature. Western legal institutions and Parliamentary methods were inaugurated, to mark a new era in the field of law and legislation. The impact of Western civilization on the East could not but leave a deep impress upon the beliefs and sentiments of the Indian people who came directly under its influence. The only parts of the country which had received some education on modem lines were the provinces of Bengal, Bombay and Madras. The number of educated men even in these provinces was small. In the work of settlement that followed the mutiny, these educated men found ample scope for their ambition. These races of *Babus* began to think like their English masters, admired and emulated everything that came from the West.

Soon, however, there was a reaction against this process of denationalisation which assumed various forms, some of a synthesis of the West and the East and others of a revivalism going to the past.

Brahmo Samaj & Prarthana Samaj

The germs of religious reform planted in the days of Rammohan Roy became widespread. Keshab Chandra Sen on whose shoulders fell the mantle of Rammohan Roy spread the gospel of the Brahmo Samaj far and wide and gave a new social orientation to its tenets. He turned his attention to the temperance movement and made common cause with the temperance reformers in England. He was largely responsible for the passing of the Civil Marriage Act III of 1872.

The Brahmo Samaj of Bengal had its repercussions all over the country. In Poona, the movement assumed the name of *Prarthana Samaj* under the leadership of M. G. Ranade, who, it will be remembered was the founder of the Social Reform movement which for long years continued to be an adjunct of the Congress. One feature, however, to this reformist movement was a certain disregard for the past and a spirit of revolt from the time-honoured and traditional beliefs of the country, which arose from an undue glamour presented by the Western institutions and heightened greatly by the political prestige associated with them.

Arya Samaj

The *Arya Samaj* in the North-West founded by the venerable *Swami Dayananda Saraswati,* and the Theosophical movement from the South furnished the necessary corrective to the spirit of heterodoxy and even heresy which the Western learning brought with it. Both of them were intensely nationalistic movements, only the Arya Samaj movement which owed its birth to the inspiration of the great Dayananda Saraswati was aggressive in its patriotic zeal, and while holding fast to the cult of the infallibility of the Vedas and the superiority of and the infallibility of the Vedic culture was at the same time not inimical to broad social reform. It thus developed a virile manhood in the Nation which was the synthesis of what is best in its heredity, with what is best in its environment. It fought some of the prevailing social evils and religious superstitions in Hinduism as much as the Brahmo Samaj had battle against polytheism, idolatry and polygamy.

Ramakrishna Mission

The latest phase of national renaissance in India prior to the Congress was inaugurated in Bengal by that great sage, *Ramakrishna Paramahansa,* who later found in Swami Vivekananda his chief apostle carrying his gospel to East and West. The Ramakrishna Mission is not merely an organisation wedded to occultism or realism, but to a profound transcendentalism which, however, docs not ignore the supreme duty of "Loke-Sangraha" or social service. This "Cyclonic Hindu", as *Vivekananda* was called in America, carried the message of India not only to America or Europe, Egypt, China and Japan but was himself influenced greatly by the West and preached a dynamic new gospel of regeneration in India, from Cape Comorin to the Himalayas. He stressed on the necessity for liberty and equality and the raising of the masses. He wanted to combine the Western progress with Indian spiritual background. The one constant refrain of his speech and writing was *Abhay* "Be fearless, be strong for weakness is sin, weakness is death."

A contemporary of Vivekananda and yet belonging to a much more later generation was *Rabindranath Tagore*. The Tagore family played a great part in various reform movements during the 19th Century in Bengal. It gave us Abhindranath Tagore and others, great spiritual leaders and artists. The influence of Tagore over the mind of India and the stamp that he has left in the domain of literature, poetry, drama, music, social and educational reconstruction and political thought is unsurpassed in its beauty and depth. It is a marvel of human personality and mind affecting and giving colour to successive generations. The contribution of Tag ore has been of a synthesis of the East and West, of the modern and the ancient and of the international with the rising national tide in the country.

These currents and movements were the real lifeblood of the new national consciousness, urge and their embodiment that took shape partly and developed from stage to stage in the form of the Indian National Congress.

The Idea of an All-India Organisation

The credit for the birth of the Congress is often sought to be given to *Alan Octavian Hume,* who with the blessings of the Viceroy, Lord Dufferin, inaugurated it. The British are thus said to be the foster parents of the Indian nationalism. It is true that Hume was the organiser of the Congress Session in 1885. But it will be seen that the Congress was the natural and inevitable production of various political, economic and social forces.

The more alert among the English administrators were not unaware of the rising unrest in the country. "A reckless bureaucratic Government sat at this time trembling upon the crumbling fragments of a mendacious budget on the one side and the seething and surging discontent of multitudinous population on the other". Mr. Hume collected widespread evidence of the imminence of a "terrible revolution" by the half-starved and desperate population and set about to find ways and means of directing the popular impulse into an innocuous channel.

He wrote a letter to "Graduates of Calcutta University" on March 1, 1883 and the "Indian National Union" was formed in 1884, in response to this, for constitutional agitation, on an all-India basis, and was to meet in Poona later. The Government who first patronised this organisation, however, found later that it outgrew their plans and the patronage was soon withdrawn. It came to be called the 'factory of sedition' in a few years and later Lord Dufferin, himself tried to twit it as a body representing "microscopic minority" of India's population.

There were various provincial political organisations that preceded the Congress. In Bengal which was at the vanguard of progress at this time, in 1843 was founded the British Indian Society to be merged later into the British Indian Association. This body had such stalwarts as Rajendralal Mitra, Ramgopal Ghosh, Peary Chand Mitter and Harish Chandra Mukherjee. In Bombay there was the Bombay Association with Jaggannath Sankerset, Dadabhai Naoroji, V. N. Mandlik and Nowrosjee Furdunjee.

Later, more popular bodies, the Indian Association in Bengal and Sarvajanika Sabha in Poona, under Ranade and Mahajana Sabha in Madras were established. Surendranath Bannerjee went on an all India tour in 1877 and succeeding years and carried a campaign about Indian Home Rule and the political questions of the day. He attended the Delhi Durbar that year, and the idea of an all-India political organisation was mooted there.

In December 1884, the Annual Convention of the Theosophical Society was held at Madras and there some leading public men met and decided to inaugurate an all-India national movement.

Thus, the ground was well prepared for the Government to take the initiative and the credit of forming the National Congress and keep it under control.

3

Early Phase of the Congress

The Indian National movement was primarily a movement for freedom from alien domina--nation. The movement has been one comprehensive effort embracing all aspects of the life of the community.

The birth of the Indian National Congress, perhaps the oldest and the biggest democratic organisation in the world, did not take place in an atmosphere of a fanfare of trumpets nor did it create a stir by passing flamboyant resolutions.

Hume's Initiative

In 1884, at the annual convention of the Theosophical Society at Adyar in Madras, Mr. Allan Octavian Hume laid bare to his friends his plan to organise the Congress. A committee was formed to make the necessary prepara-tions for a session at Poona to be held in 1885.

The committee consisted of Mr. Hume, Mr. Surendranath Bannerji, Mr. Narendranath Sen, Mr. S. Subramania Iyer, Mr. P. Ananda Charlu, Mr. V. N. Mandalik, Mr. K. T. Telag, Sardar Dayal Singh, Lala Sri Ram.

Mr. Hume, still a government servant, addressed an open letter to the graduates of Calcutta University with a fervent appeal for self help.

He said: "and if even the leaders of thought are all either such poor creatures, or so selfishly wedded to personal concern, that they dare not strike a blow for their country's sake, then justly and rightly they are kept down and trampled on, for they deserve nothing better. Every nation secures precisely as good a government as it merits. If you the picked men, the most highly educated of the nation cannot, scorning personal ease and selfish objects, make a resolute struggle to secure greater freedom for yourselves and your country, a more impartial administration, a larger share in the management of your own affairs then we, your friends arc wrong and our adversaries right, then Lord Rippon's noble aspirations for your good are fruitless and visionary, then at present at any rate, all hopes of progress are at an end, and India truly neither lacks nor deserves any better government than she enjoys.

"Only if this be so, let us hear no more factious, peevish complaints that you are kept in strings and treated like children, for you will have proved yourself such. Men know how to act. Let there be no more complaints of Englishmen being preferred to you in all important offices, for if you lack that public spirit, that highest form of altruistic devotion that leads men to subordinate private ease to the public weal that patriotism that has made Englishmen what they are-then rightly are these preferred to you, rightly and inevitably have they become your rulers. And rulers and task masters they must continue, let the yoke gall your shoulders never so sorely, until you realise and stand prepared to act upon the eternal truth that self-sacrifice and unselfishness are the only unfailing guide to freedom and happiness."

The First Session

The first session of the Congress was to meet at Poona but owing to an outbreak of cholera the venue was shifted to Bombay and the session began on the 28th December, 1885, with Mr. W. C. Bannerjee, the doyen of the Calcutta Bar in the chair, though originally, it had been decided to request Lord Reay, Governor of Bombay, to be the first President of the Indian National Congress but the idea had to be dropped as the Governor was advised by the Viceroy not to accept the offer. 72 delegates came from different parts of the country and most important among them were Dadabhai Naoroji, Ranade, Pherozeshah Mehta, K. T. Telang, Dinshaw Wacha, etc. The meeting was truly a national gathering consisting of leading men from all parts of India.

The president defined the objective of the Congress as "promotion of personal intimacy and friendship among all the more earnest workers in our country's cause in the parts of the empire and eradication of race, creed or provincial prejudice and fuller development of national unity." In its early sessions, the Congress Organisation, by and large, limited its activities only to debates.

After the Madras Session in 1887, an aggressive propaganda was started among the masses. Hume published a pamphlet entitled "An Old Man's Hope" in which he appealed to the people of England in these words: "Ah men, well-fed and happy, do you at all realise the dull misery of these countless myriads? From their births to their deaths, how many rays of sunshine think you chequer their gloom-shrouded paths? Toil, toil, toil; hunger, hunger, hunger, sickness, suffering, sorrow; these alas, alas, alas are the keynotes of their short and sad existence."

In December 1889, the Congress Session was held at Bombay under the Presidentship of Sir William Wedderburn. It was attended by Charles Bradlaugh, a member of British Parliament. He addressed the Congress in these words; "For whom should I work if not for the people? Born of the people, trusted by the people, I will die for the people, and I know no geographical or race limitation."

Dadabhai Naoroji was re-elected as the President of the Lahore Session of the Congress held in December 1893, His journey from Bombay to Lahore presented the spectacle of a procession, and Citizens at various places on the way presented him addresses. At the Golden Temple at Amritsar, he was given a robe of honour. Addressing the audience at the Session, Dadabhai Naoraji declared: "Let us always remember that we are children of our mother country. Indeed, I have never worked in any other spirit than that I am an Indian and owe duty to my work and all my countrymen. Whether I am a Hindu or a Mohammedan, a Parsi, a Christian, or of any other creed, I am above all an Indian. Our country is India, our nationality is Indian."

The Moderates

The early Congressmen who dominated the affairs of the Indian National Congress from 1885 to 1905 were known as the Moderates. They belonged to a class which was Indian in blood and colour but British in tastes, in opinions, in morals and in intellect. They were supporters of British institutions. They believed that what India needed was a balanced and lucid presentation of her needs before the Englishmen and their Parliament. They had faith in the British sense of justice and fairplay. The Moderates believed in orderly progress and constitutional agitation. They believed in patience, steadiness, conciliation and union. To quote Surendarnath Banerjee, "The triumphs of liberty are not to be won in a day. Liberty is a jealous goddess, exacting in her worship and claiming from her votaries prolonged and assiduous devotion." In 1887, Badruddin Tyabji observed: "Be moderate in your demands, just in your criticism, correct in your facts and logical in your conclusions."

The Moderates believed in constitutional agitation within the four corners of law. They believed that their main task was to educate the people, to arouse national political consciousness and to create a united public, opinion on political questions. For this purpose they held meetings. They criticised the Government through the press. They drafted and submitted memorials and petitions to the Government, to the officials of the Government of India and also to the British Parliament. They also worked to influence the British Parliament and British public opinion. The object of the memorials and petitions was to enlighten the British public and political leaders about the conditions prevailing in India. Deputations of leading Indian leaders were sent to Britain in 1889. A British Committee of the Indian National Congress was founded in 1906 and that Committee started a journal called *India*. Dadabhai Naoroji spent a major part of his life and income in Britain doing propaganda among its people and politicians.

The object before the Moderates was "wide employment of Indians in higher offices in the public service and the establishment of representative institutions."

The economic and political demands of the Moderates were formulated with a view to unifying the Indian people on the basis of a common political programme. They organised a powerful all-India agitation against the abandonment of tariff-duties on imports and against the imposition of cotton excise duties. This agitation aroused the feelings of the people and helped them to realise the real aims and purposes of British rule in India. They urged the Government to provide cheap credit to the peasantry through agricultural banks and to make avail-able irrigation facilities on a large scale. They asked for improvement in the conditions of work of the plantation labourers, a radical change in the existing pattern of taxation and expenditure which put a heavy burden on the poor while leaving the rich, especially the foreigners, with a very light load. The Moderates complained of India's growing poverty and economic backwardness and put all the blame on the policies of the British Government. They criticised the individual administrative measures and worked hard to reform the administrative system.

The Moderates opposed tooth and nail the restrictions imposed by the Government on the freedom of speech and the press. In 1897, Tilak and many other leaders were arrested and sentenced to long terms of imprisonment for spreading disaffection against the Government through their speeches and writings. The Natu brothers of Poona were deported without trial. The arrest of Tilak marked the beginning of a new phase of the Nationalist movement. The *Amrita Bazar Patrika* wrote: "There is scarcely a home in this vast country where Tilak is not now the subject of melancholy talk and where his imprisonment is not considered as a domestic calamity."

The basic weakness of the Moderates lay in their narrow social base. Their movement did not have a wide appeal. The area of their influence was limited to the urban community. As they did not have the support of the masses, they declared that the time was not ripe for throwing out a challenge to the foreign rulers. To quote Gokhale, "You do not realise the enormous reserve of power behind the Government. If the Congress were to do anything such as you suggest, the Government would have no difficulty in throttling it in five minutes." However, it must not be presumed that the Moderate leaders fought for their narrow interests. Their pro-grammes and policies championed the cause of all sections of the Indian people and represented nation-wide interests against colonial exploitation. What they wanted was to reform or liberalise the existing system of government through peaceful, gradualist and constitutional means.

The influence of the moderates, however, declined with the rise of the militants who did not believe in gradualism and who criticized the moderates for their great faith in Britain and British political institutions.

Rise of Extremism

The moderates sought to make the provincial e legislatures more representative and to increase the Indian clement in the civil services, but the process was long and the progress slow. Repelled by the unsympathetic approach of the imperial bureaucracy and enraged by the unpopular policies of Lord Curzon, the Viceroy, and particularly his decision on the partition of Bengal, the youth of India moved towards militant politics and direct action. As a protest against the partition of Bengal (October 1905), the nationalists advocated the boycott of British goods".

In 1907, Bipin Pal made the paradoxical statement, that the "viceroyalty of Lord Curzon... had been one of the most beneficent if not decidedly the most beneficent viceroyalty that India ever had," for Curzon, by pursuing his unpopular policies, had made Indians so discontented that they demanded self-government with greater determination than ever before. Aurobindo similarly declared that he considered the partition of Bengal to be a most beneficial measure because, by arousing intense opposition among the people, that measure had stirred up and strengthened national feeling.

As a result of the growing disillusionment about the activities of the British rulers and as a reaction against Curzon's proposal for the partition of Bengal; there came into existence the extremist party which advocated a policy of boycott, *swadeshi* and national education. In January 1907, Tilak declared: "We are not armed, and there is no necessity of arms either. We have a stronger weapon, a political weapon in boycott." Tilak also said: "When you prefer to accept *swadeshi.* You must boycott *videshi* (foreign) goods. Without boycott, *swadeshi* cannot flourish."

Aurobindo, Tilak, and Pal asked the people not to cooperate with the government. The basic theory of Tilak, Aurobindo and Pal, which was later put into operation on a mass scale by Mahatma Gandhi, was that as the existence of the Government depended on the cooperation of the people, the Government would cease to function or to exist the very day the people withdrew their co-operation from it.

With the rise of the militant movement the glamour of England and English institutions began to fade and English influence increasingly came to be replaced by the influence emanating primarily from the indigenous sources as also from the European literature or revolt. The study of British constitutional history had generated among the moderates a love for and faith in Dominion

Status. But such stories as how the Italians had driven the Austrians out of their land gave militant nationalists a new conception and in fact a new ideal of complete independence. Self-government under British paramountcy had been the goal of the moderate school, but the ideal of the extremist or militant school was complete autonomy and elimination of all foreign control.

Bal Gangadhar Tilak (1856-1920) and other extremist leaders, who wanted to adopt a policy of direct act and passive resistance, denounced what they called "the political mendicancy" of the moderates. During the anti partition agitation, in the first decade of the twentieth century, Tilak wrote: "The time has come to demand *Swaraj* or self-Government. No piecemeal reform will do. The system of the present administration is ruinous to the country. It must mend or end." According to him Swaraj was the birthright of every Indian.

"The term *Swaraj*," said Bipin Pal (1858-1932), another exremist leader, was not merely a political but primarily a moral concept. "The corresponding term in our language," he said, "is not non-subjection which would be a literal rendering of the English word independence, but self-subjection which is a positive concept. Self--subjection means.... complete identification of the individual with the universal."

Another Swarajist leader who, like Tilak, spoke of the ideal of *Swaraj*, was Aurobindo Ghose (1872-1950). "We of the new school, "he said, "would not pitch our ideal one inch lower than absolute *Swaraj*-Self-Government as it exists in the United Kingdom." And he added, "We reject the claim of aliens to force upon us a civilisation inferior to our own or keep us out of our inheritance on the untenable ground of a superior fitness."

Lajpat Rai (1865-1928), along with Bal Gangadhar Tilak and Bipin Pal, constituted the *swarajist* triumvirate called "Lal-Bal-Pal". Lajpat, like the other extremists, believed that India must rely on her own strength and should not look to Britain for help.

The *swarajist* said that however much Britain's rule might be improved or liberalised, it could never be as beneficial to Indians as the self-rule. Their attitude was the same as that of the Irish Sinn Fein leader Arthur Griffith, who had said: ".... In those who talk of ending British misgovernment we see the helots. It is not British misgovernment, but British government in Ireland, good or bad, we stand opposed to." The *swarajists* accordingly considered that freedom was their birthright.

The Surat Split

In 1907, there was a split in the Congress and the Moderates parted company with the Extremists. That split was due to many causes. The moderates had controlled the Congress from its very beginning and even now they were in control of it. They had their own ways of thinking and doing which were not acceptable to the younger generation who were impatient with the speed at which the Moderates were moving and leading the nation. Under the circumstances, a confrontation between the two was inevitable and that actually happened in 1907.

The seeds of the split could be traced to the Calculla Session in 1906, where the Moderates had accepted the resolutions on *Swaraj*, national education, boycott and *Swadeshi* on account of the pressure brought on them from all quarters. In their hearts, they had not accepted the new resolutions. Their fear was that the growing pace of the national struggle might lead to lawlessness and that would provide the British with an excuse to deny the reforms on the one hand and to crush all political activity on the other. They had no self-confidence. They did not believe that sustained and dignified national struggle was possible and desirable. They considered the Extremists irresponsible persons who were likely to put in danger the future of the country. The British Government also tried to win over the Moderates against the Extremists. While the Extremists were roughly handled by the Government, the Moderates were shown all the favours. Lala Lajpat Rai, Sardar Ajit Singh, Tilak and many leaders of Bengal were deported.

The break-up of the Surat Congress was no doubt an unpleasant affair. It marked a direct open breach between the Moderates and the Nationalist panics not only in Maharashtra but throughout India. For the first time in the history of the Congress, there was at Surat an open light between the delegates of the congress and some blood was drawn. But it did not stop at that. The split led to a cleavage in the sense that the name of the Indian National Congress had to be kept in abeyance for the time and a new entity called the convention was installed in its place. Of course as the name itself implies, the Convention was a stop-gap expedient, intended to function in the place of the Congress only till such time as the national Congress could meet again in its old form. The old form had this peculiarity that there was not much ceremony observed in the election of the delegates to the Congress. There were no conditions of membership. There was no constitution as such for the Congress, no election of delegates. In fact the membership was open to anyone that might choose to attend the Congress session as a delegate. There was no competition as such in the election of the delegates for the simple reason that there was no numerical allotment fixed for any province. It was an open rally of all that chose to attend.

Tilak and his party were of course ousted from the Convention because they would not sign a prescribed creed of political faith, which practically excluded the ideal of independence, if only an ideal so far. The Convention and, the Nationalist party met in two separate camps at Surat. It must be noted here that even with this definite split in the Congress each party duly affirmed its love for the Congress which alone was regarded as the true national Assembly for the country and in both the camps the hope was expressed that sooner or later there might again be held a Congress united as before.

Nobody could openly allege the break-up of the Congress as a criminal offence, but the split was taken into consideration by the government as an open challenge to the policy of constitutional agitation. After Tilak's conviction by the High Court, the National party led by him became sullen and almost went underground. For six years, from 1908 to 1914, the Nationalist Party could not decide as to what it should do about entering the Congress. There was an attempt made to call a meeting of a rival Congress at Nagpur. But while government banned the session, there was also want of unanimity in the party itself about the starting of a rival Congress which might make the split absolutely permanent. The cooler wings in the Party thought that there was no wisdom in setting up a rival to the old Congress as without unity among political parties the show as presented by separate parties was bound to be poor. A group within the Tilak Party was trying to negotiate matters with the leaders of the Moderate party for making the entry of this group and others of its persuasion into the Congress on its own terms, that is to say, without the restriction of a creed and with the old facilities for unfettered election of delegates. But the other view was more insistent and prevailed, namely, that nothing should be done in this matter until Tilak returned from Mandalay.

Allan Octavian Hume

Events like the passage of the Vernacular Press Act in 1878 and the Ilbert Bill of 1882, as well as the reduction of the age limit for the Civil Services Exams in 1876 resulted in a wave of opposition from the middle class Indians. Consequently some of them came together and formed a number of small political parties that came out in the streets for protests and rallies. The British foresaw the situation resulting in another rebellion on the pattern of the War of Independence of 1857.

To avoid such a situation, the British decided to provide an outlet to the local people where they could discuss their political problems. In order to achieve this goal, Allan Octavian Hume, a retired British civil servant, had a series of meetings with Lord Dufferin, the Viceroy. He also visited England and met people like John Bright, Sir James Caird, Lord Ripon and some members of the British Parliament. Hume also had the support of a large number of Englishmen in India, including Sir William Wedderbun, George Yule and Charles Bradlaugh.

On his return from Britain, Hume consulted the local Indian leaders and started working towards the establishment of an Indian political organization. He invited the convention of the Indian National Union, an organization he had already formed in 1884, to Bombay in December 1885. Seventy delegates, most of whom were lawyers, educationalists and journalists, attended the convention in which the Indian National Congress was established. This first session of Congress was presided over by Womesh Chandra Banerjee and he was also elected as the first president of the organization.

The Indian national flag was derived from the flag of Congress.

To begin with, Congress acted as a 'Kings Party'. Its early aims and objectives were:

1. To seek the cooperation of all the Indians in its efforts.
2. Eradicate the concepts of race, creed and provincial prejudices and try to form national unity.
3. Discuss and solve the social problems of the country.

4. To request the government, give more share to the locals in administrative affairs.

As time went by, the Congress changed its stance and apparently became the biggest opposition to the British government.

Muslims primarily opposed the creation of Congress and refused to participate in its activities. Out of the 70 delegates who attended the opening session of the Congress, only two were Muslims. Sir Syed Ahmad Khan, who was invited to attend the Bombay session, refused the offer. He also urged the Muslims to abstain from the Congress activities and predicted that the party would eventually become a Hindu party and would only look after the interests of the Hindus. Syed Ameer Ali, another important Muslim figure of the era, also refused to join Indian National Congress.

Indian National Congress Objective and Programme

The Indian National Congress was founded in the year 1885. The first session of Congress was presided over by Womesh Chandra Banerjee who was also elected as the first president of Indian National Congress party. Around seventy reputed delegates that included educationalists, lawyers, journalists etc. attended the first session of the congress when it was established. The Indian national congress was considered to be a royal party when it was established. Read on about the history of Indian National Congress.

The Indian National Congress had the following aims and objectives when it was established:

- Inculcate a feeling of national unity and try to eradicate the notion of race, creed and provincial prejudices.
- Seek the cooperation of all the Indians in its efforts and allow them to take part in the administrative affairs of the country.
- Find a solution to the social problems of the country.

The Indian National Congress had a royal air about it which faded as time passed by.

Though the Congress was made to improve India, the Muslims were opposed to the party. Muslim leaders like Sir Syed Ahmed Khan and Syed Ameer Ali got invitation to attend the conference when congress party was established but they refused. They also told other Muslims to abstain from joining the party. He predicted that Congress would become a party dominated by the Hindus. The Congress party was broadly divided among two types of members-the conservatives and the leftists. The former had a cautious approach towards the policies while the latter were more into socialism. During the moderate phase of the congress they were extremely loyal to the British but with time the party entered the extremist phase and expressed its displeasure in the policies of the British.

Indian National Movement

The East India Company had established its control over almost all parts of India by the middle of the 19th century. There were numerous risings in the first hundred years of British rule in India. They were, however, local and isolated in character. Some of them were led by the nobility who were refusing to accept the changing patterns of the time and wanted the past to be restored. But the risings developed a tradition of resistance offoreign rule, culminating in the 1857 revolt.

The Revolt of 1857, which was called a Sepoy Mutiny by British historians and their imitators in India but described as "the First War of Indian Independence" by many Indian historians, shook the British authority in India from its very foundations.

The Revolt of 1857, an unsuccessful but heroic effort to eliminate foreign rule, had begun. The capture of Delhi and the proclamation of Bahadurshah as the Emperor of Hindustan are a positive meaning to the Revolt and provided a rallying point for the rebels by recalling the past glory of the imperial city.

On May 10, 1857, soldiers at Meerut refused to touch the new Enfield rifle cartridges. The soldiers along with other group of civilians, went on a rampage shouting 'Maro Firangi Ko'. They broke open jails, murdered European men and women, burnt their houses and marched to Delhi. The appearance of the marching soldiers next morning in Delhi was a'signal to the local soldiers, who in turn revolted, seized the city and proclaimed the 80-year old Bahadurshah Zafar, as Emperor of India.

Within a month of the capture of Delhi, the Revolt spread to the different parts of the country. Kanpur, Lucknow, Benaras,

Allahabad, Bareilly, Jagdishpur and Jhansi. In the absence of any leader from their own ranks, the insurgents turned to the traditional leaders of Indian society. At Kanpur, NanaSaheb, the adopted son of last Peshwa, Baji Rao II, led the forces. Rani Lakshmi Bai in Jhansi, Begum Hazrat Mahal in Lucknow and. Khan Bahadur in Bareilly were in command. However, apart from a commonly shared hatred for alien rule, the rebels had no political perspective or a definite vision of the future. They were all prisoners of their own past, fighting primarily to regain their lost privileges. Unsurprisingly, they proved incapable of ushering in a new political order.

Government of India Act 1858

Queen Victoria issued a proclamation on November 1, 1858, placing India under direct government of the Crown, whereby:

(a) A viceroy was appointed in India
(b) Princes were given the right to adopt a son (abolition of Doctrine of Lapse)
(c) Treaties were honoured
(d) Religious freedom was restored and equality treatment promised to Indians.

The Proclamation was called the 'Magna Carta of Indian Liberty'. The British rule in India was strongest between 1858 and 1905. The British also started treating India as its most precious possession and their rule over India seemed set to continue for centuries to come. Because of various subjective and objective factors which came into existence during this era, the feeling of nationalism in Indians started and grow.

Partition of Bengal (1905)

On December 30, 1898, Lord Curzon took over as the new Viceroy of India. The partition of Bengal came into effect on October 16, 1905, through a Royal Proclamation, reducing the old province of Bengal in size by creating a new province of East Bengal, which later on became East Pakistan and present day Bangladesh. The government explained that it was done to stimulate growth of underdeveloped eastern region of the Bengal. But, actually, the main objective was to 'Divide and Rule' the most advanced region of the country at that time.

The Social Composition of Early Congress Leadership Moderates and Extremists

Pressures of Loyalism During British Rule

As has been noted by several historians of British-ruled India, the numerical presence of the British in colonized India was never very significant. Yet, the British were able to maintain a vast and stable empire in the Indian subcontinent for almost two centuries. They were able to recklessly exploit India's natural resources and drain the wealth of it's citizens through the imposition of excessive and unreasonable taxes-all without unmanageable challenges to their political authority during much of their debilitating reign.

Although there is no doubt that physical violence (including torture) were important elements of British domination in India, equally important were the successes of political strategies that took full advantage of rivalries amongst native rulers and cynically exploited divisions arising from caste, religion, class and other sectarian loyalties. Not only were the British able to garner the loyalty or acquiescence of the Indian Maharajas and other elements of the decadent feudal aristocracy, they were also able to command the support of influential sections of the British-educated new urban intelligentsia whose loyalty to the colonial empire remained unquestioned even as nationalist feelings and nationalist currents emerged with greater or lesser intensity after the defeat of 1858. Moneylenders and the landed gentry were particularly reliable allies of the British, and the new industrial class, though critical of British policies, was invariably constrained by it's conservatism in opposing British rule.

Thus, *loyalism* became a powerful political trend in British India that either countered nationalist forces outright, or attempted to diffuse their impact and efficacy through calls for political moderation, non-violence and tactical restraint. Loyalist forces made frequent and fervent appeals to the Indian masses to be patient with the British, to be content with the slow pace of political reforms, and to be grateful for minor concessions concerning self-rule. Those who demanded a more radical and confrontationist approach with the British (such as Tilak) were branded as "extremists" and dismissed as unrealistic or utopian radicals.

Rooted amongst sections of the Indian elite that feared the power of the restive masses, loyalism was not only a strong political force in Indian territories directly ruled by the British, but also had a profound impact on Princely India. Recognizing their importance, British administrators feted loyalist elements, rewarding them in accordance with their contribution to the stability of the Raj. In the decades that followed the 1857 uprising, loyalism showed up in a variety of forms (moderate or extreme), and the most anti-national of the loyalist tendencies served as a bulwark against all attempts at overthrowing or even diluting British authority in India. Not only did such elements collaborate dutifully in facilitating the sustained transfer of wealth from India to England, in their aggressively loyalist propaganda, they matched or even outdid colonial attacks on nationalist currents, spreading dis-information against even those that were politically quite moderate, and essentially reconciled to alien rule.

An archetype of such loyalist agents was Sir Salar Jung, (b, 1829, Prime Minister of the Princely State of Hyderabad in 1853), who wrote and spoke of the 1857 Mutiny with great hatred, and successfully employed Arab mercenaries on behalf of the British Resident, Colonel Davidson, in fending off mutineers in the Deccan kingdom. Leaders of the mutiny were shot dead or publicly executed. Local residents who attempted to plead on behalf of the mutinous soldiers were dispersed with canon fire.

Like elsewhere in the country, the 1857 rebellion enjoyed considerable popular appeal in the Nizam's kingdom, and in Hyderabad, there was a clamor for war against the British. In one of his briefs in praise of British General Thornhill, Salar Jung acknowledged that Hyderabad was seeped in disaffection with the British, and seeing the grave danger to British rule, acted quickly to fend off the challenges to British colonial presence. His timely and brutal actions in suppressing the mutineers was of crucial import and was duly acknowledged by Sir Richard Temple who described as *"priceless"*, his services to the British Government.

But Salar Jung was not alone in his opposition to the 1857 rebellion, which essentially took on the character of India's first War of Independence. When the troops of Indore and Mho rebelled and joined the 1857 war against the British, the Holkar Raja felt compelled to apologize to the British for the behaviour of the troops under his command, and sought to affirm his loyalty to the British in no uncertain terms. Troops in Tonk, Kota, Gwalior,

Bhopal and Bharatpur also rebelled, but their rulers remained staunchly loyal to British interests.

Even former-rulers such as Nagpur's Rani Bakabai (whose Bhosle royal clan had been earlier humiliated by the British) nevertheless threatened potential mutineers in her territory with dire consequences. Following Nagpur's annexation, the British had confiscated almost the entire Bhosle treasury, transferring 136 bags of precious metals and jewels, and other cultural valuables, to British vaults. Palace animals were auctioned off, and much of the remaining personal jewelry of the Bhosle queens was auctioned off in Calcutta. However, Rani Bakabai and other senior royals were provided a pension, and this proved sufficient to buy their loyalty.

Inspired by the rebellions in other cities-(such as at Meerut, Delhi, Lucknow, Kanpur, Sagar and Jhansi), an iregular unit at Takli near Nagpur had rebelled, but other units remained passive allowing the British to overcome the rebellion. Dildar Khan, Inayatulla Khan, Vilayat Khan and Nawab Kadar Khan of the irregular cavalry were tried and executed.

Although the masses of Nagpur were generally sympathetic to those who rebelled, the influence of the pro-British royals remained strong, and it was the pro-colonial orientation of many such Indian rulers that allowed the British to regain their confidence and regroup, and ultimately recover the territories they lost in 1857.

But even as the first Indian War of Independence came to a tragic and bitter end, the Princely States that had sided with the British, (or remained neutral) were to discover that the British were no less capable of undermining them. New and more aggressively loyalist agents were employed to weaken the independence and financial viability of the Princely States.

For instance, Sir T. Madhav Rao, (British appointed administrator of the state of Baroda) passed laws preventing the state from manufacturing or purchasing arms at will. He also pushed through laws increasing taxes on commodities of daily public use such as salt, and providing British manufacturers monopoly distribution rights. Additionally, Madhav Rao signed decrees requiring sizeable payments to the British for services that the state had no need of. Nepotism and corruption thrived in the

Madhav Rao administration, and locals who may have objected to (or resisted) laws and decrees that were inimical to the economic interests of the state were kept out. Loyalist like Madhav Rao thus became instrumental in driving the people of the state into utter helplessness and dire poverty.

Other loyalists were not as blatant, and attempted to couch their collaboration with the British administrators in a more reformist light. Sir Syed Ahmed (b. 1817) appointed a Member of the Public Service Commission by Lord Dufferin saw the British presence in India as "beneficial to the scientific modernization of the country", and saw British presence in the subcontinent as a "liberalizing" factor.

(Many others echoed such views, discounting the possibility that such advances could have very well been made by the Indian people themselves, under a political dispensation of their own choosing, and without the enormous economic drain caused by colonial rule. It is notable that countries such as Thailand, South Korea and Japan who escaped European colonization in Asia were able to adopt modern education systems and modern technology at a much faster pace than India).

In writing about the *"Causes of the Indian Revolt of 1857"*, Syed Ahmed wrote that the people of India had *"misunderstood"* the intentions of the British, and failed to comprehend the *"good points"* of the British rulers. When the Indian National Congress was launched with it's rather limited goals of ensuring greater representation for Indians in the colonial administration and gradual transformation towards home-rule within the empire, Syed Ahmed opposed the movement, and in an 1887 speech to the Mahomeddan Educational Conference, discouraged Indian Muslims from joining the Congress. Although he projected himself as a liberal and secular reformer, he opposed common electorates for all Indians, arguing for separate electorates and compartmental elections for Muslims and other non-Hindus. Though it appears from his speeches that his views were not motivated by consciously divisive or communal intent, the effects of his propagandizing sowed the seeds for the elaboration and development of the highly pernicious two-nation theory, and ultimately to the bloody partition of the Indian subcontinent. Only late in life, did he begin to realize that the British colonial rulers were incapable of treating Indians with equality. It was then that he came to recognize the value of a body such as the Congress and began to express serious doubts and reservations about the role of the British in India. But by then the damage had been done-in his public life, Syed Ahmed (like many others) had served British interests only too well.

Like Sir Ahmed, Sir Ali Imam, Sir Muhammad Shafi and Rahimatulla Mohammed Sayani (b.1847) were other prominent loyalists who played an important propagandist role in defending the empire. Lauded for his great services to the 'Raj' by Lord Harding, Ali Imam (who eventually became a judge in the Patna High Court) tried to obscure the contradictions between the Indian masses and the colonial administration by projecting Indian nationalism as being entirely compatible with loyalty to the British Sovereign and pride in the British Empire.

Muhammad Shafi attempted to argue that British and Indian interests were "similiar". Even as Shafi championed the cause of reforms in the British administration of India, he emphasized *"India's fidelity to the Empire"* adding that the empire was *"Our Common Heritage". "To my own countrymen I appeal with equal earnestness to recognize that our British fellow-subjects in India have as permanent an interest in her future well-being as ourselves, and are entitled to play, a leading part in her constitutional development. Let us realize that in their cooperation and good-will for India's regeneration lies our sure and certain success along the path of constitutional development. We too, should cast aside all distrust and, imbued with a feeling of mutual confidence, meet the British elements in this country more than half way. In union lies strength and with Indo-British union there is no height to which India may not rise."* (Quoted from the concluding portion of a series of articles published in the Civil and Military Gazette, Lahore-Eminent Mussalmans) .

The trend towards loyalism culminated in the persona of the Aga Khan (Sir Sultan Mhd. Shah, b. 1875, Karachi) who aggressively championed allegiance to the British in all it's war efforts (whether in Europe, South Africa or elsewhere), even stating that *"If they will only give me the opportunity, I will shed my last drop of blood for the British Empire".*

Continuing in the vein of Sir Syed Ahmed, the Aga Khan developed Muslim sectarian and separatist ideas much further by calling for the creation of the All India Muslim League as a political counter-weight and foil to the Congress. He also argued for the establishment of a University that would cater exclusively to the nation's Muslims. In deepening divisions between India's Hindus and Muslims, the Aga Khan could not have served the interests of the British Empire any better and was justly rewarded with great accolades in the British Press and royal circles.

However, not all eminent Muslims adopted a separatist approach. Badruddin Tyabji (b. 1844), who became President of the Indian National Congress in 1887 won the support of Indian industrialists when he argued against the abolition of import duties on cotton goods in 1879. A liberal reformer, he encouraged modern education for India's Muslims, and the lifting of *Purdah* for Muslim women when he became Secretary (and later President) of the Anjuman-i-Islam in Bombay in 1880. In 1883, he campaigned to seek equal rank for Indians employed in British-run Indian administrative services.

Tyabji was succeeded by Sir Pherozeshah Mehta (b. 1845) who headed the Congress in 1889. Like Tyabji, Pherozeshah Mehta also fought for equality for Indians in the colonial administration, and resisted European domination of the Indian University system, taking up the cudgels against Lord Curzon (who had won the editorial backing of the pro-colonial Times of India in his attempts at furthering the British domination of the Indian education system). Yet, Pherozeshah Mehta also repeatedly expressed his opposition to more radical nationalism and strived hard to keep the Congress on a loyalist track. The election of Mohd. Sayani (who had previously stayed aloof from the Congress) as President in 1896 underlined the loyalist hold on the Congress.

Sayani had been an ardent admirer of the British, and criticized those who distrusted their motives and presence in India. In a passionate speech defending the British presence in India, he argued that *"a more honest or steady nation does not exist under the sun than this English nation"*. At a time when India was reeling from famines induced by British policies in India, he defended British Rule, describing it as generally based on *"law and sympathy"*, and having given India *"peace"*. Sayani also harboured the illusion that English capital would modernize and industrialize India, and make Indians prosperous, but in fact, the Indian economy experienced zero growth in the first half of the 20th century, and the flow of capital from England to India was never more than a trickle. (Quotes taken from a speech delivered during discussion of the Financial Statement of 1898-99). But throughout this period, it was Pherozeshah Mehta who became the main rallying point for loyalists in the Congress. Mehta led the charge in humiliating and isolating the more uncompromising nationalist currents. Most onerous was his diatribe against the young nationalist, Bal Gangadhar Tilak, whom he described as a dangerous "extremist". In his attacks against Tilak, Mehta won the endorsement of the Times of India (who saw in Tilak, a serious threat to the cult of loyalism, and assiduously campaigned for the Congress to remain on the loyalist track). In 1910, in a key speech to Congress cadres, Mehta affirmed the loyalty of the Congress to British rule. The British were naturally appreciative of Mehta's politics, and duly rewarded him with knighthood. Although Mehta's strong opposition to Tilak and Bipin Chandra Pal was not entirely popular within the Congress, the Congress remained generally wedded to the creed of loyalism, and only moderates such as Gokhale were able to find an influential voice within it.

Gokhale epitomized the Congress leaders that emerged between 1895 and 1920. Acutely aware of the economic devastation that colonial rule had brought to the nation, they nevertheless repeatedly expressed their fidelity to the British-struggling only for political reforms and greater self-government within the empire. However, during the years of 1905-1908, there was an intense struggle for the soul of the Indian National Congress, with leaders like Tilak (and others such as Ajit Singh in Punjab and Chidambaram Pillay) fighting hard to intensify the struggle against British colonial domination.

"Moderates" Versus "Extremists" in the Battle for "Swaraj" and "Swadeshi"

Even as loyalist pressures cast a long shadow on political currents that were to influence the Indian elite of the late nineteenth century, rapidly deteriorating economic conditions also led to a heightened degree of radicalization amongst the most advanced sections of the new Indian intelligentsia. Ajit Singh in Punjab, Bal Gangadhar Tilak in Maharashtra, Chidambaram Pillay in Tamil Nadu and Bipin Chandra Pal in Bengal formed the nucleus of a new nationalist movement that tried valiantly, but mostly unsuccessfully to move the conservative leadership of the Indian National Congress in a more radical direction. Most charismatic amongst the new national leaders was Bal Gangadhar Tilak (b. 1856, d. 1920).

Portrayed as anti-Muslim by the Muslim-League, maligned by India's colonial rulers and British loyalists as an "extremist", and misrepresented as a sectarian Hindu revivalist by some historians, Tilak was in fact, one of the leading lights of the Indian freedom movement. Best remembered for his slogan *"Swaraj is my birth-right "*, he was one of the first to call for complete freedom from British rule, and fought a long and sometimes lonely political struggle against the forces of "moderation" that held sway over the Indian National Congress in the early part of the last century.

After the defeat of 1858, one of the most significant challenges to British imperial authority in India had appeared in the form of Vasudeo Balvant Phadke's revolt of 1879, and amongst his many youthful followers and trainees in Pune was the young Tilak. Along with Chiplunkar, Agarkar and Namjoshi, Tilak initially concentrated on launching a nationalist weekly-the *Kesari* (1881), the publishing house-*Kitabkhana*, and developing Indian educational institutions such as the Deccan Education Society (1884). Tilak and his friends saw the right kind of education as being a crucial element in the task of national regeneration, and in this respect appeared to be continuing in the tradition of Jyotirao Phule (1827-1890) and Gopalrao Deshmukh (1823-1892) who was more known by his pen-name 'Lokahitwadi'.

Foremost amongst the social revolutionaries of nineteenth century Maharashtra, Phule and his wife Savitribai, had advocated a radical restructuring of Hindu society on the basis of equality of caste, gender and creed. Phule, (who belonged to the *Mali* caste) was unsparing in his criticism of Brahminical society that looked down upon the *shudra jatis*, prevented the *atishudra* (untouchable) *jatis* from attending school, and treated young widows (particularly Brahmin widows) as outcastes. One of the first to start a school for girls (1848), Phule went on to found the first school for the *atishudras* (1851), a home for young widows (1863), and also the first to open the family well to *atishudra* women (1868). Social reformers in Maharashtra also emerged from the upper castes, such as Gopalrao Deshmukh, who although a Chitpawan Brahmin was a sharp critic of Brahminical society, and worked primarily through reformist middle-class organizations such as the Prasthana Samaj and the Arya Samaj to fight against caste inequities.

But amongst Tilak's colleagues, not all were well-disposed towards Phule and Deshmukh (Lokahitwadi). Chiplunkar was particularly vitriolic in his criticism of Phule. Tilak, on the other hand, was not unsympathetic to the need for social reforms, and was opposed to evils like child-marriage, casteism and untouchability. Many years later, (at a conference in Bombay in 1918), he was to declare: *"If God were to tolerate untouchability, I would not recognize him as God at all"*. However, he was reluctant to give precedence to social reforms over political struggle, believing that social change ought to come gradually, through the growth of enlightened public opinion, rather than through the legislative authority of an alien government. He was convinced that no significant social progress was possible in a country that wasn't politically free. He was particularly critical of loyalist or moderate "reformers" who were unwilling to practice what they preached, yet frequently baited him as being against social reforms.

Neither a sectarian religious revivalist in the mold of Chiplunkar, nor willing to confine himself exclusively to the cause of radical social reforms like Agarkar, Tilak eventually parted ways with his colleagues in 1888. Working through the *Kesari,* (and later also the *Maratha*) he gradually developed a more advanced nationalist perspective based on the pillars of nationalist education, *Swaraj* (self-rule) *and Swadeshi* (self-reliance). One of the first to take the nationalist message to the Indian masses, he played a particularly important role in organizing western Maharashtra's peasant and artisan communities during the 1897 famine under the auspices of the Sarvajanik Sabha.

By 1905, popular resistance movements had developed in both Bengal and Maharashtra, calling for the boycott of British goods and non-payment of land revenues and other taxes. Between 1905 and 1908 the national movement intensified, workers participated in strikes and work-stoppages, women and students joined the boycott movements-picketing at shops that sold imported goods, and an ever-growing mass of people began joining mass meetings and street processions.

Only too aware of the economic devastation that British rule had brought on the country, India's broad masses were responding eagerly to the nationalist message. But the nationalist movement was also becoming exceedingly divided between two poles representing radically different currents and tendencies. Whereas one side (even as it recognized the many negative aspects of alien rule) clung to the British umbilical chord, and attempted to restrict the national movement to a struggle for political reforms, the other side correctly saw British rule as an unmitigated disaster for the Indian people and called for the complete liberation from colonial rule.

Tilak eloquently and succinctly summarized the sentiments of the new and increasingly militant national movement. He spoke of British rule as having ruined trade, caused the collapse of industry, and destroyed the people's courage and abilities. Under the colonial regimen, Tilak asserted that the country was offered neither education, nor rights, nor respect for public opinion. Without prosperity and contentment, the Indian people suffered constantly from the three 'd's'-i.e. *daridra* (poverty), *dushkal* (famine) and *dravyashosha* (drain). And he saw only one remedy: for the Indian people to take political power without which Indian industry could not develop, without which the nation's youth couldn't be educated, and without which the country could win neither social reforms nor material welfare for it's people. Tilak saw colonial rule as being inimical to India's progress, and the contradictions between the British oppressors and the Indian people as being irreconcilable.

But "moderates" such as Gokhale (President of the Congress in 1905) while cognizant of how *"deplorable"* Britain's industrial domination of India was, and how the economic drain from India to Britain was *"bleeding India"*, were nevertheless all praise for the British educational system in India, ascribing to the British the virtues of introducing liberal "social reforms", governmental "peace and order" and such modern conveniences as the railways, post and telegraphs, and new industrial appliances. (That all these things benefited a miniscule Indian elite did not appear to bother such admirers of the empire, nor did it occur to them that this and much more could have just as easily been achieved under self-rule.)

Tilak and Gokhale were clearly seeing Indian reality from very different vantage points. From the point of view of the ordinary masses, British rule had already bankrupted the nation, left intolerable misery in it's wake, and offered no hope for the future. Tilak's assessment of the situation reflected bleak reality-as experienced not only by the oppressed and downtrodden Indian masses, but by an overwhelming majority of all Indians. But

Gokhale's ambivalence and his more cautiously expressed (though clearly articulated) concerns reflected the position of those who had at least partially shared in the spoils of the empire, but saw with some trepidation how the growing poverty of the nation might unravel the British empire. Reluctant to make common cause with the masses, "moderates" such as Gokhale did everything in their power to restrain the growing national movement-even branding Tilak and his allies as "extremists".

The British took full advantage of this schism, and proceeded to bring the full weight of their administrative and military might in crushing the new national movement. Communal forces such as the Muslim League were also employed in the battle to extinguish radical tendencies. The years 1905-1908 were thus extremely critical in shaping the direction of the Indian national movement. Increasingly, the Indian masses were looking to Tilak and his compatriots for direction. But, in direct opposition to the energizing of the Indian peasantry, and mass of workers and students across the country, the elite was reasserting it's loyalty to British rule.

In Punjab, the polarization was especially sharp. The boycott movement had struck deep roots within the peasantry, and made it difficult for British troops to find porters and other logistical help from the poor peasants. Roused by calls to protest the British land revenue policy, Sikh and Jat agricultural workers were becoming strongly politicized. In a rousing speech, Tilak's close associate in Punjab, Ajit Singh made a secular appeal to the masses of Punjab to rise against the British: *"Hindu brothers, Mohammedan brothers, Sepahi brothers-we are all one. The government is not even dust before us....What have you got to fear?....Our numbers are much greater. True they have guns, but we have fists...You are dying from the plague and other diseases, so better sacrifice yourselves to your motherland. Our strength lies in unity..."* (Excerpts from an April 21, 1907 speech in Rawalpindi)

On May 1, 1907, a spontaneous outburst of popular discontent shook the British administration in Rawalpindi when seething crowds, reinforced by striking workers marched through the streets-throwing mud and stones at passing Britishers, attacking government offices, cottages of Christian missionaries, British enterprises and commercial establishments. Although the uprising was effectively quelled by a large contingent of British troops who were close at hand, it shook the colonial administration enough to hastily evacuate families of colonial officials and military officers from Punjab, and extend term of the Commander-in-Chief of the British Army, Lord Kitchener. The colonial police and troops were also ruthless in crushing such uprisings in Lahore and Amritsar. Ajit Singh and Lala Lajpat Rai were summarily deported to Burma, without trial or right of appeal. Arrests and persecution of other patriots followed, and a state of emergency was declared in a number of Punjab districts.

In 1908, uprisings on a similiar scale broke out in the South, in Trivandrum, Tirunelveli, and Tuticorin. In Trivandrum, police stations were attacked, prisoners liberated, and offices of the repressive colonial state were set on fire. When Chidambaram Pillay, another important Tilak ally was put on trial, he refused to disown his national goals, and was sentenced to life imprisonment.

Russian consular official Chirkin had been quite prophetic in his May 28, 1907 report when he wrote:" The *outburst in Punjab is by it's character more dangerous than the Bengal unrest.....This outburst has roused all India."* But equally powerful forces were working to stem and reverse the radical tide that had the potential of upturning colonial rule. Bengal zamindars who had agitated against the partition of Bengal declared their loyalty to the Raj. The Maharajas not only offered armed personnel to help the British but some (such as the Maharaja of Jammu and Kashmir) themselves initiated repressive measures against those deemed "extremist".

The Congress who under the leadership of Dadabhai Naoroji had accepted the demands put forth by the Tilak group for Swaraj, Swadeshi and National Education in 1906, reneged on it's previous position, and at it's Surat session in 1907 decided to limit the struggle to a *"constitutional manner"*. *"Swaraj"* was reinterpreted to mean *"self-rule"* as a colony, and rather than fighting the colonial power, the Congress decided to cooperate with it in effecting *"reforms"*. A motion to elect Tilak (who was unquestionably the most popular leader of the national-liberation movement) was turned down, as was a compromise motion to elect Lala Lajpat Rai. The triumph of the "moderate" wing was total and complete. Gokhale's "moderate nationalism" which was simply another face of loyalism succeeded to the utter exclusion of all the popular forces aligned with Tilak, and returned the Congress to a broadly loyalist track.

Tilak and his supporters were thus compelled to regroup outside the stifling confines of the Congress and continued a vigorous struggle against the British. But in July 1908, after having removed most of Tilak's serious compatriots from the national scene, Tilak himself was brought to trial. The English majority outvoted the Indian jurors to issue a guilty verdict, and Tilak was sentenced to six years of transportation. This evoked a mass protest wave which swept a number of Indian cities culminating in a massive strike of 100,000 workers and a city-wide 'hartal' (shutdown) in Bombay. Tilak's sentence had to be commuted to simple imprisonment, but it was sufficient to deal a severe blow to the Indian freedom movement.

By 1914, the Congress had so deteriorated that a majority of it's members failed to admonish the young Mohandas Karamchand Gandhi when he embarked on a campaign to seek volunteers for the British war efforts in World War I. The man who was to repeatedly chastise the Indian masses for being insufficiently "nonviolent", had in 1914, no compunctions in seeking sacrificial lambs for a war in which India's only interest should have been for the defeat of it's colonial master. But Gandhi, who had been born the son of the Prime Minister of the princely state of Rajkot in Kathiawar, was simply following the lead of the Indian Maharajas, such as that of Bikaner-who needed little prodding in offering his troops for a war that essentially pitted Europe's older and stronger imperial powers against their emerging rivals.

Unsurprisingly, it was to Gokhale that the young Gandhi looked for inspiration, not Tilak. But others recognized his pre-eminent role in giving new direction and leadership to the Indian freedom movement. Nehru pointed out that the *"real symbol of the new age was Bal Gangadhar Tilak"*, and recognized that *"the vast majority of politically-minded people in India favoured Tilak and his group"*. This was acknowledge as much by Sir Valentine Chirol, foreign editor of the *The Times,* who noted how Tilak's imprisonment deprived India of it's most able and determined leader, perhaps the only one capable of providing the Indian national movement (with it's different and often contradictory trends), the organization and unity that had been lacking thus far. N.C. Kelkar, a biographer and follower of Tilak echoed such sentiments.

4

Partition of Bengal (1905)

The decision on the Partition of Bengal was announced on 19 July 1905 by then Viceroy of India, Lord Curzon. The partition took effect on 16 October 1905. Due to the high level of political unrest generated by the partition, the eastern and western parts of Bengal were reunited in 1911.

Origin

The province of Bengal had an area of 489,500 sq. km. and a population of over 80 million. Eastern Bengal was almost isolated from the western part by geography and poor communications. In 1836, the upper provinces were placed under a lieutenant governor, and in 1854 the Governor-General-In-Council was relieved of the direct administration of Bengal. In 1874 Assam, including Sylhet, was severed from Bengal to form a Chief-Commissionership, and the Lushai Hills were added to it in 1898.

Partition

Partitioning Bengal was first considered in 1903. There were also additional proposals to separate Chittagong and the districts of Dhaka and Mymensingh from Bengal and attaching them to the province of Assam. In a similar way, Chhota Nagpur was to be incorporated with the central provinces.

The government officially published the idea in January 1904, and in February, Lord Curzon made an official tour to eastern districts of Bengal to assess public opinion on the partition. He consulted with leading personalities and delivered speeches at Dhaka, Chittagong and Mymensingh explaining the government's stand on partition. The idea was opposed by Henry John Stedman

Cotton, Chief Commissioner of Assam 1896-1902. The Partition of Bengal in 1905 was made on October 16 by then Viceroy of India, Lord Curzon. Partition was promoted for administrative regions; Bengal was as large as France but with a significantly larger population. The eastern region was thought to be neglected and under-governed. By splitting the province, an improved administration could be established in the east where, subsequently, the population would benefit from new schools and employment opportunities. However, other motives lurked behind the partition plan. Bengali Hindus were in the forefront of political agitation for greater participation in governance; their position would be weakened, since Muslims would now dominate in the East. Hindus tended to oppose partition, which was more popular among Muslims. What followed partition, however, stimulated an almost national anti-British movement that involved nonviolent and violent protests, boycotts and even an assassination attempt against the Governor of the new province of West Bengal.

Partition barely lasted half a decade, before it was annulled in 1911. Britain's policy of *divide et impera* which lay behind partition, however, continued to impact on the re-united province. In 1919, separate elections were established for Muslims and Hindus. Before this, many members of both communities had advocated national solidarity of all Bengalis. Now, distinctive communities developed, with their own political agendas. Muslims, too, dominated the Legislature, due to their overall numerical strength of roughly twenty eight to twenty two million. Nationally, Hindus and Muslims began to demand the creation of two independent states, one to be formed in majority Hindu and one in majority Muslim areas with most Bengali Hindus now supporting partitioning Bengal on this basis. The Muslims wanted the whole province to join the Muslim state, Pakistan. In 1947, Bengal was partitioned for the second time, this time specifically on religious grounds. It became East Pakistan. However, in 1971 East Pakistan became the independent state of Bangladesh after a successful war for liberation with the West Pakistani military regime. Partition may sometimes be necessary as a pragmatic strategy to avoid bloodshed but more often than not this leads to new problems that divide even more people.

This article may contain original research. Please improve it by verifying the claims made and adding references. Statements consisting only of original research may be removed. Almost always, partition produces discontent among minorities on both sides of the border. Both partitions of Bengal saw bloodshed.

The new province would consist of the state of Hill Tripura, the Divisions of Chittagong, Dhaka and Rajshahi (excluding Darjeeling) and the district of Malda incorporated with Assam province. Bengal was to surrender not only these large eastern territories but also to cede to the Central Provinces the five Hindi-speaking states. On the western side it was offered Sambalpur and five minor Oriya-speaking states from the Central Provinces. Bengal would be left with an area of 141,580 sq. miles and population of 54 million, of which 42 million would be Hindus and 9 million Muslims.

The new province was named Eastern Bengal and Assam with Dhaka as its capital and subsidiary headquarters at Chittagong. Its area would be 106,540 sq. miles with a population of 31 million, where 18 million would be Muslims and 12 million Hindus. Administration would consist of a Legislative Council, a Board of Revenue of two members, and the jurisdiction of the Calcutta High Court would be left undisturbed. The government pointed out that Eastern Bengal and Assam would have a clearly demarcated western boundary and well defined geographical, ethnological, linguistic and social characteristics. The government of India promulgated their final decision in a resolution dated July 19, 1905 and the partition of Bengal was effected on October 16 of same year.

This created a huge political crisis. The Muslims in East Bengal had the impression that a separate region would give them more opportunity for education, employment etc. However, the partition was not liked by the people in West Bengal and a huge amount of nationalist literature was created there during this period. Opposition by Indian National Congress was led by Sir Henry John Stedman Cotton who had been Chief Commissioner of Assam, but Curzon was not to be moved. Later, Cotton, now Liberal MP for Nottingham East coordinated the successful campaign to oust the first lieutenant-governor of East Bengal, Sir Bampfylde Fuller. In 1906, Rabindranath Tagore wrote *Amar Shonar Bangla* as a rallying cry for proponents of annulment of Partition, which, much later, in 1972, became the national anthem of Bangladesh. Due to these political protests, the two parts of Bengal were reunited in 1911.

A new partition which divided the province on linguistic, rather than religious, grounds followed, with the Hindi, Oriya and Assamese areas separated to form separate administrative units. The administrative capital of British India was moved from Calcutta to New Delhi as well.

However, conflict between Muslims and Hindus resulted in new laws having to be introduced so as to satisfy the political needs of both groups.

Partition of Bengal, 1905 effected on 16 October during the viceroyalty of lord curzon (1899-1905), proved to be a momentous event in the history of modern Bengal. The idea of partitioning Bengal did not originate with Curzon. Bengal, which included Bihar and Orissa since 1765, was admittedly much too large for a single province of British India. This premier province grew too vast for efficient administration and required reorganisation and intelligent division.

The lieutenant governor of Bengal had to administer an area of 189,000 sq. miles and by 1903 the population of the province had risen to 78.50 million. Consequently, many districts in eastern Bengal had been practically neglected because of isolation and poor communication which made good governance almost impossible. Calcutta and its nearby districts attracted all the energy and attention of the government. The condition of peasants was miserable under the exaction of absentee landlords; and trade, commerce and education were being impaired. The administrative machinery of the province was understaffed. Especially in east Bengal, in countryside so cut off by rivers and creeks, no special attention had been paid to the peculiar difficulties of police work till the last decade of the 19th century. Organised piracy in the waterways had existed for at least a century.

Along with administrative difficulties, the problems of famine, of defence, or of linguistics had at one time or other prompted the government to consider the redrawing of administrative boundaries. Occasional efforts were made to rearrange the administrative units of Bengal. In 1836, the upper provinces were sliced off from Bengal and placed under a lieutenant governor. In 1854, the Governor-General-in-Council was relieved of the direct administration of Bengal which was placed under a lieutenant governor. In 1874 Assam (along with Sylhet) was severed from

Bengal to form a Chief-Commissionership and in 1898 Lushai Hills were added to it.

Proposals for partitioning Bengal were first considered in 1903. Curzon's original scheme was based on grounds of administrative efficiency. It was probably during the vociferous protests and adverse reaction against the original plan, that the officials first envisaged the possible advantages of a divided Bengal. Originally, the division was made on geographical rather than on an avowedly communal basis. 'Political Considerations' in this respect seemed to have been 'an afterthought'.

The government contention was that the Partition of Bengal was purely an administrative measure with three main objectives. Firstly, it wanted to relieve the government of Bengal of a part of the administrative burden and to ensure more efficient administration in the outlying districts. Secondly, the government desired to promote the development of backward Assam (ruled by a Chief Commissioner) by enlarging its jurisdiction so as to provide it with an outlet to the sea. Thirdly, the government felt the urgent necessity to unite the scattered sections of the Uriya-speaking population under a single administration. There were further proposals to separate Chittagong and the districts of Dhaka (then Dacca) and Mymensigh from Bengal and attach them to Assam. Similarly Chhota Nagpur was to be taken away from Bengal and incorporated with the Central Provinces.

The government's proposals were officially published in January 1904. In February 1904, Curzon made an official tour of the districts of eastern Bengal with a view to assessing public opinion on the government proposals. He consulted the leading personalities of the different districts and delivered speeches at Dhaka, Chittagong and Mymensigh explaining the government's stand on partition. It was during this visit that the decision to push through an expanded scheme took hold of his mind. This would involve the creation of a self-contained new province under a Lieutenant Governor with a Legislative Council, an independent revenue authority and transfer of so much territory as would justify a fully equipped administration.

The enlarged scheme received the assent of the governments of Assam and Bengal. The new province would consist of the state of Hill Tripura, the Divisions of Chittagong, Dhaka and Rajshahi (excluding Darjeeling) and the district of Malda amalgamated with Assam. Bengal was to surrender not only these large territories on the east but also to cede to the Central Provinces the five Hindi-speaking states. On the west it would gain Sambalpur and a minor tract of five Uriya-speaking states from the Central Provinces. Bengal would be left with an area of 141,580 sq. miles and a population of 54 million, of which 42 million would be Hindus and 9 million Muslims.

The new province was to be called 'Eastern Bengal and Assam' with its capital at Dhaka and subsidiary headquarters at Chittagong. It would cover an area of 106,540 sq. miles with a population of 31 million comprising of 18 million Muslims and 12 million Hindus. Its administration would consist of a Legislative Council, a Board of Revenue of two members, and the jurisdiction of the Calcutta High Court would be left undisturbed. The government pointed out that the new province would have a clearly demarcated western boundary and well defined geographical, ethnological, linguistic and social characteristics. The most striking feature of the new province was that it would concentrate within its own bounds the hitherto ignored and neglected typical homogenous Muslim population of Bengal. Besides, the whole of the tea industry (except Darjeeling), and the greater portion of the jute growing area would be brought under a single administration. The government of India promulgated their final decision in a Resolution dated 19 July 1905 and the Partition of Bengal was effected on 16 October of the same year.

The publication of the original proposals towards the end of 1903 had aroused unprecedented opposition, especially among the influential educated middle-class Hindus. The proposed territorial adjustment seemed to touch the existing interest groups and consequently led to staunch opposition. The Calcutta lawyers apprehended that the creation of a new province would mean the establishment of a Court of Appeal at Dacca and diminish the importance of their own High Court. Journalists feared the appearance of local newspapers, which would restrict the circulation of the Calcutta Press. The business community of Calcutta visualised the shift of trade from Calcutta to Chittagong, which would be nearer, and logically the cheaper port. The Zamindars who owned vast landed estates both in west and east Bengal foresaw the necessity of maintaining separate establishments at Dhaka that would involve extra expenditure. The educated Bengali Hindus felt that it was a deliberate blow inflicted by Curzon at the national consciousness and growing solidarity of the Bengali-speaking population. The Hindus of Bengal, who controlled most of Bengal's commerce and the different professions and led the rural society, opined that the Bengali nation would be divided, making them a minority in a province including the whole of Bihar and Orissa. They complained that it was a veiled attempt by Curzon to strangle the spirit of nationalism in Bengal. They strongly believed that it was the prime object of the government to encourage the growth of a Muslim power in eastern Bengal as a counterpoise to thwart the rapidly growing strength of the educated Hindu community. Economic, political and communal interests combined together to intensify the opposition against the partition measure.

The Indian and specially the Bengali press opposed the partition move from the very beginning. The British press, the Anglo-Indian press and even some administrators also opposed the intended measure. The partition evoked fierce protest in west Bengal, especially in Calcutta and gave a new fillip to Indian nationalism. Henceforth, the Indian national congress was destined to become the main platform of the Indian nationalist movement. It exhibited unusual strength and vigour and shifted from a middle-class pressure group to a nation-wide mass organisation.

The leadership of the Indian National Congress viewed the partition as an attempt to 'divide and rule' and as a proof of the government's vindictive antipathy towards the outspoken *Bhadralok* intellectuals. Mother-goddess worshipping Bengali Hindus believed that the partition was tantamount to the vivisection of their 'Mother province'.

'Bande-Mataram' (Hail Motherland) almost became the national anthem of the Indian National Congress. Defeat of the partition became the immediate target of Bengali nationalism. Agitation against the partition manifested itself in the form of mass meetings, rural unrest and a swadeshi movement to boycott the import of British manufactured goods. Swadeshi and Boycott were the twin weapons of this nationalism and *Swaraj* (self-government) its main objective. *Swaraj* was first mentioned in the presidential address of Dadabhai Naoroji as the Congress goal at its Calcutta session in 1906.

Leaders like surendranath banerjea along with journalists like Krishna Kumar Mitra, editor of the *Sanjivani* (13 July 1905) urged the people to boycott British goods, observe mourning and sever all contact with official bodies. In a meeting held at Calcutta on 7 August 1905 (hailed as the birthday of Indian nationalism) a resolution to abstain from purchases of British products so long as 'Partition resolution is not withdrawn' was accepted with acclaim. This national spirit was popularised by the patriotic songs of dwijendralal roy, rajanikanta sen and rabindranath tagore. As with other political movements of the day this also took on religious overtones. *Pujas* were offered to emphasise the solemn nature of the occasion.

The Hindu religious fervour reached its peak on 28 September 1905, the day of the *Mahalaya,* the new-moon day before the *puja,* and thousands of Hindus gathered at the Kali temple in Calcutta. In Bengal the worship of Kali, wife of Shiva, had always been very popular. She possessed a two-dimensional character with mingled attributes both generative and destructive. Simultaneously she took great pleasure in bloody sacrifices but she was also venerated as the great Mother associated with the conception of Bengal as the Motherland. This conception offered a solid basis for the support of political objectives stimulated by religious excitement. Kali was accepted as a symbol of the Motherland, and the priest administered the Swadeshi vow. Such a religious flavour could and did give the movement a widespread appeal among the Hindu masses, but by the same token that flavour aroused hostility in average Muslim minds. Huge protest rallies before and after Bengal's division on 16 October 1905 attracted millions of people heretofore not involved in politics.

The Swadeshi Movement as an economic movement would have been quite acceptable to the Muslims, but as the movement was used as a weapon against the partition (which the greater body of the Muslims supported) and as it often had a religious colouring added to it, it antagonised Muslim minds.

The new tide of national sentiment against the Partition of Bengal originating in Bengal spilled over into different regions in India Punjab, Central Provinces, Poona, Madras, Bombay and other cities. Instead of wearing foreign made outfits, the Indians vowed to use only *swadeshi* (indigenous) cottons and other clothing materials made in India. Foreign garments were viewed as hateful imports. The Swadeshi Movement soon stimulated local enterprise in many areas; from Indian cotton mills to match factories, glass blowing shops, iron and steel foundries. The agitation also generated increased demands for national education. Bengali teachers and students extended their boycott of British goods to English schools and college classrooms. The movement for national education spread throughout Bengal and reached even as far as Benaras where Pandit Madan Mohan Malaviya founded his private Benaras Hindu University in 1910.

The student community of Bengal responded with great enthusiasm to the call of nationalism. Students including schoolboys participated en masse in the campaigns of Swadeshi and Boycott. The government retaliated with the notorious Carlyle Circular that aimed to crush the students' participation in the Swadeshi and Boycott movements. Both the students and the teachers strongly reacted against this repressive measure and the protest was almost universal. In fact, through this protest movement the first organised student movement was born in Bengal. Along with this the 'Anti-Circular Society', a militant student organisation, also came into being.

The anti-partition agitation was peaceful and constitutional at the initial stage, but when it appeared that it was not yielding the desired results the protest movement inevitably passed into the hands of more militant leaders. Two techniques of boycott and terrorism were to be applied to make their mission successful. Consequently the younger generation, who were unwittingly drawn into politics, adopted terrorist methods by using firearms, pistols and bombs indiscriminately. The agitation soon took a turn towards anarchy and disorder. Several assassinations were committed and attempts were made on the lives of officials including Sir andrew Fraser. The terrorist movement soon became an integral part of the Swadeshi agitation. Bengal terrorism reached its peak from 1908 through 1910, as did the severity of official repression and the number of 'preventive detention' arrests.

The new militant spirit was reflected in the columns of the nationalist newspapers, notably the *Bande Mataram, Sandhya* and *Jugantar*. The press assisted a great deal to disseminate revolutionary ideas. In 1907, the Indian National Congress at its annual session in Surat split into two groups-one being moderate, liberal, and evolutionary; and the other extremist, militant and revolutionary.

The young militants of Bal Gangadhar Tilak's extremist party supported the 'cult of the bomb and the gun' while the moderate leaders like Gopal Krishna Gokhale and Surendranath Banerjea cautioned against such extremist actions fearing it might lead to anarchy and uncontrollable violence. Surendranath Banerjea, though one of the front-rank leaders of the anti-Partition agitation, was not in favour of terrorist activities.

When the proposal for partition was first published in 1903 there was expression of Muslim opposition to the scheme. The *moslem chronicle,* the central national Muhamedan association, chowdhury kazemuddin ahmad siddiky and Delwar Hossain Ahmed condemned the proposed measure. Even Nawab salimullah termed the suggestion as 'beastly' at the initial stage. In the beginning the main criticism from the Muslim side was against any part of an enlightened and advanced province of Bengal passing under the rule of a chief commissioner. They felt that thereby, their educational, social and other interests would suffer, and there is no doubt that the Muslims also felt that the proposed measure would threaten Bengali solidarity. The Muslim intelligentsia, however, criticised the ideas of extremist militant nationalism as being against the spirit of Islam. The Muslim press urged its educated co-religionists to remain faithful to the government. On the whole the Swadeshi preachers were not able to influence and arouse the predominantly Muslim masses in east Bengal. The anti-partition trend in the thought process of the Muslims did not continue for long. When the wider scheme of a self contained separate province was known to the educated section of the Muslims they soon changed their views. They realised that the partition would be a boon to them and that their special difficulties would receive greater attention from the new administration.

The Muslims accorded a warm welcome to the new Lieutenant-Governor bampfylde fuller. Even the *Moslem Chronicle* soon changed its attitude in favour of partition. Some Muslims in Calcutta also welcomed the creation of the new province. The Mohammedan literary society brought out a manifesto in 1905 signed by seven leading Muslim personalities. The manifesto was circulated to the different Muslim societies of both west and east Bengal and urged the Muslims to give their unqualified support to the partition measure. The creation of the new province provided an incentive to the Muslims to unite into a compact body and form an association to voice their own views and aspiration relating to social and political matters. On 16 October 1905 the Mohammedan Provincial Union was founded. All the existing organisations and societies were invited to affiliate themselves with it and Salimullah was unanimously chosen as its patron.

Even then there was a group of educated liberal Muslims who came forward and tendered support to the anti-partition agitation and the Swadeshi Movement. Though their number was insignificant, yet their role added a new dimension in the thought process of the Muslims. This broad-minded group supported the Indian National Congress and opposed the partition. The most prominent among this section of the Muslims was Khwaza atiqullah. At the Calcutta session of the Congress (1906), he moved a resolution denouncing the partition of Bengal. Aabdur Rasul, Khan Bahadur Muhammad Yusuf (a pleader and a member of the Management Committee of the Central National Muhamedan Association), Mujibur Rahman, AH Abdul Halim Ghaznavi, Ismail Hossain Shiraji, Mohammad Gholam Hossain (a writer and a promoter of Hindu-Muslim unity), Maulvi Liaqat Hussain (a liberal Muslim who vehemently opposed the 'Divide and Rule' policy of the British), Syed Hafizur Rahman Chowdhury of Bogra and Abul Kasem of Burdwan inspired Muslims to join the anti-Partition agitation. There were even a few Muslim preachers of Swadeshi ideas, like Din Muhammad of Mymensingh and Abdul Gaffar of Chittagong. It needs to be mentioned that some of the liberal nationalist Muslims like AH Ghaznavi and Khan Bahadur Muhammad Yusuf supported the Swadeshi Movement but not the Boycott agitation.

A section of the Muslim press tried to promote harmonious relations between the Hindus and the Muslims Ak Fazlul Huq and Nibaran Chandra Das preached non-communal ideas through their weekly *Balaka* (1901, Barisal) and monthly *Bharat Suhrd* (1901, Barisal). Only a small section of Muslim intellectuals could rise above their sectarian outlook and join with the Congress in the anti-partition agitation and constitutional politics.

The general trend of thoughts in the Muslim minds was in favour of partition. The All India Muslim league, founded in 1906, supported the partition. In the meeting of the Imperial Council in 1910 Shamsul Huda of Bengal and Mazhar-ul-Huq from Bihar spoke in favour of the partition. The traditional and reformist Muslim groups-the Faraizi, Wahabi and Taiyuni-supported the partition. Consequently an orthodox trend was visible in the political attitude of the Muslims. The Bengali Muslim press in general lent support to the partition. The *Islam Pracharak* described Swadeshi as a Hindu movement and expressed grave concern saying that it would bring hardship to the common people. The Muslim intelligentsia in general felt concerned about the suffering of their co-religionists caused by it. They particularly disliked the movement as it was tied to the anti-partition agitation. Reputed litterateurs like Mir Mosharraf Hossain were virulent critics of the Swadeshi Movement. The greater body of Muslims at all levels remained opposed to the Swadeshi Movement since it was used as a weapon against the partition and a religious tone was added to it.

The economic aspect of the movement was partly responsible for encouraging separatist forces within the Muslim society. The superiority of the Hindus in the sphere of trade and industry alarmed the Muslims. Fear of socioeconomic domination by the Hindus made them alert to safeguard their own interests. These apprehensions brought about a rift in Hindu-Muslims relations. In order to avoid economic exploitation by the Hindus, some wealthy Muslim entrepreneurs came forward to launch new commercial ventures. One good attempt was the founding of steamer companies operating between Chittagong and Rangoon in 1906.

In the context of the partition the pattern of the land system in Bengal played a major role to influence the Muslim mind. The absentee Hindu zamindars made no attempt to improve the lot of the *raiyats* who were mostly Muslims. The agrarian disputes (between landlords and tenants) already in existence in the province also appeared to take a communal colour. It was alleged that the Hindu landlords had been attempting to enforce Swadeshi ideas on the tenants and induce them to join the anti-partition movement.

In 1906, the Muslims organised an Islamic conference at Keraniganj in Dhaka as a move to emphasise their separate identity as a community. The Swadeshi Movement with its Hindu religious flavour fomented aggressive reaction from the other community. A red pamphlet of a highly inflammatory nature was circulated among the Muslim masses of Eastern Bengal and Assam urging them completely to dissociate from the Hindus. It was published under the auspices of the Anjuman-I-Mufidul Islam under the editorship of a certain Ibrahim Khan. Moreover, such irritating moves as the adoption of the *Bande Mataram* as the song of inspiration or introduction of the cult of Shivaji as a national hero, and reports of communal violence alienated the Muslims. One inevitable result of such preaching was the riot that broke out at Comilla in March 1907, followed by similar riots in Jamalpur in April of that year. These communal disturbances became a familiar feature in Eastern Bengal and Assam and followed a pattern that was repeated elsewhere. The 1907 riots represent a watershed in the history of modern Bengal.

While Hindu-Muslims relations deteriorated, political changes of great magnitude were taking place in the Government of India's policies, and simultaneously in the relations of Bengali Muslim leaders with their non-Bengali counterparts. Both developments had major repercussions on communal relations in eastern Bengal. The decision to introduce constitutional reforms culminating in the morley-minto reforms of 1909 introducing separate representation for the Muslims marked a turning point in Hindu-Muslim relations.

The early administrators of the new province from the lieutenant governor down to the junior-most officials in general were enthusiastic in carrying out the development works. Bampfylde Fuller was accused by the anti-Partition movement leaders as being extremely partial to Muslims. He, because of a difference with the Government of India, resigned in August 1906. His resignation and its prompt acceptance were considered by the Muslims to be a solid political victory for the Hindus. The general Muslim feeling was that in yielding to the pressure of the anti-Partition agitators the government had revealed its weakness and had overlooked the loyal adherence of the Muslims to the government.

Consequently, the antagonism between the Hindus and Muslims became very acute in the new province. The Muslim leaders, now more conscious of their separate communal identity, directed their attention in uniting the different sections of their community to the creation of a counter movement against that of the Hindus. They keenly felt the need for unity and believed that the Hindu agitation against the Partition was in fact a communal movement and as such a threat to the Muslims as a separate community. They decided to faithfully follow the directions of leaders like Salimullah and Nawab Ali Chowdhury and formed organisations like the Mohammedan Provincial Union.

Though communalism had reached its peak in the new province by 1907, there is evidence of a sensible and sincere desire among some of the educated and upper class Muslims and Hindus to put an end to these religious antagonisms. A group of prominent members of both communities met the Viceroy Lord Minto on 15 March 1907 with suggestions to put an end to communal violence and promote religious harmony between the two communities.

The landlord-tenant relationship in the new province had deteriorated and took a communal turn. The Hindu landlords felt alarmed at the acts of terrorism committed by the anti-partition agitators. To prove their unswerving loyalty to the government and give evidence of their negative attitude towards the agitation, they offered their hands of friendship and cooperation to their Muslim counterparts to the effect that they would take a non-communal stand and work unitedly against the anti-government revolutionary movements.

In the meantime the All-India Muslim League had come into being at Dacca on 30 December 1906. Though several factors were responsible for the formation of such an organisation, the Partition of Bengal and the threat to it was, perhaps, the most important factor that hastened its birth. At its very first sitting at Dacca the Muslim League, in one of its resolutions, said: 'That this meeting in view of the clear interest of the Mohammedans of Eastern Bengal consider that Partition is sure to prove beneficial to the Muhammadan community which constitute the vast majority of the populations of the new province and that all such methods of agitation such as boycotting should be strongly condemned and discouraged'.

To assuage the resentment of the assertive Bengali Hindus, the British government decided to annul the Partition of Bengal. As regards the Muslims of Eastern Bengal the government stated that in the new province the Muslims were in an overwhelming majority in point of population, under the new arrangement also they would still be in a position of approximate numerical equality or possibly of small superiority over the Hindus. The interests of the

Muslims would be safeguarded by special representation in the Legislative Councils and the local bodies.

Lord hardinge succeeded Minto and on 25 August 1911. In a secret despatch the government of India recommended certain changes in the administration of India. According to the suggestion of the Governor-General-in-Council, King George V at his Coronation Darbar in Delhi in December 1911 announced the revocation of the Partition of Bengal and of certain changes in the administration of India. Firstly, the Government of India should have its seat at Delhi instead of Calcutta. By shifting the capital to the site of past Muslim glory, the British hoped to placate Bengal's Muslim community now aggrieved at the loss of provincial power and privilege in eastern Bengal. Secondly, the five Bengali speaking Divisions viz The Presidency, Burdwan, Dacca, Rajshahi and Chittagong were to be united and formed into a Presidency to be administered by a Governor-in-Council. The area of this province would be approximately 70,000 sq. miles with a population of 42 million. Thirdly, a Lieutenant-Governor-in-Council with a Legislative Council was to govern the province comprising of Bihar, Chhota Nagpur and Orissa. Fourthly, Assam was to revert back to the rule of a Chief Commissioner. The date chosen for the formal ending of the partition and reunification of Bengal was I April 1912.

Reunification of Bengal indeed served somewhat to soothe the feeling of the Bengali Hindus, but the down grading of Calcutta from imperial to mere provincial status was simultaneously a blow to 'Bhadralok' egos and to Calcutta real estate values. To deprive Calcutta of its prime position as the nerve centre of political activity necessarily weakened the influence of the Bengali Hindus. The government felt that the main advantage, which could be derived from the move, was that it would remove the seat of the government of India from the agitated atmosphere of Bengal.

Lord Carmichael, a man of liberal sympathies, was chosen as the first Governor of reunified Bengal. The Partition of Bengal and the agitation against it had far-reaching effects on Indian history and national life. The twin weapons of Swadeshi and Boycott adopted by the Bengalis became a creed with the Indian National Congress and were used more effectively in future conflicts. They formed the basis of Gandhi's Non-Cooperation, Satyagraha and Khadi movements. They also learned that organised political agitation and critical public opinion can force the government to accede to public demands.

The annulment of the partition as a result of the agitation against it had a negative effect on the Muslims. The majority of the Muslims did not like the Congress support to the anti-partition agitation. The politically conscious Muslims felt that the Congress had supported a Hindu agitation against the creation of a Muslim majority province. It reinforced their belief that their interests were not safe in the hands of the Congress. Thus they became more anxious to emphasise their separate communal identity and leaned towards the Muslim League to safeguard their interest against the dominance of the Hindu majority in undivided India. To placate Bengali Muslim feelings Lord Hardinge promised a new University at Dacca on 31 January 1912 to a Muslim deputation led by Salimullah.

The Partition of Bengal of 1905 left a profound impact on the political history of India. From a political angle the measure accentuated Hindu-Muslim differences in the region. One point of view is that by giving the Muslim's a separate territorial identity in 1905 and a communal electorate through the Morley-Minto Reforms of 1909 the British Government in a subtle manner tried to neutralise the possibility of major Muslim participation in the Indian National Congress.

The Partition of Bengal indeed marks a turning point in the history of nationalism in India. It may be said that it was out of the travails of Bengal that Indian nationalism was born. By the same token the agitation against the partition and the terrorism that it generated was one of the main factors which gave birth to Muslim nationalism and encouraged them to engage in separatist politics. The birth of the Muslim League in 1906 at Dacca (Dhaka) bears testimony to this. The annulment of the partition sorely disappointed not only the Bengali Muslims but also the Muslims of the whole of India. They felt that loyalty did not pay but agitation does. Thereafter, the dejected Muslims gradually took an anti-British stance. [Sufia Ahmed]

Indian National Congress

Founded in 1885 by a narrowly based national elite, the Indian National Congress (INC) gradually transformed into a broadbased nationalist organisation from the beginning of the 20th century.

The Anglo-Indian agitation against the Ilbert Bill during ripon's viceroyalty served to underline the efficacy of an all-India political organisation as India's English educated politicians wished to speak effectively and authoritatively to the British rulers. Surendranath Benerjee, who had been playing a key role in organising nationalist forums like the Indian association (1876) and the National Conference (1883), welcomed the move of AO Hume, a retired British ICS officer, for establishing an organisation by the western educated upper class Indians to function as a 'safety valve' for the escape of growing resentment of Indians against British rule. Hume had the blessings of viceroy dufferin who accepted the idea of such an organisation as the 'loyal opposition' to the British Raj. Barrister WC Banerjee was chosen as the first president of the INC's inaugural session in Bombay in December 1885.

Surendranath Benerjee joined the INC at its second session in Calcutta in 1886. The INC was then not a full-fledged political party, rather a loose association of influential men in provincial politics trying to build up a national platform. Leading public figures such as Dadabhai Naoroji, Feroze Shah Mehta, Badruddin Tayabji, KT Telang and others associated themselves with the INC.

The Indian National Congress initially had little year round activity and was active only in its annual gatherings. Its delegates were mostly upper caste Hindus and its leaders primarily came from the legal profession. Known for their loyalty to the Raj, they did not like radical sort of political or social change and were interested in having some say in government administration and structures of political life. Until 1905 these moderate leaders confined themselves to political agitation by 'prayer-petition-protest'.

At the beginning the Muslims were not attracted to INC in significant numbers. Sir Sayyed Ahmad advised the Muslims to keep themselves away from INC in the interest of furthering Muslim solidarity. Aswini Datta, the mass leader of Barisal, described each of the sessions of the INC as 'three-day opera'. The moderate leaders of the INC believed that British rule in India was a good dispensation, which can be made better through negotiations. They shunned the violence of small groups of terrorists and revolutionaries in Bengal, the Punjab and Bombay provinces.

Viceroy Curzon's measure of partitioning the province of Bengal in 1905 evoked strong protest from the Bangali Hindu leaders and ultimately gave rise to militant politics of aurobindo ghosh, Bipin Chandra Pal, Bal Gangadhar Tilak and Lala Lajpat Rai. The Calcutta-based swadeshi movement and the programme of boycotting British goods were instrumental in creating the extremist faction within the INC. The moderate and extremist leaders openly and violently clashed in the Surat session (1907) over the 'policy of mendicancy' pursued by the moderates. The INC suffered a split as the extremists came out of it. Congressmen were divided by personal animosities, and factionalism became endemic within the INC at national, provincial and local levels. Meanwhile, the Muslim league (ML) was formed in 1906 to protect the interests of the Muslims.

When the British government involved India in Britain's war efforts in 1914 without consulting Indian opinion, strong Indian resentment against this policy brought the INC and the ML closer. The leaders of INC and ML entered into 'Lucknow Pact' (1916) to strengthen India's demand for self-government. The growing popularity of the Home Rule Leagues led by Annie Besant and B.G Tilak and the 'Lucknow Pact' persuaded the British government to promise in 1917 self-government on a gradual basis. But the political situation suddenly changed for the worse in the wake of the Jalianwala Bagh massacre in 1919.

By the 1920s the old uncertainties of imperial paternalism were gone. There were clear signs of the beginning of a more popular politics, being welded into a nationalist movement by a new leader Mohandas Karamchand Gandhi, who had experience of launching nonviolent *Satyagraha* movement in South Africa and had emerged in Indian politics at this hour with his new technique of offering resistance to injustice. He received support from the Congress leadership and also from the national revolutionaries who agreed to give him a chance of realising his stated goal of achieving 'Swaraj' (self-government) in one year's time. Gandhi utilised the grievances of the Indian Muslims over the issue of *Khilafat* for forging unity among the Hindus and the Muslims against British imperialism.

Gandhi launched in 1920 his non-cooperation movement which was the first truly national and popular political campaign against the British government. Gandhi's strategy boosted the significance of the INC in Indian politics. The INC undoubtedly owed much of its success into building itself as the organisations of mainstream nationalism in the 1920s to Gandhi and a number of other leaders like Motilal Nehru, Madan Mohan Malavya and Chitta Ranjan Das. Later emerged a new generation of leaders who were content to work with Gandhi and submit to his authority. Prominent among this group were C Raja Gopalachari, Rajendra Prasad, Jawaharlal Nehru, Abul Kalam Azad and Sardar Vallabbhai Patel. Subhas Chandra Bose was initially a part of this group but soon was unwilling to submit to Gandhi. Though the INC accepted in 1929 complete independence of India as its goal, its main aim was to force concessions from the British imperialists. Through the non-cooperation movement (1920-22) and the civil disobedience movement (1930-34) Gandhi exercised his charisma over millions of men and women to make INC a mass-based political forum.

When the British government arranged the Round Table conferences and offered the 'communal award' for reservation of seats in legislatures for different communities and scheduled castes, Gandhi resisted it by undertaking a fast unto death, but the superior skill of political dialogue and divisive strategy of the British imperialism ultimately got Gandhi and the INC outwitted. The Government of India Act (1935) did not introduce full responsible government at the central level but introduced responsible autonomy at the provincial level. There was much resentment within the INC against the proposed federation with the 'native states' and the formidable 'special power' in the governor general's hand.

An inner pressure group of leftists and socialists within the INC was formed in 1934 styled as the Congress Socialist Party (CSP) with Acharya Narendra Dev as chairman and Jayaprakash Narayan as general secretary. Nehru and Subhas Bose sympathised with the cause of socialism but did not formally join the CSP. The leaders and workers of the Communist Party of India, which was banned at that time, worked through the CSP. The group of MN Roy and the Krishak Sabha maintained close contact with the INC and the CSP. The consolidation of leftist forces within the INC caused some consternation in Gandhi and the rightist camp of the INC.

In the elections held in 1937 under the Government of India Act 1935, the INC achieved great successes in the general seats and formed its own government in six Hindu-majority provinces. It failed electorally in Sindh and the Punjab and became the single largest party in Assam, Bengal and NWFP. In Bengal the INC's decision to reject the coalition offer from Ak Fazlul Huq's Krishak Praja party paved the way for the Muslim League-Krishak Praja Party coalition. The ML's desire to form a coalition government with the INC in UP was also sabotaged by Nehru's insistence on ML accepting the 'congress creed'. In order to take the wind out of the leftist sail Gandhi nominated the leftist leader Subhas Bose as the Congress president at the Haripura session (1938). Bose refused to be an obedient disciple of Gandhi, and showed dynamic leadership bent on a massive struggle against imperialism and laying the broad principles of planned economic development of India. Gandhi and the rightist leaders refused to re-elect Bose for the next year, but their nominee was defeated by Bose with the help of the leftists. This confrontation eventually pushed Bose out of the INC. Meanwhile, the ML adopted the Lahore resolution (1940) calling for establishing independent Muslim states in the subcontinent. In 1941, Bose left India to Europe and from there to the East Asian war theatres to launch armed struggle against British imperialism.

Gandhi launched the quit India movement in August 1942, which went in a violent way and was suppressed quickly. This was followed by a series of negotiations between the British government, the INC and the ML for transfer of power. Viceroy Wavell called all concerned parties to the Simla Conference in June-July 1945, but nothing concrete emerged. The search for a consensus between the INC and ML proved illusive.

Between December 1945 and February 1946 fresh elections were held in which the Indians were found to be clearly divided in their allegiance to the INC and the ML. Meanwhile there was a massive popular upsurge against British rule in the wake of the trial of the officers of Indian National Army of Subhas Bose, followed by revolts in the Royal Indian Navy in February 1946 and also wide discontent in the army, police and civil service. The British Prime Minister Attlee announced the appointment of a high power cabinet mission for negotiation with the Indian leaders. The mission recommended a Constituent Assembly and a responsible interim government to be formed by Indian ministers. The ML's demand for Pakistan was not accepted, but a grouping of provinces was recommended to accommodate the demand for powerful provinces on the communal divide. Both the Congress and the League grudgingly accepted the recommendations, but the whole plan was ruined as Nehru indiscreetly asserted the INC's rights to proceed on constitution making without any precondition. This attitude alienated Mohammed Ali Jinnah and the ML which began sabotaging Nehru's interim cabinet and organised violent campaigns to force the British government to concede the demand for partition of India in early 1947. Attlee sent lord Mountbatten as the new viceroy and set the deadline of June 1948 for ending British rule in India. Things now began moving fast. The partition of India took place on 14 August 1947.

Partition of Bengal

The opening years of the twentieth century were stormy. That was the time when the greatest catastrophe of history took place. The political scenario was undergoing a change. The British were beginning to feel a bit uneasy. Discontentment was brewing. Political discontent was growing due to the inability of the government to organize effective relief during the period of plague and famine. In order to stem the discontent, the British played the political trump card with great aplomb. For the first time, they used their divide-and-rule political game with great force. From 1870 onwards, the British started inciting the Hindus and the Muslims to form their own political parties to establish their distinct religious identities. That was perhaps, the beginning of the communalisation of politics. The British not only encouraged the two communities to form political parties along religious lines, they took various constructive steps to create a situation whereby Hindus and Muslims would be forced to think in a way as if their religious identity is at peril. This effort culminated in the partition of Bengal in 1905. West Bengal, Orissa and Bihar was on one side and the erstwhile east Bengal and Assam was on the other. The partition was made along communal lines. This partition provided an impetus to the religious divide and, as a result of that, All India Muslim League and All India Hindu Mahasabha was formed. Both the organisations aimed at fanning communal passions.

The main reason for the Partition was purely political. The Hindus were in a better position in terms of economic status, professional qualities etc., than the Muslims. During the pre-Sepoy Mutiny period, section of Hindu traders greatly helped the British while their Muslim counterparts did not. The British were angry. With the spread of Western education Hindus made a big way, but the Muslims could not. A sense of deprivation crept in. Perhaps, the sense of deprivation was engineered. When the discontentment grew in the beginning of this century, the British capitalised on this sense of deprivation. A feeling of inferiority was there. The British merely added fuel to fire. Suddenly both the communities became aware of their religious identities. The net result is the Partition of Bengal. The sear of Partition is yet to heal.

Partition

Lord Curzon, the viceroy of India decided to partition Bengal for administrative purposes, creating a new province of East Bengal and Assam, with a population of 31 million people and with its capital at Dhaka. The Brahmaputra and the Padma (the Ganges) rivers physically defined this first partition of Bengal. East Bengal prospered, Dhaka assumed its old status as capital and Chittagong became an important sea port.

Given below is the proclamation of partition:

- The Governor-General is pleased to constitute the territories at present under the administration of the Chief Commissioner of Assam to be for the purposes of the Indian Councils Act 1861... a province to which the provisions of that Act touching the making of laws and regulations for the peace and good order of the presidencies of Fort St. George and Bombay shall be applicable and to direct that the said province shall be called and known as the province of Eastern Bengal and Assam....
- The Governor-General in Council is pleased to specify the sixteenth day of October, 1905 as the period at which the said provisions shall take effect and 15th as the number of councillors whom the Lieutenant-Governor may nominate for his assistance in making laws and regulations.
- The Governor-General in Council is further pleased to declare and appoint that upon the constitution of the said province of Eastern Bengal and Assam, the districts of Dacca, Mymensingh, Faridpur, Backergunge, Tippera, Noakhali, Chittagong, the Chittagong Hill Tracts,

Rajashahi, Dinajpur, Jalpaiguri, Rangpur, Bogra, Pabna, and Malda which now form part of the Bengal Division of the Presidency of Fort William shall cease to be subject to or included within the limits of that Division, and shall thenceforth be subject to and included within the limits of the Lieutenant-Governorship of the province of Eastern Bengal and Assam.

The reason behind the partition that was officially announced was that the Bengal province was too large to be administered by a single governor and therefore was partitioned on administrative purpose. But the real reason behind the partition was political and not administrative. East Bengal was dominated by the Muslims and West Bengal by the Hindus. Partition was yet another part of the 'Divide and rule' policy. The following excerpts from Curzon's letter of 2 February 1905 to St. John Brodrick, Secretary of State for India, give an idea of his aims in partitioning Bengal:

"Calcutta is the centre from which the Congress Party is manipulated throughout the whole of Bengal, and indeed the whole of India. Its best wire pullers and its most frothy orators all reside here. The perfection of their machinery, and the tyranny which it enables them to exercise are truly remarkable. They dominate public opinion in Calcutta; they affect the High Court; they frighten the local Government, and they are sometimes not without serious influence on the Government of India. The whole of their activity is directed to creating an agency so powerful that they may one day be able to force a weak government to give them what they desire. Any measure in consequence that would divide the Bengali-speaking population; that would permit independent centres of activity and influence to grow up; that would dethrone Calcutta from its place as the centre of successful intrigue, or that would weaken the influence of the lawyer class, who have the entire organization in their hands, is intensely and hotly resented by them. The outcry will be loud and very fierce, but as a native gentleman said to me – 'my countrymen always howl until a thing is settled; then they accept it'."

Lord Curzon

George Curzon was the eldest son of Baron Curzon. He was perhaps the most important British politician in modern times that failed in his quest to become prime minister. He was born in 1859 and proved to be a brilliant student. Curzon was an ambitious man who tended to see issues in stark terms. He took strong positions and would rarely acknowledge any middle ground. He became a force in the Conservative Party and served as Viceroy of India. He introduced reforms angering Lord Kitchner—head of the British Army in India. He was at the time a firm believer in Empire and Britain's imperial mission. Interestingly, today he is chiefly remembered for extending Western knowledge of Indian art, archeology, and literature. Before and after World War I, he led the fight against women's' suffrage which is part of the reason he never achieved his goal of becoming prime minister.

George was a brilliant student. He attended the prestigious Eton public (private) school. At Eton College, he won a record number of academic prizes. He entered Oxford University in 1878. He was elected president of the Oxford Union in 1880—a considerable honour. Although George did not earn a first he was made a fellow of All Souls College in 1883.

The Marquis of Salisbury in November 1891, appointed Curzon as his secretary of state for India. Curzon lost this post when Earl of Rosebery formed a Liberal Government in 1894. The General Election of 1895 returned the Conservative Party to power. Curzon was given the post of under secretary for foreign affairs. Three years later the Marquis of Salisbury granted him the title, Baron Curzon of Kedleston, and appointed him Viceroy of India. Once in India, Curzon introduced a series of reforms that upset the British and civil service in India. He also angered Lord Kitchener, who had became the commander of the Indian Army in 1902. Lord Curzon was one of the most important English Viceroys. He was a seasoned politician and very young, only about 40 at the time of his appointment. He was both energetic and capable. His understanding of the Asian affairs was better than that of other British statesman of the time. He understood Indian problems and addressed most of them. His goal was to strengthen British Empire in India. Many such as measures to deal with plague and to protect farmers were of great benefit to Indians. A measure to divide Bengal proved very unpopular. He was at the time a firm believer in Empire and Britain's imperial mission. Interestingly, today he is chiefly remembered for extending Western knowledge of Indian art, archeology, and literature. One of his reforms was to preserve Indian archeological treasures. His many reforms disturbed many British leaders who chief interest was to maintain the established order with a minimum of local unrest. The new leader of the Conservative Party, Arthur Balfour, began to question Curzon's judgment. Curzon in 1905 was forced out of office.

Anti-Partition Movement

The first part of a news item, which appeared in the Amrita Bazar Patrika of 17 October 1905 entitled "Calcutta in Mourning-A Unique Sight", describing the situation in Calcutta on 16 October 1905, the day Bengal was partitioned, is given below.

'Yesterday was one of the most memorable days in the history of the British administration of India. It being the day on which the Bengal Partition scheme took effect, the day on which our unsympathetic government forced a measure by a proclamation in the official gazette against the wishes of the whole population, the day on which our rulers tried to separate the Bengali speaking people of the East Bengal from those of the West Bengal, the people of Calcutta, irrespective of nationality, social position, creed and sex, observed it as a day of mourning. The leaders of the Bengali community-Hindus and Mohammedans-did not however silently mourn and weep. They as a legacy to posterity and as a landmark to British administration laid the foundation of the Federation Hall. They also took a practical step towards the furtherance of the Swadeshi movement by opening the National Fund.'

Sixteenth of October 1905 was observed as the day of mourning. Right from the morning thousands of people began taking dip in Ganges. Hindus and Muslims tied Rakhis to each other to show their indestructible unity. People in Calcutta walked bare-foot in the streets shouting the slogan 'Vande Mataram'. Such was effect of the slogan that the British prohibited the use of it in Bengal.

The partition of Bengal led many youths to resort to arms. In different parts of the country a number of secret societies sprang up, particularly in Bengal and Maharashtra. To terrorize the British officers, they trained members, mostly students in the use of fire-arms. In this, Aurobindo Ghosh and his associates Bengal and one Chapekar brother and the Savarkar brothers in Maharashtra were quite active. By assassinating unpopular British officials and their Indian agents, their main method was to spread terror. Attempts were made on the lives of Lt. Governor of Bengal and the Viceroy.

Khudiram Bose, a 16 year old fired a shot at a district judge on April 30, 1908, which accidentally killed two English women instead. He was caught, flogged and hanged. But the main consequence of the Partition of Bengal was the Swadeshi and Boycott movement.

It was with the sense of a need for organisation, the sense of intense bitterness at the Congress, and the realisation that the liberation of India would have to be won by force, that led to the emergence of the revolutionary terrorists. Many Swadeshi movement radicals joined the movement: among them, Ajit Singh's group in Punjab and the Tirunelveli radicals after the arrest of Pillai and Siva. These early revolutionaries' special contribution was in putting forward a conscious alternative path of struggle to the Congress's peaceful petitioning. Jugantar (which along with Bande Mataram and Sandhya was one of the leading magazines representing this trend) wrote about the police assault on the peaceful Barisal conference:

"The 30 crores of people inhabiting India must raise their 60 crores of hands to stop this course of oppression. Force must be stopped by force."

Though the revolutionary terrorists did not lead mass struggles against the British, their heroic acts and sacrifices won them enormous popularity among the common people. Among the major groups were the Abhinav Bharat (centres in Nasik, and led by V. Savarkar), the Anushilan Samity (based in Dacca and led by Pulin Das), the Jugantar group (led by Jatindranath Mukherji) and the group led by Rash Behari Bose and Sachindranath Sanyal. These groups carried out several armed raids to raise funds, executions of English officials (especially of sadistic and racist district magistrates), and a few spectacular attempts on the lives of major officials. Some of their more famous actions included the unsuccessful attempt in 1907 on the life of the lieutenant governor of Bengal, the 1908 attempt on the life of the notorious Muzaffarpur district magistrate Kingsford, the 1909 execution of the Nasik district magistrate, the 1909 London execution of the India Office bureaucrat Curzon-Wyllie, and the 1912 attempt on the life of the Viceroy Lord Hardinge.

The sheer heroism of these men, who carried out these acts in the face of certain death, moved the people. The would-be assassins of Kingsford (their bomb instead killed two

Englishwomen and left Kingsford unscathed), Prafulla Chaki and Khudiram Bose, became heroes of Bengal. Chaki shot himself in captivity while Bose was tried and hanged. Folk songs in their memory were composed and sung all over the country.

Swadeshi & Boycott Movement

The spark for the Swadeshi Movement was the British decision to partition Bengal. Viceroy Curzon's scheme, ostensibly for "administrative convenience", to divide Bengal into Eastern and Western provinces, was indeed a major provocation. First, the Congress, and political activity in general, were strongest in Bengal. Moreover, Curzon had an obsessive hatred of the Congress: "The Congress", he wrote to the Secretary of State, "is tottering to its fall, and one of my great ambitions while in India is to assist it to a peaceful demise." His Secretary of State, on the other hand, differed. Congress leaders, of course, were unhappy with Curzon's hostility, and compared him unfavourably with earlier, more liberal, Viceroys. Gokhale complained, "The bureaucracy was growing frankly selfish and openly hostile to national aspirations. It was not so in the past."

Swadeshi, which means of ones own country, implied that people should use only the goods produced in India and boycott foreign goods. On August 7, 1905, in a public meeting at the Calcutta Town Hall, the Boycott Resolution was passed. Tilak had attempted a boycott of foreign cloth in 1896, but failed to elicit such response. The response in Bengal was overwhelming: By September 1905, the sale of British cloth in some districts fell to between 6 and 20 per cent of original levels. Public burning of foreign cloth and the setting up of village Samitis took place spontaneously. One of these Samitis, the Swadesh Bandhab Samiti of Barisal, headed by the schoolteacher Aswinikumar Dutt, attained remarkable popularity for its social and humanitarian work among the largely Muslim peasantry. It was reported even in 1909 to have 175 village branches.

The Swadeshi movement also saw a remarkable upsurge in labour organisation, with the added feature of active public sympathy with the strikers. Among the strikes of this period (1905-8) in Bengal were those of clerical staff, Calcutta tram workers, jute workers, railway workers (of various categories, from clerical staff to coolies), and press workers. The Swadeshi movement in

Bengal also saw the emergence of labour unions and professional agitators. Bombay, Madras and Punjab also witnessed the growth of a spontaneous anti-imperialist labour movement-the most famous example being the 1908 strike of Bombay textile workers in protest against Tilak's arrest.

Among the many lasting achievements of the Swadeshi movement were its contribution to anti-imperialist culture-whether in Rabindranath Tagore's earlier writings, in Subramania Bharati's poems, or, most importantly, in the vast number of extremely popular patriotic folk songs, folk plays, and other forms of people's art. The writings of "extremist" journalists also philosophically advanced the Indian liberation struggle. For instance, as Indian "extremists" started building contacts with Irish radicals, a sense of the worldwide anti-imperialist movement (which had, of course, nourished the beginnings of Swadeshi-as in its drawing inspiration from China and the Russian Revolution) was getting enunciated.

Bande Mataram wrote (in 1909, by which time it was being brought out from Europe by Madame Cama), "Dhingra's pistol shot has been heard by the Irish Cottier in his forlorn hut, by the Egyptian fellah in the field, by the Zulu labourer in the dark mine..."

While Aurobindo Ghosh's fanatic Hinduism severely limited his anti-imperialist politics and ultimately led him, for fear of British repression, into the safety of ashram life, other groups had no such limitations. The pamphlet Oh Martyrs (1907), for instance, evokes the memory of 1857, when "the Firinghee rule was shattered to pieces and the swadeshi thrones were set up by the common consent of Hindus and Mohammedans..." When Madame Cama unfurled the flag of "free" India at the Stuttgart Congress of the Second International, the design contained, besides the words "Bande Mataram", both Hindu and Muslim symbol.

Education

The year 1905 was in many ways a turning point. Its immediate impact was political. Bengal at that time was a hot bed of anti British political activity. Though for some time a partition of the huge province was being contemplated for administrative convenience, Curzon decided to kill two birds with one stone. By dividing the Bengali speaking population on communal grounds, he hoped to break the nationalist movement. But what happened was just the opposite. The anti-British feeling did not fizzle out. Instead, a new wave of patriotism swept through the province. The protest snowballed to such proportions that finally the partition had to be annulled in 1911. But the protesters had to pay a price. From Calcutta, the capital was shifted to Delhi.

Saha, Bose and their contemporaries who later made significant contributions in science grew up in this atmosphere of inspired idealism. Children along with their elders roamed the streets singing patriotic songs, burning of foreign goods became a rage- "Boycott British goods, buy Swadeshi" was the popular slogan. The reason why many good students of the generation opted for science was again this vague sense of patriotism. They felt it was possible to improve things, to bring about development through science. It was against this background that India's first crop of brilliant scientists came up – the celebrated 1909 batch of Presidency College, about whom P C Ray has waxed eloquent in his autobiography. They all happened to be the students of P C Ray, though many changed over to mathematics or physics later. They were, apart from Saha and S N Bose- J.N. Ghosh, J.N.Mukherjee, Maniklal De, Sailen Ghosh, N.R.Sen, Pulinbehari Sarkar, Amaresh Chakravarty and Prankrishna Parija. Though the 1909 batch was the brightest in the history of that college, there were others destined for greatness. P C Mahalanobis, N R Dhar and S K Mitra were a few years senior to this group. Other illustrious people like Subhas Bose and Rajendra Prasad were students around this period. The teaching faculty was also outstanding, with P C Ray, J C Bose, D N Mullick, C E Cullis, Surendranath Maitra, P C Ghosh, Manmohan Ghosh, H M Percival and others. This combination of excellent teachers and receptive pupils brought about a new period in the history of science in India.

One manifestation of the Swadeshi spirit was the Indianisation of education. There was a feeling that along with the boycott of British goods the students should turn to their own culture and tradition. English education only resulted in alienation from their roots.. From boycott of British goods the next step was boycott of the Calcutta University. Alternatives had to be worked out. The National Education movement gathered momentum, but there were serious differences of opinion about what measures should be adopted. One group led by Gooroodas Bannerjee, Satish Chandra Mukherjee and Rabindranath Tagore wanted to have a completely

Indian structure of education under Indian control. The other group was of opinion that extreme nationalism could not take them very far. Led by eminent people like Taraknath Palit and Nilratan Sircar, they wanted to add courses in scientific and technical education as well. The difference between the two camps led to two different institutions – the National Council of Education and the Society for the Promotion of Technical Education. But none of these institutions could attract enough students. Eventually Sir Taraknath handed over all his assets to Sir Asutosh Mookerjee, the Vice Chancellor of Calcutta University about whom Lord Minto had said, " I know no pilot more capable of steering the ship of learning through educational shoals and quick-sands than Dr. Mookerjee." It was a prophetic statement. Sir Asutosh did more for higher education in Bengal than all other educationalists put together.

By an Act of 1904, the University was now to be a teaching university and not just an examining body. It was now empowered to appoint professors and lectures. Under the able guidance of Sir Asutosh who believed that changes could be made within the framework of the existing structure, Calcutta University became a thriving centre for research. Princely donations from eminent jurists and other wealthy patrons helped Asutosh in creating professorships and scholarships. With such support the University College of Science came into being. With uncanny insight, Asutosh spotted talents and brought many deserving people under the same umbrella. The new Science College soon acquired a character of it's own. A stipulation for the endowment chairs clearly laid down the rule that all the posts were only for Indians. So starting off as an ally of the British, Asutosh was able to achieve the objectives of the National School. By and by an attitude of hostility developed between the government and the university. In those crucial times, a man of the courage and stature of Sir Asutosh was needed to steer things with a firm hand. When the government rejected the request for more funds, Asutosh said we would rather go from door to door with a begging bowl rather than accept the government's terms. A galaxy of stars assembled round Asutosh, P C Ray as the Palit Professor of Chemistry, D M Bose as the Ghosh Professor and C V Raman in the Physics chair. Raman belonged to the Indian Audits and Accounts Service and carried on research during off-hours in the Indian Association for the Cultivation of

Science. It goes to the great credit of Sir Asutosh that this officer was inducted into the University with complete freedom to work in the I A C S., work which finally won him the Nobel Prize in Physics.

National Flag

On August 7, 1906, the first anniversary of the anti-partition movement, a big rally was organised at Parsi Bagan Square (Greer Park) in Calcutta. For the first time a tricolour flag was unfurled there. The moving spirit behind the design of this flag was Schindra Prasad Bose, a close follower of Sir Surendranath Banerjee and the son-in-law of the moderate Brahmo leader, Krishna Kumar Mitra. The flag they designed had open lotuses on the top green, yellow and red. It had eight half open lotuses on the green stripe, Vande Mataram in blue on the middle yellow stripe, and the sun and moon (crescent) in white on the bottom red stripe. This flag was for the first time hoisted at the Parsi Bagan Square on August 7, 1906, which was observed as Boycott Day to protest against the partition of Bengal, Narendranath Sen ceremonially the flag and sang a song. Sir Surendranath Banerjee, who hoisted this flag with the bursting of a hundred and one crackers.

Literature

The sufferings of the motherland and the passion for independence inspired many Bengali writers, novelists, poets and play weights to show their protest against the colonial rule.

'Bangamangal' was written by the poet Karunanidhan Bandopadhyay, and was published in 1901. In some of these poems, Satyendranath Dutta too wrote about the Swadeshi Movement. It was the Swadeshi Movement which gave a new dimension to the Bengali literature of that time. A number of ballad songs were written by the famous poet Mukunda Das. These songs became very popular t that time of the Anti-Partition Movement, and were great source of inspiration to the freedom fighters.

The turbulent movement against the partition of Bengal came in the sphere of drama and plays too. 'Sirajdaullah' (1906), 'Mirkasim' (1907) and 'Chhatrapati' (1908) were the important plays by Girishchandra Ghosh whose patriotism was reflected in them. Apart from Girishchandra, the historical plays by D.L. Roy like 'Mewar Patan (the downfall of the Mewar), 'Shahjahan',

'Pratapsinha' etc. had the Swadeshi flavour. Not only by his plays, D. L. Roy showed his emotions for his motherland by many of his patriotic songs. Rajanikanta Sen and Atulprasad Sen – these two names are also remarkable for their patriotic songs. Dwijendranath Tagore's name is also remarkable in this perspective.

In 1905, Sri Aurobindo Ghosh wrote 'Vawani Mandir'. In this book, he stated the plans and programmes of the Revolutionary Terrorist groups. Abinashchandra Bhattacharya discussed the guerilla strategy in his book 'Bartaman Rananiti' (the present war policy). But above all it was the novel called 'Pather Dabi' by Saratchandra Chattopadhay. Where a vivid sketch of the passion, the strategy and the spirit of the Revolutionary Terrorists was revealed. The character of the main protagonist of the novel, Sabyasachi, was inspired by many great revolutionists of that time like Rasbehari Basu, Manabendranath Roy and many others. This novel was about the Revolutionary Terrorist group of Bengal which was working outside India especially in Burma to eradicate the foreign rule from their motherland. Though some critics think that the importance of romance and personal emotions were much prominent in this novel than the detailings of the revolutionary activities, but it can't be denied that the revolutionary flavour in this novel was so much that it was banned by the contemporary British Government immediately after its publication in 1926.

It is impossible to avoid Rabindranath Tagore concerning the Swadeshi Movement in Bengali literature, especially when his 'Gora' (1910) came out just in this period.

Vande Mataram

Created on 7th November, 1875, the next few years saw Vande Mataram being accepted and appreciated in the literary circles of Bengal. However, the masses better conceived it through a novel written by Bankimchandra himself: The Anandmath. This novel started appearing in the magazine, Banga Darshan, during 1880 to 1882. Its concept itself generated ripples in people's minds, as it was a novel, which speaks of revolutionaries who live and die for their motherland. So naturally was the song incorporated in it, that its prior creation seems unlikely.

The year 1905 was memorable to Vande Mataram in many ways. In this year the song crossed the boundaries of Bengal, spread like a jungle fire throughout the nation which would oust the British rule. No sooner than the Partition of Bengal was declared, thousands of angry Bharatiyas protested the decision in a unanimous voice: Vande Mataram.

Bengal was a province rich enough in resources. The then viceroy Lord Curzon had ulterior motives in separating Bengal into two. Although portrayed to be an 'administrative convenience', the partition aimed at segregating the Hindu and Muslim populations on the basis of cast, creed and language.

Mild protests didn't change the decision and time came to revolt. On 7th of August 1905, a huge mob gathered for protest. Somebody just loudly said, the words Vande Mataram and the miracle happened. Thousands echoed it in one voice. Indian freedom struggle had got it's march song. The whole incidence is witnessed and chronicled by a great spiritual and revolutionary person-Shri Aurobindo Ghosh.

It took the year 1905 and the events narrated above when the British government realized the potential and nuisance value of Vande Mataram. Saraladevi Chaudharani, niece of Ravindranath Tagore, sung it despite protest in the 1905 Congress convention. The very next year 1906 saw a massive blood-shed, because of Vande Mataram. A regional youth convention of the Congress was originated at Barisal (now in Bangladesh). Strict orders were issued that Vande Mataram should not be rehearsed in any way in the convention, in any procession or even in a public place. The eminent leaders present-Surendranath Banerjee and the editor of Amrit Bazar Patrika, Mr. Motilal Ghose discussed the issue with delegates.

On the 14th April 1906, neglecting the orders issued, a full procession wearing Vande Mataram badges gathered. Before it could proceed, the police charged them in the cruelest manner with police sticks. Neither Shri Aurobindo nor Surendranath could escape the attack. Their bodies were covered with blood. Again, the next day of the convention began with the Vande Mataram song. After concluding, every volunteer returned with Vande Mataram in his mind.

Origin

Vande Mataram inspired a true sense of patriotism amongst Bharatiyas. These were the very words, which ultimately avoided the partition of Bengal, and these were the words recited in the end, by numerous Bharatiya revolutionaries while facing the gallows. It will be appropriate to glance over the inspirations of its writer poet-Bankimchandra Chattopadhay, in creating such a great song. Although a sudden flux of energy made him write it instantly, many events have acted as trigger.

The first runner of the Indian National Congress was a gathering started in 1867-The Hindu Mela. In its second convention (11th April 1868), Bankimchandra heard a song 'Jai Bharat, Jai' and was greatly influenced by its content. He started thinking on a need of a universal, patriotic message to fellow Bharatiyas. Bankim felt sad about this mindset of his countrymen. In his times, Vande Mataram did not acquire so much importance in Indian hearts, as compared to later years. But surely, it provided a common chord of brotherhood provided the right stimuli for the Indians. Ancient Indian tradition worships 'Mother' asa sacred deity, a mother, her love and affection towards her children, the pains she takes to bring up the child, have given this unparalleled position in our culture. Obviously, Bankim portrayed the nation as the 'Mother' itself and hailed her. In fact, he was searching for the right words. Words, with power and zeal, which will chant the ultimate praise of the motherland. The year was 1875. Not even in the creations (poems) of the great poets like Bhavabhuti, Kalidasa that such powerful words could he find.

On the 7th of November, 1875 he was quietly meditating in a house on the banks of Ganga, night was tranquil and flux of full moon was showering on the waters of Ganga. Suddenly Bankimda could hear the folklore of Bengal's fishermen. It was saying that "for us, the river Ganga is nothing else but mother Durga. Easily will we sacrifice our lives for her, within her." That was the right tone, the right feeling Bankimchandra was looking for. Durga is the warrior goddess, with the lion as the chariot. Although a mother, a woman she is, destroying the enemy with a weapon in hand. This stance of the mother was what was needed.

Thus was born the Indian national song Vande Mataram. The day was 7 November 1875 Kartik Shuddha Navami, Hindu year 1797.

Partition of Bengal (1905)

The Partition of Bengal in 1905, was made on October 16, by then Viceroy of India, Lord Curzon. Partition was promoted for administrative regions; Bengal was as large as France but with a significantly larger population. The eastern region was thought to be neglected and under-governed. By splitting the province, an improved administration could be established in the east where, subsequently, the population would benefit from new schools and employment opportunities. However, other motives lurked behind the partition plan. Bengali Hindus were in the forefront of political agitation for greater participation in governance; their position would be weakened, since Muslims would now dominate in the East. Hindus tended to oppose partition, which was more popular among Muslims. What followed partition, however, stimulated an almost national anti-British movement that involved nonviolent and violent protests, boycotts and even an assassination attempt against the Governor of the new province of West Bengal.

Partition barely lasted half a decade, before it was annulled in 1911. Britain's policy of *divide et impera* which lay behind partition, however, continued to impact on the re-united province. In 1919, separate elections were established for Muslims and Hindus. Before this, many members of both communities had advocated national solidarity of all Bengalis. Now, distinctive communities developed, with their own political agendas.

Muslims, too, dominated the Legislature, due to their overall numerical strength of roughly twenty eight to twenty two million. Nationally, Hindus and Muslims began to demand the creation of two independent states, one to be formed in majority Hindu and one in majority Muslim areas with most Bengali Hindus now supporting partitioning Bengal on this basis.

The Muslims wanted the whole province to join the Muslim state, Pakistan. In 1947, Bengal was partitioned for the second time, this time specifically on religious grounds. It became East Pakistan. However, in 1971, for cultural reasons, East Pakistan became the independent state of Bangladesh. Partition may sometimes be necessary as a pragmatic strategy to avoid bloodshed but more often than not this leads to new problems that divide even more people. Almost always, partition produces discontent among minorities on both sides of the border. Both partitions of Bengal saw bloodshed, ruined lives and made the world a less united place. A partitioned world will not be able to make our planet a common home, so that it becomes a shared, not a contested space. As a race, people need to find ways of building bridges instead of barriers.

Reason for Partition

Partitioning Bengal was first considered in 1903. There were also additional proposals to separate Chittagong and the districts of Dhaka and Mymensingh from Bengal, attaching them to the province of Assam. The government officially published the idea in January 1904, and in February, Lord Curzon the Governor-General of India made an official tour to eastern districts of Bengal to assess public opinion on the partition.

He consulted with leading personalities and delivered speeches at Dhaka, Chittagong and Mymensingh, explaining the government's stand on partition. Curzon explained the reason for partition as an administrative improvement; "under the British the province of Bengal was as large as France, with a population of seventy-eight and a half million, nearly as populous as contemporary France and Great Britain combined," says Hardy. The province included Bihar and Orissa and the eastern "region was notoriously under-governed." According to Hardy, Curzon did not intend to divide Hindus, who were the majority in the West, from Muslims, the majority in the East but "only Bengalis." The plan was to re-unite the eastern region with Assam (which had been part of Bengal until 1874) and to form a "new province with a population of thirty-one millions, of whom 59 percent would be Muslims."

The plan also involved Bengal ceding five Hindi-speaking states to the Central Provinces. It return, it would receive, on the western side, Sambalpur and five minor Oriya-speaking states from the Central Provinces. Bengal would be left with an area of 141,580 sq. miles and a population of 54 million, of which 42 million would be Hindus and 9 million Muslims. However, Bengali speakers would be a minority in the West "in relation to Biharis and Oriyas." Administration of the new province would consist of a Legislative Council, a Board of Revenue of two members, and the jurisdiction of the Calcutta High Court would be left undisturbed. The government pointed out that Eastern Bengal and Assam would have a clearly demarcated western boundary and well defined geographical, ethnological, linguistic and social characteristics. The government of India promulgated their final decision in a resolution dated July 19, 1905, and the partition of Bengal was effected on October 16 of the same year.

Reaction to the Plan

As details of the plan became public knowledge, prominent Bengalis began a series of demonstrations against partition and a boycott of British products. While protest was mainly Hindu-led the Muslims *nawab* of Dhaka was also initially opposed to the plan, even though Dhaka would serve as capital of the new province. Baxter suggests that the "divide and rule" policy was the real reason for partition. Lord Curzon said, "Bengal united is a power; Bengali divided will pull in several different ways." Bengalis were the first to benefit from English education in India and as an intellectual class were disproportionately represented in the Civil Service, which was, of course, dominated by colonial officials. They were also in the forefront of calls for greater participation in governance, if not for independence. By splitting Bengal, their influence would be weakened. This would also, effectively, divide the nationalist movement. Bengalis, who regarded themselves as a nation, did not want to be a linguistic minority in their own province. Indeed, many of those Hindus who were considered "unfriendly if not seditious in character" lived in the east and dominated "the whole tone of Bengal administration." Since Muslims would form the majority in the east under the plan, their power would be undermined. Baxter is thus, unlike Hardy, of the view that playing Hindu and Muslims off against each other did lie behind the partition plan. Calcutta, the capital of the united province, was still at this point also the capital of British India, which meant that Bengalis were at the very centre of British power. At the same time, the Muslims of Bengal were considered loyal to the British since they had not joined the anti-British rebellion of 1857-8, so they would be rewarded.

Partition

Partition took place October 1905. It resulted in a huge political crisis. The Muslims in East Bengal after initial opposition tended to be much more positive about the arrangement, believing that a separate region would give them more opportunity for education, employment, and so on. However, partition was especially unpopular by the people of what had become West Bengal, where a huge amount of nationalist literature was created during this period. Opposition by Indian National Congress was led by Sir Henry Cotton who had been Chief Commissioner of Assam, but

Curzon was not to be moved. His successor, Lord Minto, also though it crucial to maintain partition, commenting that it "should and must be maintained since the diminution of Bengali political agitation will assist to remove a serious cause of anxiety... It is," he continued, "the growing power of a population with great intellectual gifts and a talent for making itself heard which is not unlikely to influence public opinion at home most mischievously." Sir Andrew Fraser, formerly Lt. Governor of Bengal stayed on as Governor of West Bengal and was especially targeted by anti-partition agitators, who derailed his train in 1907. He retired in 1908. Support for the anti-partition cause came from throughout India, where the partition of an historic province was regarded as an act of colonial arrogance and blamed on the divide and rule policy. "Calcutta," says Metcalf, "came alive with rallies, bonfires of foreign goods, petitions, newspapers and posters." Anti-British and pro-self-rule sentiment increased. In fact, the Swadeshi movement itself emerged from opposition to Partition, which was regarded as "a sinister imperial design to cripple the Bengali led nationalist movement."

Later, Cotton, now Liberal MP for Nottingham East coordinated the successful campaign to oust the first lieutenant-governor of East Bengal, Sir Bampfylde Fuller. In 1906, Rabindranath Tagore wrote Amar Shonar Bangla as a rallying cry for proponents of annulment of Partition, which, much later, in 1972, became the national anthem of Bangladesh. The song "Bande Mataram" which Tagore set to music became the "informal anthem of the nationalist movement after 1905." Secret terrorist organizations began to operate, for whom Bengal as their mother-land was epitomized by the goddess Kali, "goddess of power and destruction, to whom they dedicated their weapons."

Bengal's Partition Rescinded

Due to these protests, the two parts of Bengal were reunited in 1911. A new partition which divided the province on linguistic, rather than religious, grounds followed, with the Hindi, Oriya and Assamese areas separated to form separate administrative units. The administrative capital of British India was moved from Calcutta to New Delhi as well.

Dhaka, no longer a capital, was given a University as compensation, founded in 1922. Curzon Hall was handed over to the new foundation as one of its first building. Built in 1904, in preparation for partition, Curzon Hall, which blends Western and Mughal architectural styles, was intended to be the Town Hall.

Legacy

East and West Pakistan before 1911, following Bengal's second partition in 1947.

Although protest had been largely Hindu-led, such eminent leaders of the Indian nationalist movement at Nazrul Islam and Rabindranath Tagore stressed Hindu-Muslim unity. Although some opponents to partition gave it a religious aspect by identifying closely with Kali, others stressed the unity of the Bengali nation, not religion. Divine and rule, however, continued as a British policy. In 1919, they created different electorates for Muslims, Hindus and for other distinctive communities. A new award of seat allocation in 1932 increased Muslim representation.

This encouraged Muslims to develop as a "social-cultural group" so that even in Bengal where, culturally, Muslims shared much in common with Hindus, they began to regard themselves as a separate nation. As Indian nationalism gained momentum, Muslims and Hindus began to demand a new partition, more radical than that of 1905. This one would divide Hindu-majority areas from Muslim majority areas to form the independent states of India and Pakistan. Yet, as plans for Pakistan were set in motion, many people assumed that the Muslims of Bengal would not want to join the proposed state, partly because of its geographical distance from the other main centres of Muslim majority population over one thousand miles to the West but also due to the strength of Bengali nationalism.

The proposed name for the new Muslim state, Pakistan, was formed from Punjab, Afghania (North-West Frontier Province), Kashmir, Sindh, and Baluchi*stan,* thus, Bengal was not included. The United Bengal Movement did champion a separate, united state for all Bengalis on the eve of the 1947 partition but failed to attract enough support. If the 1905 partition had not happened, Bengali nationalism would probably have been strong enough to resist partition when this was once more placed on the agenda. The consequences, however, of the 1905 partition and of subsequent British divide and rule inspired policies seriously undermined Bengali solidarity cross-faith solidarity. This time, it was Hindus who supported partition, largely because, after the Communal Award of 1932, Muslims had dominated the Legislature in a coalition government with European support. Hindus now saw their future within India, where Hindus would be a majority. For Hindus, a separate Bengali state was no longer an attractive option, despite the appeal of Bengali solidarity. Bengali Muslims, for their part, did not want to live in a United India.

London mandated that the Legislature meet in two sections, one comprising delegates from Hindu-majority districts and the other from Muslim districts. A majority in favour of partition from either section would determine the outcome. On June 20 1947, 166 to 35 in the East Bengal section actually voted against partitioning Bengal and in favour of the whole province joining Pakistan. A vote in the Western region favoured partition by 58-21, with the West joining India and the East Pakistan.

Almost certainly due to the wedge that Britain's divide and rule policy had driven between Hindus and Muslims in Bengal, partition followed more or less along the same demographic lines as it had in 1905, except that only the Muslim Sylhet region of Assam voted to join (by a majority of 55,578 votes) what was to become East Pakistan. Partition followed, although only a minority of the whole province wanted this. Hundreds of thousands of casualties resulted from riots and during mass population transfers.

Having religion in common with West Pakistan, however, over a thousand miles away, did not prove strong enough to glue the two provinces of the new nation together. In 1971, after a bloody Bangladesh War of Independence, the East became a separate sovereign state for reasons that had to do with culture and language and Bengali nationalism. A nation was born that, although majority-Muslim, declared all its citizens, regardless of religion, equal before the law with "nationalism" as a principle of state.

Lord Curzon and the Partition of Bengal

"I am not a politician, and still less can I be said to be a party-man: but I have a hatred of tyranny, and a contempt for its tools; and this feeling I have expressed as often and as strongly as I could." These are the opening words of Hazlitt's Preface to his Political Essays. They could as well have been the words of Rabindranath. Without ever identifying himself with any political organization or 'ism' he did the same as Hazlitt through his writings. But on one occasion he came out on the street to actively protest and agitate against an administrative measure which had hurt the Bengali sentiment most – the 1905 Partition of Bengal.

The sense of indignation among the Bengalis was unprecedented, their protest spontaneous and almost universal and their agitation taking forms that often transgressed the limits set by law. The Partition had ultimately to be revoked but not before Curzon, the perpetrator of this arbitrary act, left in defeat and disappointment, apparently resigning his Viceroyalty over a row with the Commander-in-Chief Kitchener. Traditionally on retirement every Viceroy used to be awarded an earldom. An exception was made in the case of Curzon. Instead, from a powerful potentate reigning over a vast empire consisting of many extensive provinces his Lordship now became the petty Chancellor of the prestigious yet small university of Oxford which consisted only of a few colleges. Never a fall could have been greater. And when in 1912, the very year when the Partition was set aside and a year before he received the Nobel Prize, Rabindranath visited Britain with his manuscript *Gitanjali* the British intellectual world received him with enthusiasm quite uncharacteristic of the British. A friend of Rothenstein informally proposed for the award of an Oxford degree on Rabindranath. But Curzon as Chancellor turned down that proposal. He had obviously not recovered from the injuries of his great fall nor forgotten the man who had played a leading role in the anti-Partition agitation which, among other things, led to that fall.

An imperialist to the tips of his fingers Curzon was the rising hope of the imperialist wing of the Conservative Party. In his student days as President of the Oxford Union he had merited the doggerel:

My name is George Nathaniel Curzon,
I am a most superior person,
My cheek is pink, my hair is sleek,
I dine at Blenheim once a week.

To a man like Churchill – another bird of the same feather, albeit of a lighter shade, not from conviction but for convenience– who belonged to the same party, Curzon was one of those 'superior Oxford prigs', to whom democracy, even of the Tory variety, was anathema. Under the unbridled capitalist system,-the lessez faire economy – of Victorian England the evils of industrialization had manifested themselves in their ugliest forms. In the words of Disraeli the country was divided into 'Two Nations'. In the midst of plenty there was poverty and squalor. At one extreme there were the upper classes – the landed aristocracy and the manufacturer magnates – who virtually owned all the properties and enjoyed all the material comforts and powers and privileges. On the other extreme were 'the lower orders of society' – the burgeoning industrial workers, miners, the lower-middle class and the poor – who wallowed in untold misery both physical and spiritual. Such a society supplied Marx and Engels with ample materials for their formulation of a new philosophy of revolution and the time would not be far away when the weapon they forged in the living laboratory of industrial Britain would burst upon an inherently exploitative world with a shattering impact. Dickens, the most popular novelist of the day, also faithfully documented and depicted this appalling social scene in his works.

This 'deep-seated vulgarity' in the very heart of a high civilization caused widespread indignation among the sufferers as well as among the reformers. Organizations like the Social Democratic Federation (1881) based on Marxist ideas, the Fabian Society (1883) and the Independent Labour Party (1893) sprang up and the behaviour of the poor and the pauperized no longer remained disciplined and deferential but became riotous and rebellious. The Utilitarians like Bentham and Mill were arguing for 'the greatest good of the greatest number' – the extension of democracy in all spheres of society – economic, social and political. The vested interests represented chiefly by the Conservative Party felt threatened.

One of the Eminent Victorians of Lytton Strachey, Dr. Arnold of Rugby school fame, must have echoed the sentiments of the Conservatives when he wrote in his letter to his son Matthew about the famous Hyde Park riot, "the old Roman way of dealing with that (i.e. rioting) is always the right one; flog the rank and file, and fling the ring-leaders from the Tarpeian Rock!" One section of that Party however appreciated the inevitability of democratization in the changed circumstances and thought it prudent for the sake of survival as a political party to accept at least a 'democratic Toryism' if not the democracy of the Liberals.

Others there were, however, the hard-boiled reactionaries, one of whom Curzon undoubtedly was, who failed to read the signs of the time and saw in the rising tide of democracy a high tide of anarchy which would eventually swamp what was best in the British society – their traditional culture and institutions. They felt that if this could not be averted at home they could do it abroad in their empire overseas. They could invest their imperialism with a moral purpose. They made themselves believe that their empire had a mission to fulfil – the mission of civilizing their dominions where their superior culture could be transplanted, preserved and protected from the onslaught of philistinism.

That was 'the white man's burden' as the troubadour of their imperialism Kipling sang. These people seem to have despaired of the grown up but not of the growing up Briton, for a ceremony called the 'Empire Day' was introduced in British schools calculated to inculcate in the young the virtues of the chauvinism of imperialism. It consisted in the hoisting and waving of flags, recitation of appropriate poems of Kipling, mass singing of 'Rule Britannia', playing on gramophone Dame Clara Butt singing Elgar's 'Land of Hope and Glory', some speechifying, letting off fire-crackers around a bonfire in the evening, all followed by a full holiday. Also in collaboration with some liberals, now disillusioned by democracy, they formed in 1884 an Imperial Federation League with the object of bringing about the political integration of the British Empire. At first what they had in mind was not the non-white part but the white part of the empire, the so-called 'settlement colonies' of Canada, South Africa, Australia and New Zealand.

Though still conscious of their British origin and racial ties with the mother country these dominions had by that time developed an awareness of their separate national identities and were reluctant to give up their political privilege of self-government. Trevelyan has traced the hardening of colour prejudices also to this period.

Thus frustrated in their attempt to test their pet scheme in the white part of the empire they now fastened their attention on the coloured part, that is India. Curzon wrote two long letters to his great political patron, the last peer-Prime Minister Lord Salisbury, seeking the Viceroyalty which no other aspirant to the post had done before. He had realized that the white part formed a part of the empire only in name, the real empire was the non-white part which was to be preserved in perpetuity at any cost for the preservation of the superior culture of the British. When, therefore, he came to India as Viceroy on his own seeking he set himself to his task with a missionary zeal from the very outset. He made his intentions abundantly clear when on the eve of his assumption of office he declared: "India is the pivot of Empire, by which I mean that outside the British Isles we could, I believe, lose any portion of the dominions of the Queen and yet survive as an Empire; while if we lost India, I maintain that our sun would sink to its setting".

It therefore logically follows that in whatever he thought or said or did his sole aim was the administration of the empire as an efficient system for its preservation and perpetuation. In his foreign policy his object was the removal of all external threats to India to make it a safe base from which to operate the empire system.

His domestic policy was to do away with red-tapism, to modernize India, to make the country strong from within as a strong base for the same empire system. If he did any good to India, it was an offshoot of the good that he did for the empire. If he did any right thing he did it for the wrong reason. If he came down with a heavy hand on those who committed any atrocity on any Indian he did so in the spirit of a magnanimous autocrat or a benevolent despot. The Indian deserved his protection only as a subject but not as a matter of right as a citizen. Did not his monarch advise him at Balmoral not to allow the feelings of her Indian subjects to be trampled on, they needed special protection as children do and they should be taught the virtues of obedience? The Indian princes were his partners in the empire to be suitably educated and trained for the purpose. As for the common Indian his case was altogether different.

The viceroyalty of Curzon is said to have marked the apogee of this empire system. But the halo of the high noon of empire seems to have blinded the arrogant imperialists. They failed to recognize the emergence of the English educated middle class and appreciate its significance. Macaulay thought that English education would create "a class of persons Indian in blood and colour, but English in taste, in opinions, in morals and in intellect". In Bengal English education generated an unprecedented intellectual ferment which ushered in a renaissance and gave it a cultural and intellectual primacy that prompted Gokhale to remark: "What Bengal thinks today India thinks tomorrow". A Bengali of the time could well feel like saying with Wordsworth:

"Bliss it was in that dawn to be alive

But to be young was very heaven".

The initial impact of Western civilization produced a middle class Bengali whose main concern was education and culture and not politics. Bankim has paid him a rich tribute by making a model of his kind in the character of Amarnath in the novel Rajani published in 1877. When we meet this character in the drawing room of the hero of the novel we find him opening his conversation with social and political topics, turning the pages of Shakespeare Gallery, discussing the characters of Desdemona and Juliet as well as the characters of Indian classical literature like Sakuntala, Sita, Kadambari, Vasavadatta,, Rukmini and Satyabhama. Next he takes up ancient historiography and gives a masterly exposition of classical historians like Tacitus, Plutarch, Thucydides and others.

Contemporary philosophers and thinkers like Comte, Mill, Huxley, Owen, Darwin, Buchner and Schopenhauer also form the subjects of his discussion. Five years later in Bankim's Anandamath, published in 1882, we find the emergence of a different kind of Bengali – a political man and a man of action with a burning passion for political emancipation from the foreign yoke, ready to sacrifice not only the security and comforts of a settled family life but even his very life. He is no longer effeminate and cowardly but courageous enough to form a secret society and take up arms against his alien oppressors. From among such people arose the hawks who resented the placidity of the first political organization formed in 1885 which met more as a social club to pass resolutions praising the ruling power and praying for some small pittance through constitutional means. Soon they were to turn Bankim's 'Vande Mataram' into their war cry.

Macaulay had also visualized a day which would be the proudest day for the English when the Indians "having become instructed in European knowledge" would "demand European institutions". This ideal of ultimate self-government by the natives was never quite disavowed by the British, but the day of its realization remained a kind of a movable feast. Thus when in the closing decade of the 19th century the English educated Indian middle class had grown self-confident and claimed that the day had arrived the British disputed it. In their arrogance they could never bring themselves to believe that the Indians would ever attain adulthood and would be able to govern themselves if they got a chance to do so. So long they were under the tutorship and now they should be under the trusteeship of the British. Self-government would be granted to them in some future which was however subject to extension ad infinitum. When therefore in the ambivalent Congress the Young Turks in their toga virilis grew restive and showed signs of militancy Curzon expressed his great ambition to give that body a decent burial. To achieve that end he took a number of measures which were provocatively reactionary and retrograde. The most mischievous of them all was his scheme of partitioning of Bengal.

The question of territorial reorganization of the Indian empire never engaged the attention of Curzon. He had an occasion to deal with it when he was required to settle the administrative disposition of Berar after it was wrested through his gunboat diplomacy from the dominions of the Nizam of Hyderabad. All British conquests and annexations were gradual in nature. The shapes and sizes of their provinces were therefore the results more of historical accidents than of any deliberate scheme or policy, the political exigencies of the hour being the main deciding factors. Bengal was a classic case where an administrative unit initially consisting of a few districts had grown over the years into a province too large to be effectively administered by a Lt. Governor. Earlier the position was worse.

The Governor-General of India himself was directly responsible for its administration. It was Dalhousie who first divested himself of its charge and created for it a separate post of Lt. Governor. In 1874 Assam was separated. Still it contained Bihar and Orissa. Some of Curzon's predecessors had made attempts to further relieve the overburdened Bengal administration but had to shelve them as they found the scheme to be very costly and not so easy to implement. But Curzon now rushed in where his forebears feared to tread, specially when he convinced himself that bureaucratic sloth had delayed the implementation of a scheme designed to achieve administrative efficiency for which he was a great stickler.

In his famous 'round and round' minutes he roundly blamed the bureaucracy and determined to show off his own efficiency.

Red tape, which he greatly abhorred, did to him what a red rag does to a bull. For formulation of the scheme he found some boon companions and helpmates, a band of yesmen and courtly cronies, who were eager to please him and pamper his whims than to give him sound advice. Chief among them were Fraser and Risley, respectively the Lt. Governor of Bengal and the Home Secretary to the government of India.

In Curzon's time it took the scheme of partition of Bengal three long years to mature. To follow the course of its development we may quote from the masterly summary of Sumit Sarkar given in his The Swadeshi Movement in Bengal:

"After the Orissa famine of 1866, Sir Stafford Northcote suggested a reduction in the size of the vast presidency of Bengal (which included, apart from Bengal proper, the whole of Bihar, Orissa and Assam) on grounds of administrative efficiency. In 1874 Assam was separated and made into a chief commissioner's province: Sylhet, a predominantly Bengali speaking area, was transferred along with it despite some local opposition. In 1892, in connection with a proposal for the transfer of the South Lushai Hills from Bengal to Assam, some officials in the foreign department suggested that the whole of Chittagong division (comprising the districts of Chittagong, Chittagong Hill Trcts, Noakhali and Tippera) should also be transferred.

The latter idea was discussed in detail during 1896-97, in course of which William Ward, the chief commissioner of Assam, for the first time put forward the idea that the Dacca and Mymensingh districts should go along with Chittagong division into Assam, thus making of that province a unit big enough for a separate administrative cadre. Sir Henry Cotton, Ward's successor, vehemently opposed the whole plan, and with Mackenzie, the lieutenant-governor of Bengal, also rather lukewarm, the Indian government decided on 29 April 1897 to transfer South Lushai Hills only for the time being. In 1901, the question of Bengal's boundaries was revived, at first purely on the departmental level, in connection with Sir Andrew Fraser's (the then chief commissioner of the Central Provinces) suggestions for some adjustments along the Bengal-CP border so as to solve the problem of Sambalpur, an Oriya enclave in a Hindi-speaking province. The file on the subject reached the viceroy only fourteen months later, provoking Curzon into his famous outburst against 'departmentalism' – the

'Round-and-round' note of 24 May 1902. The same note referred to "the approaching incorporation of Berar in British India", in connection with which Curzon had already "suggested in council that we would take up the question of readjustment of boundaries all around". In the discussion which followed, Fraser in his note of 28 March 1903 strongly urged the transfer of both Chittagong division and Dacca and Mymensingh, and for the first time highlighted the political benefits of the scheme. His ideas were accepted by Curzon, and embodied in the viceroy's Minute on Territorial Redistribution in India (19 May-1 June 1903) which its author fondly hoped would "fix the administrative boundaries of India for a generation".

The minute, suitably edited for public consumption, formed the basis of Risley's letter of 3 December 1903 proposing transfer of Chittagong division, Dacca and Mymensingh to Assam.

Now began a process of expansion, which soon transformed a scheme for transfer of certain districts into a full-scale partition of Bengal. In the last week of December 1903 Fraser suggested that Bakargunj and Faridpur should also be annexed to Assam, converting the latter into a full-scale lieutenant's province. Curzon in course of his East-Bengal tour (February 1904) hinted rather vaguely that "a more ambitious" scheme "for a larger readjustment in the east of Bengal" was being considered. While for the next year a half the general public was permitted to hear little about the matter – so much so that the impression spread that the whole idea had been dropped – the officials went on merrily with the game of switching about other people's lands.

The list of transferable districts steadily expanded – the Bengal government on 6 April 1904 added Rangpur, Bogra, Pabna; five months later Simla even more generously annexed Rajshahi, Dinajpur, Malda, Jalpaiguri and Cooch-Behar state to the new province. Curzon on his return from England sent off this final scheme in his dispatch to the secretary of state of 2 February 1905. The secretary of state gave his consent in the dispatch of 9 June, and on 19 July 1905 the government of India announced its decision to set up a new province of 'Eastern Bengal and Assam' comprising the Chittagong, Dacca and Rajshahi divisions, Hill Tippera, Malda and Assam. The formal proclamation came on 1 September 1905, and on 16 October 1905 Bengal was partitioned." Thus what had begun as a proposal for transfer of a few districts finally became a scheme of a full-scale partition of Bengal apparently to achieve administrative efficiency but really to gain a political end of a sinister kind. The Hindu majority western Bengal was separated from the Muslim majority eastern and northern Bengal with a new capital at Dacca. The motive was to create a Muslim opposition within the Bengalis themselves and to isolate and weaken the Bengali middle class which was preponderantly Hindu and spearheaded all political agitations. It was also calculated to reduce the importance of Calcutta as the centre of all seditious activities. The Bengali middle class had become very assertive and troublesome. It was perceived as a potent threat to the empire. It had to be kept in check. The proposed administrative reorganization offered to the imperialists a golden opportunity to divide the Bengalis both territorially and racially along communal lines. Moreover, the tagging of one portion of Bengal to Bihar and Orissa and the rest to Assam politically relegated the position of the Bengalis in both the new provinces from one of predominance to insignificance.

This 'divide and rule' policy was not only machiavellian but also mephistophelean. Till the partition Bengal enjoyed the unique distinction of being communally the least disturbed province. The partition marks the date from which communal disturbances began to occur with increasing frequency. For the creation of this monster of communalism the entire credit goes to Curzon and his cronies like Fraser and Risley. The government of India itself later in its dispatch of 25th August 1911 was to recognize a growing estrangement between the two communities as a result of the partition.

The initial Muslim response to the partition was neither widespread nor enthusiastic. Curzon made extraordinary personal efforts to generate larger support from that community. Through numerous tours and lectures in Muslim majority districts he coaxed and tried to convince the Muslims about the advantages that would accrue to them from the partition. He also made them many promises much of which proved empty in the years to come. He set much store by the support of the Nawab of Dacca who himself was dogged by family feuds and had very little influence over his coreligionists. His estates were also in the red and to keep this personage financially afloat as a prop of his diabolical scheme Curzon threw all financial principles and proprieties to the winds to grant him a huge advance which was more in the nature of gratuitous relief than a loan.

A renowned historian like Trevelyan has called Curzon great. It cannot be said that Curzon was born great. He was indeed the scion of one of the landed aristocratic families of England which could trace their history back to the days of the Conqueror, but the Curzons of Kedleston could boast of no distinction whatsoever in their long history of eight hundred years before Curzon. He seems to have determined to make good this deficiency in his family tradition. But one who follows his career dispassionately can hardly agree with those who claim that he succeeded in his efforts.

As a student he did not fare so extraordinarily well as to be called brilliant. One of his teachers who considered him so and remained his lifelong admirer was a homosexual and it is arguable whether his admiration was due to his student's scholarship or good looks. Nayana Goradia in her recent study, Lord Curzon: The Last of the British Mughals, has found traces of masochism in him. He used to enjoy caning by his governess as well as by his teachers. The anonymous author of the doggerel quoted earlier appears to have been an accurate observer of his character. A first rate snob he was fond of pomp and ceremony and always gave himself an air of superiority. This irked his friends and foes alike. To a man like Churchill he was a prig. He was anti-democratic and a reactionary of reactionaries. Even his own party-men did not trust him and were to play a cruel trick on him when he was deprived of the premiership which was his due as the seniormost member after the retirement of Bonar Law on health grounds. The King also seems to have developed a dislike for him. As Prince of Wales he had an opportunity during his Indian tours to see for himself the high-handed manner of Curzon's administration as viceroy. Curzon was to have the mortification of being summoned by the King all the way from his country home to London only to be told that even though he was the seniormost leader of his party after Bonar Law he could not be made the next premier.

During the first term of his viceroyalty, however, Curzon gave a fairly good account of himself and earned praises specially for his vigour and drive. But his efforts were actually no more than the continuation of the works of his predecessors and had little innovative or original about them. Because of his despotic nature he was intolerant of the views of others. His impatience made him incapable of sustained efforts so that by the second term he began to lose hold of his reins. For his supercilious attitude he antagonized the bureaucracy and Woodruff does not have very many good words to spare for him in The Men Who Ruled India.

He failed to find an able hand in the ICS which had become a legend in its time. On the contrary he succumbed to the weakness of flattery to which people whose heads are turned by power are prone and became fond of two questionable characters of the service, Fraser and Risley. Though he was forewarned of the character of the latter he made him his Home secretary. He was a poor judge of men and could not suspect that these two 'poor tape worms' would eat into his vitals and egg him on to undertake measures that would ultimately bring him to grief. He exhibited his poor judgement again in the selection of Kitchener as his army chief.

His controversy with this man was to become the immediate cause of Curzon's downfall. And in the supreme test of a ruler he miserably fails. In his heart he did never keep the interest and well being of the people he ruled nor paid any heed to their feelings and aspirations. He suffered from a sense of racial superiority of the worst kind. For this Curzon though was not alone to blame because this feeling had begun to develop among the British ruling class right from the time of Macaulay whose acerbic comments about the Bengalis in general are not only vulgar but in sheer bad taste. This superiority complex was to culminate in the writings of Kipling and the ideas of that dyspeptic son of a Scottish stone mason turned messiah, Carlyle, who was an ardent lover of German philosophy and propounded the theory of dominant 'Superman' in his Heroes and Hero Worship and the life of Frederick the Great. While in world history an Austrian corporal was to become the villain of the piece for racial hatred and holocaust it may well be asked if the likes of Carlyle and Curzon can ultimately escape the culpability for such crimes. The treatment meted out by Hitler to the Jews and others are different only in degree but not in kind from the treatment which the 'black niggers' of India received at the hands of their British rulers. It is not for nothing that Curzon has been called a xenophobe.

Curzon did not inherit greatness nor could he achieve it, but greatness was thrust upon him when he was made the viceroy of

India. He however failed to measure up to that greatness for he was man who was really very little. The fault did not lie in his stars but in himself. With his limited intelligence clouded by unlimited arrogance he failed to see the changes which were in the air during the closing years of the 19th century. Not only a new century was dawning but also a new world was being born. It was a time when Waterloos could no longer be won on the playing fields of Eton nor could a few salvos from the canons of a Clive decide a Battle of Plassey.

The days of far-flung empires of vast territorial possessions were coming to a close. Their death knell was first rung by the war of 1914-18. Barely 25 years later the greedy European shopkeepers were to wage a more fierce war among themselves that not only gave a burial to their empires but also brought the world itself to the brink of total destruction. As the very personification of anachronism Curzon went out like a medieval knight-errant to give a quixotic battle to save a dying feudal world where a few landed aristocratic families could monopolise political power through a rotten electoral system that denied voting rights to the unpropertied masses.

At home the men of his class ultimately met with defeat. In this country his reactionary measures met with the same fate but rendered a signal service to the nascent nationalist movement by giving it a sharp edge which it so long lacked. He provided the nationalists with a good cause for militant action. Swadeshi and terrorism made the position of the British in India increasingly untenable. From the anti-partition agitation our freedom movement gathered a new momentum and the imperialists had to accept defeat. The partition of Bengal had to be revoked and Curzon had to leave this country in shame to spend a considerable part of his political career in the wilderness. In fact Curzon's viceroyalty marks the beginning of the end of the British empire in India which he so sedulously wanted to perpetuate. In his farewell speech Curzon had said, 'Let India be my judge'.

Today that judgement is – he harmed both himself and the empire, the very opposite of what he had intended to achieve; he unwittingly infused with new vigour the very freedom movement he wanted to suppress. And India cherishes a bitter memory of his lasting contribution in politics – the use of communalism as a political weapon, which ultimately led to the partition of India.

He was more a petty politician than a statesman. To compare him with the great is to insult the great. He totally lacked that large vision of great rulers like Akbar and others who have worked for harmony and not for chaos among the people they ruled. He was unable to avail of the opportunity which is rarely granted by destiny to any ruler to achieve greatness by cementing with cultural unity the unprecedented political unity which the British had achieved in India. Instead he permanently poisoned the relationship between the two major religious communities of this country. He also exacerbated the racial hatred and enmity between the Indians and the British. A small man as he was it was not given to him to realize the poet's conception of India as a place of pilgrimage for nations where various races and religions have met through the ages to commingle in a single body of humanity:

Swadeshi Movement emanated from the partition of bengal, 1905 and continued up to 1908. It was the most successful of the pre-Gandhian movements. Initially the partition plan was opposed through an intensive use of conventional 'moderate' methods of press campaigns, numerous meetings and petitions, and big conferences at the Calcutta town hall in March 1904 and January 1905. The evident and total failure of such techniques led to a search for new forms-boycott of British goods, *rakhi bandhan* and *arandhan*.

Theoretically, two major trends can be identified in the *Swadeshi* (Swadeshi) Movement-'constructive Swadeshi' and political 'extremism'. 'Boycott' was the weapon to make Swadeshi movement successful. Constructive Swadeshi was the trend of self-help through Swadeshi industries, national schools and attempts at village improvement and organisation. This found expression through the business ventures of Prafulla Chandra Roy or Nilratan Sarkar, national education movement laid down by Satishchandra Mukherjee, and constructive work in villages through a revival of the traditional Hindu *samaj* sketched out by rabindranath tagore. *Swadesh Bandhav Samity* of Aswini Kumar datta also played a major role in the effort for reconstruction. Rabindranath called such a perspective of development *atmashakti* (self-strengthening).

This, however, had little appeal to the excited educated youth of Bengal who were drawn much more to the creed of political 'extremism'. Their fundamental difference with the preachers of constructive Swadeshi was over methods, and here the classic statement came from aurobindo ghosh in a series of articles in April 1907, later reprinted as 'Doctrine of Passive Resistance'. He visualised a programme of 'organised and relentless boycott of British goods, officialised education, justice and executive administration', (backed up by the positive development of Swadeshi industries, schools and arbitration courts), and also looked forward to civil disobedience, 'social boycott' of loyalists, and recourse to armed struggle if British repression went beyond the limits of endurance.

Another controversy arose over cultural ideas, between modernistic and Hindu revivalist trend. The Swadeshi mood in general was closely linked with attempts to associate politics with religious revivalism. Surendranath Banerjea claimed to have been the first to use the method of Swadeshi vows in temples. National education plans often had a strong revivalist content and 'boycott' was sought to be enforced through traditional caste sanctions. Such aggressive Hinduism often got inextricably combined in the pages of *Bande Mataram, Sandhya* or *Yugantar* while Brahmo journals like *Sanjibani* or *Prabasi* were critical of this view.

The Hindu revivalist trend, together with the British propaganda that the new province would mean more jobs for Muslims did achieve considerable success in swaying upper and middle class Muslims against the Swadeshi movement. Despite eloquent pleas for communal unity propagated by an active group of Swadeshi Muslim agitators like Ghaznavi, Rasul, Din Mohammed, Didar, Liakat Hussain etc. there were communal riots in East Bengal. Some Hindu zamindars and *mahajans* started levying an *Ishvar brtti* for maintaining Hindu images. So a large section of the Muslim community in Bengal remained aloof from the Swadeshi movement and Hindu *bhadralok,* whether believing in moderate or extremist politics, took leading part in the movement. Such a limitation of the spontaneity of the movement caught the attention of Rabindranath and other men of letters. Rabindranath, though considerably swayed by revivalism for some years, under the impact of communal strife, pointed out in a series of remarkably perceptive articles in mid 1907 that simply blaming the British for the riots was quite an inadequate response.

Together with these cultural limitations, the history of boycott and Swadeshi movement vividly illustrated the limits of an intelligentsia movement with broadly bourgeois aspirations but without as yet real bourgeois support. Boycott achieved some initial success-thus the Calcutta collector of customs in September 1906 noted a decline in Manchester cloth sales. This decline had a lot to do with a quarrel over trade terms between Calcutta Marwari dealers and British manufacturers. It is significant also that the sharpest decline was in items like shoes and cigarettes where the demand was mainly from middle class Indian gentlemen.

In spite of such limitations the Swadeshi mood did bring about a significant revival in handloom, silk weaving, and some other traditional crafts. Also a number of attempts to promote modern industries were taken. Thus the 'Banga Lakshmi Cotton Mills' was launched in August 1906 and there were some fairly successful ventures in porcelain, chrome, soap, matches and cigarettes.

A considerable variety may be noticed within the national education efforts in Swadeshi Bengal, ranging from plans for vernacular technical teaching to Santiniketan of Rabindranath and dawn society of Satish Mukherjee. These were plans to combine the traditional and the modern in a scheme for 'higher culture' for selected youths. National Society of Education was set up as a parallel university in March 1906. Though National Education with its negligible job prospects failed to attract the bulk of students, still some institutions like Bengal National College or Bengal Technical Institute survived after a couple of years.

The emergence of Samitis was an achievement of the Swedeshi age. By 1908, most of these Samitis were quite open bodies engaged in a variety of activities-physical and moral training of members, social work during religious festivals, preaching the Swadeshi message through multifarious forms, organising crafts, schools, arbitration courts and village societies, and implementing the techniques of passive resistance.

Swadeshi Movement

The Swadeshi movement, part of the Indian independence movement, was a successful economic strategy to remove the British Empire from power and improve economic conditions in India through following principles of *swadeshi* (self-sufficiency). Strategies of the swadeshi movement involved boycotting British products and the revival of domestic-made products and production techniques.

Swadeshi Movement emanated from the partition of bengal, 1905 and continued up to 1908. It was the most successful of the pre-Gandhian movements. Chief architects were Aurobindo Ghosh, Veer Savarkar, Lokmanya Bal Gangadhar Tilak, and Lala Lajpat Rai.

Swadeshi, as a strategy, was a key focus of Mahatma Gandhi who described it as the soul of *Swaraj* (self rule).

The Swadeshi Jagaran Manch is an organisation committed to the promotion of Swadeshi (Indigenous) industries and culture.

Mahatma Gandhi described Swadeshi as "a call to the consumer to be aware of the violence he is causing by supporting those industries that result in poverty and harm to workers and to humans and other creatures."

Gandhi believed that alienation and exploitation often occur when production and consumption are divorced from their social and cultural context, and that local enterprise is a way to avoid these problems.

"Swadeshi is that spirit in us which requires us to serve our immediate neighbours before others, and to use things produced in our neighbourhood in preference to those more remote. So doing, we serve humanity to the best of our capacity. We cannot serve humanity by neglecting our neighbours.

5

The Swadeshi Movement of 1905

The Swadeshi Movement of 1905 started as an Anti-Partition agitation against the British Government's decision to partition Bengal, to break up the unity and solidarity of the Bengali people standing at the vanguard of India's national resurgence. In spite of vehement protests from the press and the platform all over Bengal, the bureaucratic government of Lord Curzon paid no heed to it and despisingly boycotted the united Bengali public opinion. 'A boycott of one kind was therefore sought to be met by a boycott of another', as Satis Chandra Mukherjee put it, as the last legitimate weapon of a disarmed people. As facts stand at present, the idea of Boycott of British goods was not the work of a particular man nor was it devised in the country fIrst in 1905. It was an organized expression of the national will and 'the mind of the whole community' made its contributions to its final emergence.

The Boycott Technique

From the I.B. Records of the Government of West Bengal we learn that on the eve of the Swadeshi Movement a powerful protagonist of the idea of boycotting British goods was Tahal Ram Ganga Ram (an inhabitant of North Western India and belonging to the Arya Samaj) who visited Calcutta during February-March, 1905, delivering inflammatory speeches every evening before the students in the College Square, and asking them to go in for Boycott of British goods in favour of indigenous products. His lectures made a deep impression on many young men of Calcutta at that time. This is corroborated by the Bengali Autobiography of Krishna Kumar Mitra, one of the great stalwarts of the Swadeshi Movement. In the exciting times of the Anti-Partition agitation Krishna Kumar Mitra's call for Boycott through his weekly organ, the Sanjivani (July 13, 1905) found a ready response in the country. 'When she (Bengal) declared the Boycott', wrote Aurobindo in 1908, 'she did so without calculation, without reckoning chances, without planning how the Boycott could succeed. She declared it. Was the intellect at work when she declared it? Was it her leaders who planned it as a means of bringing the British to their knees? Everybody knows that it was Kishoregunj, it was Magura, the obscure villages and towns of East Bengal which fIrst declared the Boycott. What brain planned it, what voice fIrst uttered it, history will never be able to discover. None planned it, but it was in the heart of the nation and God revealed it.'

The Boycott scheme which was first applied to the economic field extended before long to other departments involving a totalitarian scheme of Boycott-the Boycott of British goods, British schools, British courts and British bureaucratic administration. Even the idea of social Boycott of persons purchasing foreign articles was insisted upon. But for practical reasons the idea of 'no tax to the government' was temporarily held in abeyance.

The Idea of Swadeshi

Boycott was after all a negative concept. Its positive counterpart was the Swadeshi, first applied to the economic field involving the use of Swadeshi or indigenous goods 'even at a sacrifice'. Like Boycott, Swadeshi also soon became an all-comprehensive category. The idea of economic Swadeshi was advocated, among other things, in Bengal as early as the days of the Hindu Mela (functioning since 1867). In the seventies of the 19th century a Swadeshi movement was initiated in Gujarat and the Deccan. Almost about the same time, thanks to the enthusiasm of the Arya Samaj, a similar movement came into existence in the Punjab also.

So far as Bengal is concerned, it should be clearly borne in mind that the spirit of industrial Swadeshi was abroad for a long time past, particularly since the early nineties of the 19th century. Barrister Jogesh Chandra Chaudhury was 'one of the earliest pioneers' in the field of industrial revival. It was he who 'first started an industrial exhibition of Swadeshi articles as an annex to the Indian National Congress in December 1901.'

Early in the 20th century Satis Chandra Mukherjee founded the Dawn Society (July, 1902) in the premises of the present Vidyasagar College and organized a Swadeshi Stores under its auspices for the promotion of indigenous manufactures. The efforts of the Dawn Society to popularize the cause of Swadeshi goods by lectures and exhibitions, organized sale and propaganda through its journal, the Dawn, were remarkable and together served as a prelude to the Swadeshi Movement of 1905. Rabindra Nath Tagore was deeply impressed by Satischandra's selfless and total dedication to nationbuilding activities.

The Swadeshi Movement, observed Satis Mukherjee in 1906, 'is patriotic in the first instance and only economic or industrial in the second. A purely economic movement would not have proved itself to be a whole people's or a nation's business, but its activities would have been confined amongst a comparatively limited class of people with industrial instincts and business capacities. The Swadeshi Movement, it must therefore be understood, is not an industrial movement, in its essence, but is essentially a moral movement, in the larger sense of the word, concerning itself with rousing the moral sense of a whole people in its relations with a bureaucratic power.'

Bipin Chandra Pal, the foremost architect of the Swadeshi Movement of 1905, also characterized the national upsurge as a 'spiritual movement'. In his article on 'The Bed-Rock of Indian Nationalism', he wrote thus in 1908: 'The strength of the new movement in India lies in its supreme idealism. It is not a mere economic movement, though it openly strives for the economic resurrection of the country. It is not a mere political movement, though it has boldly declared itself for absolute political independence. It is an intensely spiritual movement having for its object not simply the development of economic life or the attainment of political freedom but really the emancipation, in every sense of the term, of the Indian manhood and womanhood.'

The Demand for Swaraj

The fourth idea closely associated with the Swadeshi Movement of 1905 was the aspiration after complete political independence or the separation of India from the British Empire. In the 19th century or even at the dawn of the 20th, the Indian politicians in general continued to believe in the paramountcy and justice of the British rule in this country and considered it an 'irrevocable necessity' for the furtherance of their national interests. In the pre-Swadeshi days (1903-04) even Bipin Chandra Pal and Upadhyay Brahmabandhab cherished the same complacent belief. But with the outbreak of the Swadeshi Movement, the old idea of mendicant politics was rapidly losing its hold on the imagination of the younger generation A larger and more ennobling ideal for political endeavour was found increasingly intoxicating. The overhauling of the entire Congress, both its ideal and its line of action, was deemed imperative by the more advanced political party, called the New Party or the Nationalist Party, in contradistinction to the old guards of the Congress or the Moderates.

The New Party in Bengal counted among its foremost protagonists men like Upadhyaya Brahmabandhab, Bipin Chandra Pal and Aurobindo Ghose. It was mainly organized and set in motion in Bengal by Aurobindo. Before the appearance of Aurobindo in Bengal politics, there were certainly many kindred spirits (like his) in the country, but there was no New Party. It was Aurobindo who, more than anybody else, was instrumental in organizing the men with Extremist leanings in the country into the New Party and animating it along with Bipin Pal with the intoxicating ideal of Purna Swaraj or complete Independence for India. And this marked a veritable revolution in the realm of our political thought. The New Party sketched and developed this invigorating ideal with the greatest fidelity to the people's will. It had its organs in journals like the Kesari, the New India, the Sandhya, the Yugantar and the Bande Mataram, which played a very remarkable role in those days in directing the national mind along the lines of complete political emancipation from foreign thraldom. Instead of trusting the alien bureaucracy, the New Party sought its strength in the revived manhood of the nation. It declared in no uncertain voice that 'political freedom is the life-breath of a nation; to attempt social reform, educational reform, industrial expansion, the moral improvement of the race without aiming first and foremost at political freedom is the very height of ignorance and futility' (Aurobindo). And this ideal was officially accepted by the Congress in its memorable session held at Calcutta in December,1906.

It was at the Calcutta session that the political goal of India was defined as 'Self-Government or Swaraj like that of the United Kingdom or the Colonies' by the President himself, Dadabhai Naoroji, that old, veteran politician who, only a year ago in 1905, in a series of letters addressed to the Congressmen, could not envisage any ideal beyond 'Self-Government under British paramountcy' as goal for India's political struggle. This significant change in the mental attitude of Dadabhai Naoroji was certainly due to the pressure of the Extremist forces that had developed within and outside the

Congress During 1905-06

But what was a mere high-sounding ideal with Dadabhai Naoroji became the creed and the motto of the New Party to which absolute independence or Purna Swaraj was the only ideal worth living and dying for. But this Swaraj, as Aurobindo said, must not be an importation of the European article; it must be a Swadeshi Swaraj.

Again, during 1905-06 there took place not only a revolutionary change in our political ideal, but also a revolution in our political technique. The New Party rejected the mendicant politics of 'prayer, petition and protest' of the Moderates and advocated instead an organized Boycott or 'Passive Resistance' on the part of the people to render the alien Government unworkable in the land. In the words of Aurobindo, Bipin Pal was 'the prophet and first preacher of Passive Resistance,' which Pal defined as 'not non-active, but non-aggressive' but he never intended it to be a shield for moral cowardice or inaction in relation to the adversary.

This was also the view of Aurobindo. What Aurobindo preached through his brilliant editorials in the Bande Mataram, was disseminated all over the country by the maddening eloquence of Bipinchandra whose was then the mightiest voice preaching sedition against the British Government. The discovery of 'Passive Resistance' was the most potent and fruitful contribution of Bengal school of politics to India as a whole during the Swadeshi times. But this was not the only technique by which the battle for freedom was fought and won. Aurobindo, unlike Bipin Pal, was an advocate of violence to make nonviolence also more effective in political struggle.

While the Extremists or the New Party had been advocating the technique of passive or defensive resistance, the more enthusiastic members of the Extremist fraternity began to advocate the philosophy of the bomb. Thus within the New Party further extremism developed and soon assumed the form of terrorism or violence. The party of terrorism was fathered by Bal Gangadhar Tilak and Aurobindo Ghose and found its powerful champions in Bengal in men like Barindra Kumar Ghose, Bhupendra Nath Datta, Abinash Chandra Bhattacharya and many others. While their goal was the same as that of the Passive Resisters, viz., the attainment of unqualified Swaraj for India, their technique of the struggle was different. The terrorists did not believe in 'passive resistance' and prescribed a sanguinary and revolutionary battle with the bureaucracy to realize the supreme objective. They had their own mouthpiece in the revolutionary Bengali weekly, the Jugantar, (founded on 15 March, 1906) which was insistent on its advocacy of the policy of triumph through terror.

The Demand for National Education

The Swadeshi Movement also advocated a movement for India's cultural autarchy which took shape in the National Council of Education or the N.C.E.which was something like a National University established by the greatest men of our country on 11 March, 1906. The demand for National Education with its revolutionary contents became an integral part of the Swadeshi Movement. Its supreme objective was the establishment of a three-dimensional system of education-literary, scientific and technical combined-conducted on national lines and under national control for the realization of the national destiny.

Under the National Council of Education was set up in Calcutta the Bengal National College and School (Aug, 1906) with Aurobindo Ghosh as the Principal and Satis Mukherjee as the Superintendent. Vernacular was adopted as the medium of instruction from the lowest to the highest stages, while English was retained as a compulsory second language as an instrument of world culture. Provisions were made for the study of Hindi and Marathi languages as well as Sanskrit, Pali and Persian as sources for the firsthand historical researches. Arrangement was also made for the study of French and German as aids to the study of modern science and philosophy as well as European methods in the study of Indian culture. Systematic provisions were made not only for technical education, but also for the study of physical, natural or positive sciences along with liberal arts, culture and humanism.

Research into ancient Indian history, philosophy, economics, politics, arts and sciences was also encouraged. These disciplines constituted a revolutionary ideology for Young Bengal of 1905-06.

And the whole of it was conceived as a grand project for moral and spiritual resurgence of the country. 'The return to ourselves', observed Aurobindo in 1908, 'is the cardinal feature of the national movement. It is national not only in the sense of political self-assertion against the domination of foreigners, but in the sense of a return upon our old national individuality'.

The influence of the National Council outstripped the limits of Bengal and forged ahead in Bombay and Madras Presidencies and the province of Berar. Outside Bengal, B.G. Tilak and Lajpat Rai were the most outstanding advocates of National Education. To condemn the educational ideas of the N.C.E. as based on a 'decaying and corrupt metaphysics' or 'on the basis of the most antiquated religion and religious superstitions', as Rajani Palme Dutt and Jawaharlal Nehru would have us believe, is entirely misleading. Judged by the standard of the times, the educational planning of the National Council, far from being conservative or reactionary, marked a revolutionary leap forward in the march of the Indian nation. Its chief advocates repeatedly stressed that foreign things and models India must accept, but not as a whole and undigested, not by selling herself off to the powers that be, but by retaining her individuality as a nation. Paradharma Bhayabaha-so runs the ancient warning of the Gita. It is equally valid for today, tomorrow and day after tomorrow.

Let us now turn our attention to the second aspect of the question, viz. the consideration of the deeper import and character of the Swadeshi Movement in our national life. There was an unparalleled outburst of Bengali genius and creativity in every walk of life. The Swadeshi Movement helped Bengal leap forward miles ahead by a single bound.

The upheaval of 1905 not revivalist and reactionary Many scholars and writers have often complained that with the march of time the national upheaval of 1905 assumed a religious and reactionary character. In support of their contention they point to the repeated appeal made by the popular leaders in those days to the religious sentiment of the masses through their writings and speeches, by the annual celebration of the Shivaji Festival, by the frequent reference which the great leaders, including Aurobindo Ghose, made to the Gita, the Mahabharata and such other Hindu classics, as well as by the constant use of the slogan Bande Mataram supposed to signify the worship of the goddess Kali. Valentine

Chirol states in his India Old and New (London, 1921) observes: 'The old invocation to the goddess Kali, 'Bande Mataram,' or 'Hail to the Mother', acquired a new significance and came to be used as the political war-cry of Indian Nationalism.' And on the basis of these alleged religious tendencies he has drawn the conclusion that the spirit of Hindu revivalism-revivalism of Hindu orthodoxy and social conservatism-that ultimately alienated the Muslims from the general movement.

Chirol's views on this point are more or less representative of the Anglo-Indian or official views on the subject. In subsequent times this notion found wide currency in this country and beyond and became the stock argument of the critics of the Congress movement. But a close scrutiny of facts will hardly warrant such a conclusion. In the first place, we should remember that a revivalist movement does not necessarily mean a reactionary movement. As Prof. Hiren Mukerjee has correctly observed in course of his speech at the world famous Deutsche Akademie of Germany (1967), that a revivalist movement may have progressive as well as regressive aspects.

The so-called Hindu revivalist movement in our country since the seventies and eighties of the 19th century was not an all-out conservative or reactionary movement. Even its greatest protagonist, Dayananda Saraswati, the founder of the Arya Samaj, did not aspire after a complete return to the Vedic status quo. When he said, 'Back to the Vedas', he simply meant 'Forward with the Vedas'. He did not condemn modern science and knowledge. What he mainly sought to effect was the careful preservation of what was best in Hindu thought and tradition, emancipating the minds of his countrymen from the hypnotic influence of Christian civilization whose rank exponents in those days constantly made arrogant claims to superiority.

He cried halt to this dehumanizing tendency then powerfully working in the country and restored the self-confidence which the nation had lost as a result of long political and economic emasculation. With Dayananda Hindusim was reborn as an 'aggressive' and dynamic religion and the old apologetic attitude of the Brahmo Samaj vis-a-vis Christianity was now changed into one of boldness and robust optimism. Swami Vivekananda's manly stand in the matter deserves serious consideration. This moral and mental re-awakening of the Indians with the restoration of their ancient source of power became the prelude to an all-round national resurgence at the dawn of the 20th century, to which Swamiji's contributions were very vital and powerful. It is sheer folly to think that the desire for revivalism necessarily means an invitation to conservative and life-degenerating process. Would anybody dare call the Italian Renaissance of the 15th century a conservative and reactionary movement on account of its passionate cry and adoration for the Classical treasures of ancient Greece and ancient Rome?

Secondly, we should bear in mind that a mere association of religious sentiment with political movement does not necessarily suggest a conservative or reactionary trend just as the conduct of a political movement on a purely non-religious basis does not always imply a progressive or radical tendency. A movement of great dimensions, particularly a people's movement, is always a complex phenomenon, made up of pluralistic strands, partly conservative or reactionary, partly liberal or reformistic, and partly radical or revolutionary. The nature of a movement has to be judged not on the basis whether it has in it a religious tinge or not, but more appropriately on the basis of its predominant tendency. The primary or predominant trend of the Swadeshi Movement of 1905 was, beyond the shadow of a doubt, political. The redress of the burning political question of the day, the annulment of Bengal Partition, accompanied by the rising clamour for Swaraj or complete independence for India by means of an organized passive resistance to alien despotism, or by other methods if necessary, was central to the Swadeshi Movement. The introduction of religious idealism into the scene, the frequent tendency to appeal to the glories and exploits of ancient and medieval India was not so much the outcome of social conservatism or religious orthodoxy as part of political strategy, designed to intensify and popularize the movement by linking it with the historic traditions of the soil. Tilak was the first great leader of Indian thought who strove to Indianize the Congress politics in the nineties of the 19th century, and he was the political Extremist of the day. What was begun first by him in Maharashtra found a greater fulfilment in the Swadeshi days.

The intermingling of religious passion with political idealism did not detract from the progressive and political character of the movement; it simply lent a new momentum and driving force to the awakened feelings of patriotism and thus transformed the

Anti-Partition agitation into vigorous channels. Thirdly, we should remember that the participation of the orthodox classes of society (like the landed aristocracy and the priestly order) did not render the national movement of 1905 an orthodox or conservative agitation; it simply expressed the deeper truth that even these orthodox classes could not escape the impact of the New Spirit then working in the country.

Fourthly, the top-ranking leaders of the Swadeshi Movement (like Bal Gangadhar Tilak, Lajpat Rai, Bipin Chandra Pal and Aurobindo Ghose) did never allow the subordination of politics to religion. The I.B. Records, West Bengal, repeatedly assert that Aurobindo Ghose 'first conceived the idea of training missionaries to be sent forth in Sannyasi garb to all ends of India to preach the new religion, which was the worship of the motherland'.

In his speeches and journalistic propagandism of those days, the political trend is too palpable to be ignored even by the casual observers. His editorial articles in the Bande Mataram, the greatest and most influential mouthpiece of the Extremists of the time, provide the best answer to the question. True, there was noticeable in his writings the frequent use of such expressions as Sri Krishna, Chaitanya, Kali and the Bhawani Mandir, but these expressions were very often used by him not in their ordinary and literal senses, but in a figurative way.

Fifthly, it is a gross mistake to think that the cultural outlook of the Extremist leaders of the time was conservative and reactionary. They did neither condemn modern science and technology nor did they ever seek to build up the national movement on a corrupt and outworn social system.

The cultural aspect of the Swadeshi Movement as embodied in the National Education Movement, was, far from being conservative or reactionary, a radical ideal and it breathed a revolutionary fire in those days in the realm of education and culture. The courses and curricula of the National Council of Education, Bengal, were far in advance: of what then existed or even now exist in the Indian universities.

Sixthly, Chirol's interpretation of Bande Mataram is fundamentally fallacious. Bande Mataram was never invoked for the worship of the goddess Kali nor did this worship ever become 'the political warcry of Indian Nationalism'. The slogan meant the worship of the Mother, and the Mother was no other than the

Motherland herself. This was a new conception of patriotism of which Bankim Chandra Chatterjee was the seer and prophet, and Aurobindo Ghose the high priest. Seventhly, when the Swadeshi Movement first began, both Hindus and Muslims joined it in very large numbers. At a later stage, however, the Muslims began to stand aloof from the Congress movement and even in opposition to it. Nawab Salimullah of Dacca, who was originally a staunch anti-partitionist, became before long the strongest supporter of Partition. He then dubbed the Congress a Hindu organization swayed by Hindu revivalist sentiment. And this later change in the attitude of the Muslims towards the Swadeshi Movement was not really due to the association of so-called Hindu revivalism, but fundamentally due to certain other forces, of which the British imperialist policy of divide and rule by working upon the religious sentiments of the Muslims may be counted as the foremost. Even when the Congress was all-too moderatist in outlook and constitution, when there was no introduction of the Shivaji Festival and the like in Indian political life, the National Congress came to be branded as a Hindu assembly and the Congress movement as a Hindu movement as early as the year 1886 (Vide the official Report of the Congress for 1886).

Sir Syed Ahmed Khan, the father of Muslim separatist politics and leader of Muslim opposition to the Congress, was at first a protagonist of 'one indivisible Indian nation' comprising both the Hindus and the Muslims as children of the same mother. But after his elevation to the Knighthood the sheet anchor of his policy became, under strong official influences, an opposition to the Hindus and close collaboration with the British. The members of the Aga Khan deputation to the Viceroy at Simla (1906) were the ideological successors of Syed Ahmed Khan, and advanced against the Congress and the national movement the same line of criticism as adopted by their great predecessor about two decades earlier. Nawab Salimullah of Dacca was the most redoubtable champion of Muslim separatist politics during the Swadeshi days.

It is fair to admit in this connection that the Muslim bitterness in the matter of Boycott agitation was not entirely groundless. The constant cry of the anti-partitionists for Boycott of British goods and the use of Swadeshi articles 'even at a sacrifice' (the supply of which was certainly below the minimum level) estranged the general bulk of the poor Muslims of the New Province of Eastern Bengal and Assam from the Hindu-dominated Swadeshi

Movement. This economic aspect of Muslim bitterness was closely noticed by Stuart Becker, the D.I.G. of the New Province, towards the end of 1906. But a historian must be careful to note at the same time that although a great bulk of the Muslim community withdrew from the Swadeshi Movement in 1906-07, yet numerous Muslims, particularly of the lower classes, still continued to pay their allegiance to the Swadeshi cause.

The Muslim peasants of Backergunje, in particular, under the leadership of Aswini Kumar Dutt continued to work for the national cause during the fateful years of 1906-07. Hence the total alienation of the Muslims from the Hindus in the national movement of 1905 was not a reality. The British journalist Nevinson in his memorable work, The New Spirit in India (1908), has recorded many startling news regarding Muslim role in the Swadeshi Movement.

It is worthwhile to observe that if any religion was preached at all by the Extremist political leaders of that time, it was the religion of patriotism of which Aurobindo Ghose was the greatest apostle. This new and invigorating ideal of Indian Nationalism was not based nor was ever intended to be based on rotten and decadent social ideas. It aimed at the liberation of India from alien subjection by whatever means the circumstances could suggest, and sought through India's liberation the salvation of humanity.

The Glorious Bengali Revolution of 1905

Thus the Swadeshi Movement of 1905 with its ideologies of Boycott, Swadeshi, Swaraj and National Education, far from being conservative or reactionary, marked a revolutionary advance in India's journey towards political and cultural freedom. And these alterations were effected with such an overpowering sense of suddenness as to elevate the national upheaval of 1905 to the rank of a revolution. The concept of revolution signifies change, though the converse is not true. It means, in the first place, not ordinary and superficial changes, but implies by its very nature a thoroughgoing transformation both of the social pattern and process. A revolution worth the name is marked not merely by qualitative changes; it has also a quantitative aspect. In other words, the changes introduced must not be confined to a few individuals but be 'massive in quantity and variety.' On its qualitative side, the Swadeshi Movement brought about a radical change in our whole mental attitude towards the British Raj. The hypnotic spell of the magic mantra that the British rule in India was a divine dispensation-a long-cherished illusion-was now rudely shattered. It was now keenly realized by the nation that overshadowed by a foreign culture and as a subordinate part of a foreign empire, India could have no future.

Again, in its quantitative aspect, the upheaval of 1905 affected the lives and destinies of millions of our countrymen. It was not a party rising nor a class upsurge but a gigantic national movement in which both classes and masses stood combined in opposition to alien despotism. Nor was the movement confined to Bengal alone. Other parts of India also were deeply stirred by this epoch-making upheaval. The maddening speeches of Bipin Chandra Pal at the Madras Sea Beach in 1907 on Boycott, Swadeshi, Swaraj and National Education had the miraculous impact of awakening Madras and the whole Deccan to the magic mantra of Indian Nationalism emanating from Bengal. Sarvepalli Radhakrishnan was one among the countless young men listening with devouring passion to Bipin

Pal's Oratorical Hypnotism of 1907

Another very significant characteristic of revolution is to be found in the element of suddenness. Even in 1902, at the Ahmedabad Congress, Surendra Nath Banerjea declared from the presidential chair that 'We plead for the permanence of the British rule in India'; but ere three years had passed when turbulent voices of opposition to the continuance of the British rule in India became clearly audible. When the Swadeshi Movement first began in Bengal and the doctrine of Boycott or comprehensive Passive Resistance was resorted to as the last legitimate instrument of retaliation, the whole of India was deeply astonished at this sudden change in Bengal's mental attitude to the British Government. Even the Anglo-Indians or the Europeans also were taken by surprise. In the writings of Alfred Lyall and Valentine Chirol one will easily fed a corroboration of the point. The last but not least important accompaniment of a political revolution is the element of force, violence, bloodshed, a feature which manifested itself very conspicuously in course of the Swadeshi Movement. The terrorisitic (more correctly, revolutionary) tendency already working in the country rapidly crystallized itself after 1905 into a new party with its concomitant philosophy of the bomb. The revolutionaries were advocates of violent methods and believed in 'purification by blood and fire' for the country's freedom covering all sides of national life. Thus all the essential features of a revolutionary movement marked the course and progress of the national upheaval of 1905. It is not for nothing that the late Prof. Benoy Kumar Sarkar repeatedly called it 'the Glorious Bengali Revolution of 1905'.

Dr. Bhupendra Nath Datta the renowned Marxist sociologist, who was also the Editor of the revolutionary Yugantar weekly, holds an identical view with Prof. Benoy Sarkar in this matter. Reviewing the political situation in India in 1907, Lord Minto, the Viceroy, while discussing 'The Seditious Meetings Bill' in the Legislative Council sounded a note of caution (2nd November, 1907) when he said: 'The Government of India would be blind indeed to shut its eyes to the awakening wave which is sweeping over the Eastern world, overwhelming old traditions, and bearing on its crest a flood of new ideas.'

To conclude, if the Swadeshi Movement of 1905 has left any message for India and mankind, it is the message of uttermost self-sacrifice for the country conceived as the Mother of which Aurobindo was the most shining figure during the Swadeshi days, but that spirit of noble dedication and self-sacrifice gradually gave way to self-seeking politics and 'maddening chase for... purse' in the closing years of Indian Independence Movement.

Fifty-nine years after Independence, as a close observer of the turns and realities of Indian politics I, as an octogenarian, often feel today, very sad and agonized at the corrupt and degrading political scenario of India. The political leadership, by and large, has gone bankrupt. Those who are constantly crying themselves hoarse for freedom, democracy, secularism and other noble virtues are, in the words of Dr. S. Radhakrishnan, 'more anxious to build themselves than to build the nation'. No nation or country can ever be built by this type of ignoble and self-seeking leadership. India will no doubt rise again to the full height and depths of her greatness when the present self-seeking leadership will be overthrown root and branch by the organized idealism and vigorous action of a truly dedicated hand of young men such as Bengal once produced during the fiery Swadeshi times.

6

The Economic and Political Aspect of Swadeshi Movement

Educated liberal Muslims who came forward and tendered support to the anti-partition agitation and the Swadeshi Movement. Though their number was insignificant, yet their role added a new dimension in the thought process of the Muslims. This broad-minded group supported the Indian National Congress and opposed the partition. The most prominent among this section of the Muslims was Khwaza atiqullah. At the Calcutta session of the Congress (1906), he moved a resolution denouncing the partition of Bengal Abdur Rasul, Khan Bahadur Muhammad Yusuf (a pleader and a member of the Management Committee of the Central National Muhamedan Association), Mujibur Rahman, AH Abdul Halim Ghaznavi, Ismail Hossain Shiraji, Muhammad Gholam Hossain (a writer and a promoter of Hindu-Muslim unity), Maulvi Liaqat Hussain (a liberal Muslim who vehemently opposed the 'Divide and Rule' policy of the British), Syed Hafizur Rahman Chowdhury of Bogra and Abul Kasem of Burdwan inspired Muslims to join the anti-Partition agitation. There were even a few Muslim preachers of Swadeshi ideas, like Din Muhammad of Mymensingh and Abdul Gaffar of Chittagong. It needs to be mentioned that some of the liberal nationalist Muslims like AH Ghaznavi and Khan Bahadur Muhammad Yusuf supported the Swadeshi Movement but not the Boycott agitation.

A section of the Muslim press tried to promote harmonious relations between the Hindus and the Muslims. Ak Fazlul Huq and Nibaran Chandra Das preached non-communal ideas through their weekly Balaka (1901, Barisal) and monthly Bharat Suhrd

(1901, Barisal). Only a small section of Muslim intellectuals could rise above their sectarian outlook and join with the Congress in the anti-partition agitation and constitutional politics.

The general trend of thoughts in the Muslim minds was in favour of partition. The All India Muslim league, founded in 1906, supported the partition. In the meeting of the Imperial Council in 1910 Shamsul Huda of Bengal and Mazhar-ul-Huq from Bihar spoke in favour of the partition.

The traditional and reformist Muslim groups-the Faraizi, Wahabi and Taiyuni-supported the partition. Consequently an orthodox trend was visible in the political attitude of the Muslims. The Bengali Muslim press in general lent support to the partition. The Islam Pracharak described Swadeshi as a Hindu movement and expressed grave concern saying that it would bring hardship to the common people. The Muslim intelligentsia in general felt concerned about the suffering of their co-religionists caused by it. They particularly disliked the movement as it was tied to the anti-partition agitation. Reputed litterateurs like Mir Mosharraf Hossain were virulent critics of the Swadeshi Movement. The greater body of Muslims at all levels remained opposed to the Swadeshi Movement since it was used as a weapon against the partition and a religious tone was added to it.

The economic aspect of the movement was partly responsible for encouraging separatist forces within the Muslim society. The superiority of the Hindus in the sphere of trade and industry alarmed the Muslims. Fear of socioeconomic domination by the Hindus made them alert to safeguard their own interests. These apprehensions brought about a rift in Hindu-Muslims relations. In order to avoid economic exploitation by the Hindus, some wealthy Muslim entrepreneurs came forward to launch new commercial ventures. One good attempt was the founding of steamer companies operating between Chittagong and Rangoon in 1906.

In the context of the partition the pattern of the land system in Bengal played a major role to influence the Muslim mind. The absentee Hindu zamindars made no attempt to improve the lot of the raiyats who were mostly Muslims. The agrarian disputes (between landlords and tenants) already in existence in the province also appeared to take a communal colour. It was alleged that the

Hindu landlords had been attempting to enforce Swadeshi ideas on the tenants and induce them to join the anti-partition movement.

In 1906, the Muslims organised an Islamic conference at Keraniganj in Dhaka as a move to emphasise their separate identity as a community. The Swadeshi Movement with its Hindu religious flavour fomented aggressive reaction from the other community. A red pamphlet of a highly inflammatory nature was circulated among the Muslim masses of Eastern Bengal and Assam urging them completely to dissociate from the Hindus. It was published under the auspices of the Anjuman-I-Mufidul Islam under the editorship of a certain Ibrahim Khan. Moreover, such irritating moves as the adoption of the Bande Mataram as the song of inspiration or introduction of the cult of Shivaji as a national hero, and reports of communal violence alienated the Muslims. One inevitable result of such preaching was the riot that broke out at Comilla in March 1907, followed by similar riots in Jamalpur in April of that year. These communal disturbances became a familiar feature in Eastern Bengal and Assam and followed a pattern that was repeated elsewhere. The 1907 riots represent a watershed in the history of modern Bengal.

While Hindu-Muslims relations deteriorated, political changes of great magnitude were taking place in the Government of India's policies, and simultaneously in the relations of Bengali Muslim leaders with their non-Bengali counterparts. Both developments had major repercussions on communal relations in eastern Bengal. The decision to introduce constitutional reforms culminating in the morley-minto reforms of 1909 introducing separate representation for the Muslims marked a turning point in Hindu-Muslim relations.

The early administrators of the new province from the lieutenant governor down to the junior-most officials in general were enthusiastic in carrying out the development works. Bampfylde Fuller was accused by the anti-Partition movement leaders as being extremely partial to Muslims. He, because of a difference with the Government of India, resigned in August 1906. His resignation and its prompt acceptance were considered by the Muslims to be a solid political victory for the Hindus. The general Muslim feeling was that in yielding to the pressure of the anti-Partition agitators the government had revealed its weakness and had overlooked the loyal adherence of the Muslims to the government. Consequently, the antagonism between the Hindus and Muslims became very acute in the new province. The Muslim leaders, now more conscious of their separate communal identity, directed their attention in uniting the different sections of their community to the creation of a counter movement against that of the Hindus. They keenly felt the need for unity and believed that the Hindu agitation against the Partition was in fact a communal movement and as such a threat to the Muslims as a separate community. They decided to faithfully follow the directions of leaders like Salimullah and Nawab Ali Chowdhury and formed organisations like the Mohammedan Provincial Union.

Though communalism had reached its peak in the new province by 1907, there is evidence of a sensible and sincere desire among some of the educated and upper class Muslims and Hindus to put an end to these religious antagonisms. A group of prominent members of both communities met the Viceroy Lord Minto on 15 March 1907 with suggestions to put an end to communal violence and promote religious harmony between the two communities.

The landlord-tenant relationship in the new province had deteriorated and took a communal turn. The Hindu landlords felt alarmed at the acts of terrorism committed by the anti-partition agitators. To prove their unswerving loyalty to the government and give evidence of their negative attitude towards the agitation, they offered their hands of friendship and cooperation to their Muslim counterparts to the effect that they would take a non-communal stand and work unitedly against the anti-government revolutionary movements.

In the meantime the All-India Muslim League had come into being at Dacca on 30 December 1906. Though several factors were responsible for the formation of such an organisation, the Partition of Bengal and the threat to it was, perhaps, the most important factor that hastened its birth. At its very first sitting at Dacca the Muslim League, in one of its resolutions, said: 'That this meeting in view of the clear interest of the Mohammedans of Eastern Bengal consider that Partition is sure to prove beneficial to the Muhammadan community which constitute the vast majority of the populations of the new province and that all such methods of agitation such as boycotting should be strongly condemned and discouraged'. To assuage the resentment of the assertive Bengali Hindus, the British government decided to annul the Partition of

Bengal. As regards the Muslims of Eastern Bengal the government stated that in the new province the Muslims were in an overwhelming majority in point of population, under the new arrangement also they would still be in a position of approximate numerical equality or possibly of small superiority over the Hindus. The interests of the Muslims would be safeguarded by special representation in the Legislative Councils and the local bodies.

Lord hardinge succeeded Minto and on 25 August 1911. In a secret despatch the government of India recommended certain changes in the administration of India. According to the suggestion of the Governor-General-in-Council, King George V at his Coronation Darbar in Delhi in December 1911 announced the revocation of the Partition of Bengal and of certain changes in the administration of India. Firstly, the Government of India should have its seat at Delhi instead of Calcutta. By shifting the capital to the site of past Muslim glory, the British hoped to placate Bengal's Muslim community now aggrieved at the loss of provincial power and privilege in eastern Bengal. Secondly, the five Bengali speaking Divisions viz The Presidency, Burdwan, Dacca, Rajshahi and Chittagong were to be united and formed into a Presidency to be administered by a Governor-in-Council. The area of this province would be approximately 70,000 sq. miles with a population of 42 million. Thirdly, a Lieutenant-Governor-in-Council with a Legislative Council was to govern the province comprising of Bihar, Chhota Nagpur and Orissa. Fourthly, Assam was to revert back to the rule of a Chief Commissioner. The date chosen for the formal ending of the partition and reunification of Bengal was I April 1912.

Reunification of Bengal indeed served somewhat to soothe the feeling of the Bengali Hindus, but the down grading of Calcutta from imperial to mere provincial status was simultaneously a blow to 'Bhadralok' egos and to Calcutta real estate values. To deprive Calcutta of its prime position as the nerve centre of political activity necessarily weakened the influence of the Bengali Hindus. The government felt that the main advantage, which could be derived from the move, was that it would remove the seat of the government of India from the agitated atmosphere of Bengal.

Lord Carmichael, a man of liberal sympathies, was chosen as the first Governor of reunified Bengal. The Partition of Bengal and the agitation against it had far-reaching effects on Indian history and national life. The twin weapons of Swadeshi and Boycott adopted by the Bengalis became a creed with the Indian National Congress and were used more effectively in future conflicts. They formed the basis of Gandhi's Non-Cooperation, Satyagraha and Khadi movements. They also learned that organised political agitation and critical public opinion can force the government to accede to public demands.

The annulment of the partition as a result of the agitation against it had a negative effect on the Muslims. The majority of the Muslims did not like the Congress support to the anti-partition agitation. The politically conscious Muslims felt that the Congress had supported a Hindu agitation against the creation of a Muslim majority province. It reinforced their belief that their interests were not safe in the hands of the Congress. Thus they became more anxious to emphasise their separate communal identity and leaned towards the Muslim League to safeguard their interest against the dominance of the Hindu majority in undivided India. To placate Bengali Muslim feelings Lord Hardinge promised a new University at Dacca on 31 January 1912 to a Muslim deputation led by Salimullah.

The Partition of Bengal of 1905 left a profound impact on the political history of India. From a political angle the measure accentuated Hindu-Muslim differences in the region. One point of view is that by giving the Muslim's a separate territorial identity in 1905 and a communal electorate through the Morley-Minto Reforms of 1909 the British Government in a subtle manner tried to neutralise the possibility of major Muslim participation in the Indian National Congress.

The Partition of Bengal indeed marks a turning point in the history of nationalism in India. It may be said that it was out of the travails of Bengal that Indian nationalism was born. By the same token the agitation against the partition and the terrorism that it generated was one of the main factors which gave birth to Muslim nationalism and encouraged them to engage in separatist politics. The birth of the Muslim League in 1906 at Dacca (Dhaka) bears testimony to this. The annulment of the partition sorely disappointed not only the Bengali Muslims but also the Muslims of the whole of India. They felt that loyalty did not pay but agitation does. Thereafter, the dejected Muslims gradually took an anti-British stanc

Rasul, Abdur (1872-1917) nationalist leader and lawyer. Abdur Rasul was born in 1872 in a landed family of Guniauk, a village in Brahmanbaria district. He lost his father Golam Rasul in his childhood but his mother raised him well. He was sent to England for higher studies after he had passed the Entrance Examination in 1888. He took the BA degree in 1896 and the MA degree in 1898. Abdur Rasul was called to the Bar at the Middle Temple in 1898. While in London, he became acquainted with noted Indians like Ali Imam, Syed Hasan Imam, aurobindo ghosh and others. Returning to India he got himself enrolled at the Calcutta High Court in 1899. Abdur Rasul was made an honorary lecturer in International Law at the university of Calcutta.

Abdur Rasul was opposed to the partition of bengal, 1905. He presided over the Bengal Congress Conference held at Barisal in 1906. In collaboration with Abdul Halim Ghaznavi

Dawn Society, The (1902-1906) was founded in Calcutta by Satish Chandra Mukherjee, a proponent of national education, in 1902. Satish Chandra had earlier established *Bhagabat Chatuspathi* in 1896. This was dedicated to the study of Indian religion and philosophy primarily and to Indology in general. The objective was to satisfy the quest for national identity. Its classes were held in the Metropolitan Institution (Modern Vidyasagar College) in the evening. At the same time, the famous Dawn Magazine was also launched. Many articles on Indology appeared in its pages till 1902 when it became the mouthpiece of the Dawn society.

Satish Chandra Mukherjee was a legendary teacher and a mentor of contemporary young men. Men like Binoy Kumar Sarkar, Radha Kumud Mukherjee, Haran Chandra Chakladar, Rabindranarayan Ghosh, Kishori Mohan Gupta and others flocked around him and became the mainstays of the Dawn Society. The society was critical of the colonial education imparted by the university of Calcutta which, according to it, was "all-too-literary, all-too-academic, unscientific and un-industrial" in nature. The Dawn Society wanted to promote education for man-making and nation-building purpose. In its curriculum, therefore, history, geography, economics, and political science were included in the Arts and Sciences & Technology were introduced. Apart from the above mentioned disciples, stalwarts like J.C. Bose, Nilratan Sarkar, Ramendrasundar Trivedi and even Rabindranath were invited to deliver lectures to the society while Ramakanta Roy and

Kunjabehari Sen lectured in the technology section. Students were expected to take notes from lectures and submit their notes to teachers concerned for scrutiny. Then there would be discussion on the subject in which the students were supposed to take part. They were also encouraged to submit their essays to the Dawn magazine for publication. The technology section had an elementary and a secondary course, which was backed up by workshop activities. In the workshop, all types of mechanical work were taught, along with chemical processes such as soap making and oil making. Modern weaving methods were also taught. The products of the students were sold in a *swadeshi* shop in Barabazar. Technical education was one of the main planks of the swadeshi education offered by the Dawn Society. This was advancement upon the curriculum of the Indian association for the cultivation of science, which was solely concerned with scientific pursuits.

The Dawn Magazine was not only the mouthpiece of the Society, it also reflected the ends and objectives of national education. Its purpose was to restore the heritage of India and to analyse its political, social and economic problems and to suggest remedies for them. A special section of the magazine was devoted to Indian subject, and the motto of the magazine was that it was essential to know one's own country to promote nationalism. To this effect Satish Chandra himself and his select band of disciples wrote incessantly on all subjects concerning India. In deed, *Dawn Magazine* became the mirror of the contemporary Bengali mind and Indian nationalism. The journal ran from 1896 to 1913, over-arching the Dawn society, which merged into the National Council of Education in 1906. [Chittabrata Palit]

Dawn Society, The (1902-1906) was founded in Calcutta by Satish Chandra Mukherjee, a proponent of national education, in 1902. Satish Chandra had earlier established *Bhagabat Chatuspathi* in 1896. This was dedicated to the study of Indian religion and philosophy primarily and to Indology in general. The objective was to satisfy the quest for national identity. Its classes were held in the Metropolitan Institution (Modern Vidyasagar College) in the evening. At the same time, the famous Dawn Magazine was also launched. Many articles on Indology appeared in its pages till 1902 when it became the mouthpiece of the Dawn society. Satish Chandra Mukherjee was a legendary teacher and a mentor of contemporary young men. Men like Binoy Kumar Sarkar, Radha Kumud Mukherjee, Haran Chandra Chakladar, Rabindranarayan Ghosh, Kishori Mohan Gupta and others flocked around him and became the mainstays of the Dawn Society. The society was critical of the colonial education imparted by the university of Calcutta which, according to it, was "all-too-literary, all-too-academic, unscientific and un-industrial" in nature. The Dawn Society wanted to promote education for man-making and nation-building purpose. In its curriculum, therefore, history, geography, economics, and political science were included in the Arts and Sciences & Technology were introduced. Apart from the above mentioned disciples, stalwarts like J.C. Bose, Nilratan Sarkar, Ramendrasundar Trivedi and even Rabindranath were invited to deliver lectures to the society while Ramakanta Roy and Kunjabehari Sen lectured in the technology section.

Students were expected to take notes from lectures and submit their notes to teachers concerned for scrutiny. Then there would be discussion on the subject in which the students were supposed to take part. They were also encouraged to submit their essays to the Dawn magazine for publication. The technology section had an elementary and a secondary course, which was backed up by workshop activities. In the workshop, all types of mechanical work were taught, along with chemical processes such as soap making and oil making. Modern weaving methods were also taught. The products of the students were sold in a *swadeshi* shop in Barabazar. Technical education was one of the main planks of the swadeshi education offered by the Dawn Society. This was advancement upon the curriculum of the Indian association for the cultivation of science, which was solely concerned with scientific pursuits.

The Dawn Magazine was not only the mouthpiece of the Society, it also reflected the ends and objectives of national education. Its purpose was to restore the heritage of India and to analyse its political, social and economic problems and to suggest remedies for them. A special section of the magazine was devoted to Indian subject, and the motto of the magazine was that it was essential to know one's own country to promote nationalism. To this effect Satish Chandra himself and his select band of disciples wrote incessantly on all subjects concerning India. In deed, *Dawn Magazine* became the mirror of the contemporary Bengali mind and Indian nationalism. The journal ran from 1896 to 1913, overarching the Dawn society, which merged into the National Council of Education in 1906. [Chittabrata Palit]

Mukherjee, Satish Chandra (1865-1948) nationalist writer, was born in a Brahmin family on 5 June 1865 at Bandipur in Hughli district. His father, Krishnanath Banerjee, worked as a translator at the Calcutta High Court. Satish Chandra's early education began at South Suburban School, Bhowanipore. In 1884 he passed BA from Presidency College, Kolkata on a government scholarship. After completing his MA in English in 1886, he began teaching at Metropolitan Institution, Kolkata. In 1887 he joined Berhampore College. After obtaining the BL degree in 1890, he started practising law at the Calcutta High Court. In 1895 he established an educational institution called Bhagavat Chatuspathi Bijoy Krishna Goswami was his spiritual guru.

Asutosh Mookerji was Satish Chandra's classmate. Satish Chandra maintained a close contact with contemporary personalities such as shibnath shastri, Brajendra Nath seal, Rabindranath Tagore, Bipin Chandra Pal, Aswini Kumar datta, and swami vivekananda by whom he was influenced variously. In 1902 he established the dawn society as an example of self-reliance in education and became its secretary. Dawn Society was a non-political cultural organisation founded in protest against the Report of Indian Universities Commission. Its aims included providing Bengali students with an ideal education, imparting religious and moral lessons to them, extending their intellectual capacities and building their character. Moreover, it also believed in imbuing students with a sense of nationalism and patriotism while imparting practical technical education and developing indigenous industries.

Dawn Society contributed to the introduction of nationalism in education. It arranged a meeting on 5 November 1905 to inaugurate national education. Rabindranath Tagore, Satish Chandra and Hirendranath Dutta delivered speeches at this vast gathering. Satish Chandra called upon students to leave Calcutta University and boycott its examinations.

Satish Chandra established the Council of National Education (NEC) in 1906. Aurobindo Ghosh became principal of the newly founded Bengal National College under the NCE and Satish Chandra became its Caretaker. In 1907 Aurobindo resigned and

Satish Chandra was appointed principal. But he also resigned the next year because of ill health.

Satish Chandra also protested against the Carlyle Circular of 10 October 1905 the intention of which was to keep students away from the swadeshi movement. Dawn Society worked for the revitalization of indigenous industries long before the formal beginning of the movement in 1905. The monthly *Dawn* (1897), edited by Satish Chandra, served as the mouthpiece of the Society in awakening and propagating nationalism.

Satish Chandra also contributed to the English magazine *Bandemataram*. The non-cooperation movement (1922) of Gandhi influenced him greatly. When Mahatma Gandhi was arrested, Satish Chandra fled to Sabarmati and for two months assisted in the management and publication of *Young India*. In 1930 he visited Dr. Rajendra Prasad's Vihar Vidyapith and stayed there for some time.

Satish Chandra was a profoundly religious man. At the same time he did not believe in religious superstitions and the caste system and was against provincialism. He died on 18 April 1948

Santiniketan began as an *ashram* in 1863. Maharshi Debendranath Tagore founded it on twenty bighas of land purchased from Bhubanmohan Sinha, landlord of Raipur. The *ashram,* located near Bolpur in the Birbhum district of West Bengal, was intended as a retreat for householders, where they could spend their time in prayer, away from their worldly preoccupations. The Santiniketan Trust, established by the Maharshi in 1888, provided for a guest house, a prayer hall, and a library dedicated to religious literature.

The Swadeshi Movement: The partition of Bengal in 1905 had far reaching repercussion and accelerated the pace of freedom movement in India. The event led to the launch of swadeshi movement and boycott of British goods. It also resulted in the split of the Indian National Congress into two factions, the moderates and the extremists and gave birth to revolutionaries clubs and Muslim League. The Partition of Bengal: The province of Bengal consisted of Bengal proper, Bihar and Orissa, with a population of 78 million people. In East Bengal, Muslims were in a majority while Hindus predominated in West Bengal as well as in Bihar and Orissa. Way back in 1896, William Ward, an official had prepared a scheme of partition of Bengal for administrative convenience. But due to financial constraints it was abandoned. The scheme attracted the attention of Viceroy Curzon and he decided to implement it. In February 1904, Curzon toured East Bengal and roped in Nawab Salimullah Khan of Dacca by promising him a loan at nominal interest and the latter succeeded in assembling a huge gathering of Muslims to cheer the Viceroy's plan for a Muslim province. But the Bengali intelligentsia and the Indian nationalists opposed the partition on the ground that it undermined the traditions, history and language of the Bengalis and divide them on the basis of religion. Curzon had admitted during his tour of East Bengal that one object of the partition proposal was to create a Mohammedan province where Islam could be predominate.

The Boycott movement: The new province of East Bengal was inaugurated on 16th October 1905. The leaders of the anti-partition movement made a public declaration that the day of inauguration would be observed as a day of national mourning. A detailed programme was drawn up for the day. Food would not be cooked, except for the sick and invalid; business would be suspended and people would walk barefoot and bathe in the Ganga in the morning to purify themselves. To symbolise the unity among the Bengalis, the programme of tying a red band round the wrists of the people was undertaken. Streets was echoed with the cry 'Vande Mataram' and a national fund for carrying on the agitation was started and in a few hours Rs. 10,000 was collected through subscriptions. Earlier in a public meeting held at Ripon College in Calcutta under the leadership of S.N.Banerjee on 17th July 1905, a resolution asking the people to boycott all British goods till partition was undone had been passed. On the occasion of a religious festival in August 1905, about 50,000 people took a vow before goddess Kali not to buy foreign articles and not to employ foreigners for jobs for which suitable Indians are available. The boycott movement was not a new thing. Way back in 1849, Gopal Rao Deshmukh, better known as 'Lokahitawadi' of Bombay urged the use of indigenous goods. In 1873, Bholanath Chandra preached the establishment of indigenous Banks, Companies, Corporations, Mills and Factories and denounced the practice of preferring foreign goods to home made manufacturers. Swami Dayananda Saraswati also emphasized on swadeshi. Similarly the Tagore family also lent their full support to the use of swadeshi goods. Rabindranath Tagore started the 'Swadeshi Bhandar' in 1897 and 'Sarala Devi Lakshmi Bhandar' in 1903. During the anti-partition agitation, Swadeshi stores sold homemade goods in retail and student volunteers peddled them. In consonance with the boycott call, contents of the ships arriving with foreign goods were dumped; bags of Liverpool salt were pulled out of boats and thrown into the river. The priests refused to perform religious ceremonies with foreign articles. Those found wearing foreign clothes including Europeans were jeered at. So vehement was the public opinion that nobody would think of buying foreign clothes and those who went in for its cheapness would buy only at night. At an examination hall in Rippon College, students refused to touch answer papers of foreign make and country made sheets had to be substituted. A five-year old granddaughter of S.N.Banerjee returned a pair of shoes sent to her by a relative because they were made abroad. Similarly another girl aged six though suffering from fever refused to take any foreign medicine. If any foreign-made presents were given during marriages they were returned. Guests would refuse to participate in festivities in which foreign salt or sugar was used.

Karnataka and Swadeshi movement: Karnataka enthusiastically responded to the call of swadeshi. On 5th May 1905 a public meeting presided by Gurunatha Rao Patak was held in the Victoria Theatre at Dharwad to protest against the partition of Bengal and to encourage swadeshi industries. The meeting resolved that everyone should vow not to use foreign cloth, except in unavoidable circumstances in order to encourage Indian artisans and trade in Indian goods. To spread the message of swadeshi and boycott, Tilak toured North Karnataka in 1905-06. Alur Venkata Rao, Sakkari Balachar, Krishna Rao Mudvedkar, Anantha Rao Dabade and others undertook extensive tours and delivered speeches on Swarajya, Swadeshi, Boycott and National Education. Swadeshi industries arose in many places.

Vittal Rao Deshpande of Hebbal started a weaving factory at Kittur. Another factory was built in Badami. Cloths made here were sent even to Bengal. Rama Rao Alagvadi opened a Match factory at Dharwad, while in Laxmeswar a Porcelain factory was established. Factories for manufacturing bangles, pencils and many other articles of common use arose in many places. A Karnataka Industrial Conference met at Dharwad in 1907 to chalk out plans to develop Swadeshi industries in Karnataka. New Banks were established to help these industries. Boycott of British goods: Apart from wide support to swadeshi movement, people of Karnataka wholeheartedly participated in the boycott of British goods. Ranibennur witnessed one of the biggest bonfires of foreign cloth. Textile dealers in Belgaum decided not to import foreign cloth and in Dharwad, grocers decided not to purchase Daboti and Johnson sugar. In Alnavar it was decided to smoke batti's instead of bidis and anyone found breaking the rule was fined. Hoteliers stopped the sale of tea and people poured kerosene into gutters and instead began to use indigenous oil for lighting. In one instance after it was noticed that a bangle seller had sold foreign bangles saying that it was Indian, the bangle seller was not only abused but also had to forego money. In Belgaum, along with swadeshi movement, prohibition was also advocated and toddy contractors had to incur heavy loss.

For picketing liquor shops in Belgaum nine persons were awarded one-week imprisonment and fined Rs. 680 in June 1908. Though a prominent person of Belgaum offered to pay the fine, the youths refused his help and preferred imprisonment. On 8th August 1908 a public meeting was held in Bagalkot, which was addressed by Jayarao Nargund, Jainapur, Yalagurdrao, Dharwadkar and others. It was proposed to establish a Swadeshi Vyaparottejak Samshtha in Bagalkot. The movement also saw the establishment of National Schools in various parts of Karnataka. Alur Venkata Rao started the Nutana Vidyalaya at Dharwad with arts and crafts also as subjects in the curriculum. Another national school arose at Navalgund by the efforts of Dundopanth Sahasrabuddhe.

In Belgaum Kaka Kalelkar established the Ganesh Vidyalaya, while Jaya Rao Nargund started another at Bagalkot. Similar schools were established at Hanagal, Agadi and other places. The government however saw that these schools close down one by one. In South Kanara district, Ammembala Srinivasa Pai was the moving spirit in the boycott of foreign goods and the spread of swadeshi. Men like K.P.Rao and Panje Mangesha Rao assisted him, while Kolachalam Venkata Rao and Sabhapathi Mudaliar were the leaders of the freedom movement in Bellary.

The Revolutionary Activities: The youth of Bengal had greatly contributed to the success of the anti-partition movement. They organized meetings, arranged demonstrations, roused enthusiasm, and provided volunteers for Swadeshi-Boycott propaganda and for picketing. Many were fined, expelled, beaten and flogged. But the harsher their treatment the more rebellious became their mood. The restriction on their public activities compelled them to form secret societies to achieve their aims.

Moreover the Englishmen in the past had taunted the Bengalis that they were a race of weaklings, cowardly and lacking in manly virtues. By forming revolutionary clubs called 'Samitis', the Bengali youth proved that they did not lack courage. Newspapers like 'Jugnatara', 'Bhawani Mandir', 'Bande Mataram' and 'Sandhya' were launched to preach the cult of revolutionary violence. Some youths of Karnataka like Dr.Handoor, Baburao Gani and Bheema Rao Bevoor kept up a close correspondence with the revolutionaries of Bengal.

Seeds of Separatism sown: Inspired by Muslim revolutionary activities in Egypt, Iran and Turkey, Abul Kalam Azad came into contact with Shyamsunder Chakravarthi of the Bande Mataram, met Aurobindo and joined one of the revolutionary bodies. He not only dissipated the anti-Muslim suspicious of the revolutionaries but helped in extending their activities outside Bengal and Bihar. The above development made Lawrence, the private secretary to Curzon and journalist like Valentine Chirol and Sidney Low to warn the then Viceroy Minto of the danger of the Hindu-Muslim accord. Theodore Morrison, the former principal of the Aligarh College warned the government against the possibility of Muslim sympathies going over to the Congress party. Colonel Dunlop Smith, the Private Secretary to Viceroy Minto wrote to William Archbold the then principal of Aligarh College that the Viceroy would be happy to receive a Muslim deputation.

The principal asked Nawab Mohsinul Mulk, the secretary of the college to act quickly and to press for introducing the system of nomination or granting representation on religious lines. On 1st October 1906 a deputation led by Aga Khan met Viceroy Minto at Shimla and demanded that seats in the Central Legislative Assembly be reserved for the Muslim community not only on the basis of their population but on the basis of their political importance and their services in the defence of the Empire. Minto readily accepted the demand for according them separate electorates. After their successful deputation, the Muslim leaders mooted the idea of forming an association to look exclusively after the interests of the Muslim community. On 30th December 1906 the All India Muslim League was formed to promote the political and other rights of Indian Muslims and to promote among Indian Muslims the feeling of loyalty towards the British government. The true political ideas of the Muslim League became apparent from Nawab Waqar-ul-Mulk's speech delivered at Aligarh. He said "God forbid, if the British rule disappears from India, Hindus will lord over it and there will be constant danger to our life, property and honour. The only way for the Muslims to escape this danger is to help in the continuance of the British rule. If the Muslims are heartily with the British, then that rule is bound to endure. Let the Muslims consider themselves as a British army ready to shed blood and sacrifice their lives for the British Crown". The League achieved its first success when the British government introduced separate electorates for Muslims in the 1909 Act.

Bengal Partition

Partition of Bengal, 1905 effected on 16 October during the viceroyalty of lord curzon (1899-1905), proved to be a momentous event in the history of modern Bengal. The idea of partitioning Bengal did not originate with Curzon. Bengal, which included Bihar and Orissa since 1765, was admittedly much too large for a single province of British India. This premier province grew too vast for efficient administration and required reorganisation and intelligent division.

The lieutenant governor of Bengal had to administer an area of 189,000 sq. miles and by 1903 the population of the province had risen to 78.50 million. Consequently, many districts in eastern Bengal had been practically neglected because of isolation and poor communication, which made good governance almost impossible. Calcutta and its nearby districts attracted all the energy and attention of the government. The condition of peasants was miserable under the exaction of absentee landlords; and trade, commerce and education were being impaired. The administrative machinery of the province was understaffed. Especially in east Bengal, in countryside so cut off by rivers and creeks, no special attention had been paid to the peculiar difficulties of police work till the last decade of the 19th century. Organised piracy in the waterways had existed for at least a century. Along with administrative difficulties, the problems of famine, of defence, or of linguistics had at one time or other prompted the government to consider the redrawing of administrative boundaries. Occasional efforts were made to rearrange the administrative units of Bengal. In 1836, the upper provinces were sliced off from Bengal and placed under a lieutenant governor. In 1854, the Governor-General-in-Council was relieved of the direct administration of Bengal, which was placed under a lieutenant governor. In 1874 Assam (along with Sylhet) was severed from Bengal to form a Chief-Commissionership and in 1898 Lushai Hills were added to it.

Proposals for partitioning Bengal were first considered in 1903. Curzon's original scheme was based on grounds of administrative efficiency. It was probably during the vociferous protests and adverse reaction against the original plan, that the officials first envisaged the possible advantages of a divided Bengal. Originally, the division was made on geographical rather than on an avowedly communal basis. 'Political Considerations' in this respect seemed to have been 'an afterthought'.

The government contention was that the Partition of Bengal was purely an administrative measure with three main objectives. Firstly, it wanted to relieve the government of Bengal of a part of the administrative burden and to ensure more efficient administration in the outlying districts. Secondly, the government desired to promote the development of backward Assam (ruled by a Chief Commissioner) by enlarging its jurisdiction so as to provide it with an outlet to the sea. Thirdly, the government felt the urgent necessity to unite the scattered sections of the Uriyaspeaking population under a single administration. There were further proposals to separate Chittagong and the districts of Dhaka (then Dacca) and Mymensigh from Bengal and attach them to Assam. Similarly Chhota Nagpur was to be taken away from Bengal and incorporated with the Central Provinces.

The government's proposals were officially published in January 1904. In February 1904, Curzon made an official tour of the districts of eastern Bengal with a view to assessing public opinion on the government proposals. He consulted the leading personalities of the different districts and delivered speeches at Dhaka, Chittagong and Mymensigh explaining the government's stand on partition. It was during this visit that the decision to push through an expanded scheme took hold of his mind. This would involve the creation of a self-contained new province under a

Lieutenant Governor with Legislative Council, an independent revenue authority and transfer of so much territory as would justify a fully equipped administration.

The enlarged scheme received the assent of the governments of Assam and Bengal. The new province would consist of the state of Hill Tripura, the Divisions of Chittagong, Dhaka and Rajshahi (excluding Darjeeling) and the district of Malda amalgamated with Assam. Bengal was to surrender not only these large territories on the east but also to cede to the Central Provinces the five Hindi-speaking states. On the west it would gain Sambalpur and a minor tract of five Uriya-speaking states from the Central Provinces. Bengal would be left with an area of 141,580 sq. miles and a population of 54 million, of which 42 million would be Hindus and 9 million Muslims.

The new province was to be called 'Eastern Bengal and Assam' with its capital at Dhaka and subsidiary headquarters at Chittagong. It would cover an area of 106,540 sq. miles with a population of 31 million comprising of 18 million Muslims and 12 million Hindus. Its administration would consist of Legislative Council, a Board of Revenue of two members, and the jurisdiction of the Calcutta High Court would be left undisturbed. The government pointed out that the new province would have a clearly demarcated western boundary and well defined geographical, ethnological, linguistic and social characteristics. The most striking feature of the new province was that it would concentrate within its own bounds the hitherto ignored and neglected typical homogenous Muslim population of Bengal. Besides, the whole of the tea industry (except Darjeeling), and the greater portion of the jute growing area would be brought under a single administration. The government of India promulgated their final decision in a Resolution dated 19 July 1905 and the Partition of Bengal was effected on 16 October of the same year.

The publication of the original proposals towards the end of 1903 had aroused unprecedented opposition, especially among the influential educated middle-class Hindus. The proposed territorial adjustment seemed to touch the existing interest groups and consequently led to staunch opposition. The Calcutta lawyers apprehended that the creation of a new province would mean the establishment of a Court of Appeal at Dacca and diminish the importance of their own High Court. Journalists feared the appearance of local newspapers, which would restrict the circulation of the Calcutta Press. The business community of Calcutta visualised the shift of trade from Calcutta to Chittagong, which would be nearer, and logically the cheaper port. The Zamindars who owned vast landed estates both in west and east Bengal foresaw the necessity of maintaining separate establishments at Dhaka that would involve extra expenditure.

The educated Bengali Hindus felt that it was a deliberate blow inflicted by Curzon at the national consciousness and growing solidarity of the Bengali-speaking population. The Hindus of Bengal, who controlled most of Bengal's commerce and the different professions and led the rural society, opined that the Bengali nation would be divided, making them a minority in a province including the whole of Bihar and Orissa. They complained that it was a veiled attempt by Curzon to strangle the spirit of nationalism in Bengal. They strongly believed that it was the prime object of the government to encourage the growth of a Muslim power in eastern Bengal as a counterpoise to thwart the rapidly growing strength of the educated Hindu community. Economic, political and communal interests combined together to intensify the opposition against the partition measure.

The Indian and specially the Bengali press opposed the partition move from the very beginning. The British press, the Anglo-Indian press and even some administrators also opposed the intended measure. The partition evoked fierce protest in west Bengal, especially in Calcutta and gave a new fillip to Indian nationalism. Henceforth, the Indian national congress was destined to become the main platform of the Indian nationalist movement. It exhibited unusual strength and vigour and shifted from a middle-class pressure group to a nation-wide mass organisation.

The leadership of the Indian National Congress viewed the partition as an attempt to 'divide and rule' and as a proof of the government's vindictive antipathy towards the outspoken Bhadralok intellectuals. Mother-goddess worshipping Bengali Hindus believed that the partition was tantamount to the vivisection of their 'Mother province'. 'Bande-Mataram' (Hail Motherland) almost became the national anthem of the Indian National Congress. Defeat of the partition became the immediate target of Bengali nationalism. Agitation against the partition manifested itself in the form of mass meetings; rural unrest and a swadeshi movement to boycott the import of British manufactured goods. Swadeshi and Boycott were the twin weapons of this nationalism and Swaraj (self-government) its main objective. Swaraj was first mentioned in the presidential address of Dadabhai Naoroji as the Congress goal at its Calcutta session in 1906.

Leaders like surendranath banerjea along with journalists like Krishna Kumar Mitra, editor of the Sanjivani (13 July 1905) urged the people to boycott British goods, observe mourning and sever all contact with official bodies. In a meeting held at Calcutta on 7 August 1905 (hailed as the birthday of Indian nationalism) a resolution to abstain from purchases of British products so long as 'Partition resolution is not withdrawn' was accepted with acclaim. This national spirit was popularised by the patriotic songs of Dwijendralal Roy, Rajanikanta Sen and Rabindranath Tagore. As with other political movements of the day this also took on religious overtones. Pujas were offered to emphasise the solemn nature of the occasion.

The Hindu religious fervour reached its peak on 28 September 1905, the day of the Mahalaya, the new-moon day before the puja, and thousands of Hindus gathered at the Kali temple in Calcutta. In Bengal the worship of Kali, wife of Shiva, had always been very popular. She possessed a two-dimensional character with mingled attributes both generative and destructive. Simultaneously she took great pleasure in bloody sacrifices but she was also venerated as the great Mother associated with the conception of Bengal as the Motherland. This conception offered a solid basis for the support of political objectives stimulated by religious excitement. Kali was accepted as a symbol of the Motherland, and the priest administered the Swadeshi vow. Such a religious flavour could and did give the movement a widespread appeal among the Hindu masses, but by the same token that flavour aroused hostility in average Muslim minds. Huge protest rallies before and after Bengal's division on 16 October 1905 attracted millions of people heretofore not involved in politics.

The Swadeshi Movement as an economic movement would have been quite acceptable to the Muslims, but as the movement was used as a weapon against the partition (which the greater body of the Muslims supported) and as it often had a religious colouring added to it, it antagonised Muslim minds. The new tide of national sentiment against the Partition of Bengal originating in Bengal spilled over into different regions in India Punjab, Central Provinces, Poona, Madras, Bombay and other cities. Instead of wearing foreign made outfits, the Indians vowed to use only swadeshi (indigenous) cottons and other clothing materials made in India. Foreign garments were viewed as hateful imports. The Swadeshi Movement soon stimulated local enterprise in many areas; from Indian cotton mills to match factories, glass blowing shops, iron and steel foundries. The agitation also generated increased demands for national education. Bengali teachers and students extended their boycott of British goods to English schools and college classrooms. The movement for national education spread throughout Bengal and reached even as far as Benaras where Pandit Madan Mohan Malaviya founded his private Benaras Hindu University in 1910.

The student community of Bengal responded with great enthusiasm to the call of nationalism. Students including schoolboys participated en masse in the campaigns of Swadeshi and Boycott. The government retaliated with the notorious Carlyle Circular that aimed to crush the students' participation in the Swadeshi and Boycott movements. Both the students and the teachers strongly reacted against this repressive measure and the protest was almost universal. In fact, through this protest movement the first organised student movement was born in Bengal. Along with this the 'Anti-Circular Society', a militant student organisation, also came into being.

The anti-partition agitation was peaceful and constitutional at the initial stage, but when it appeared that it was not yielding the desired results the protest movement inevitably passed into the hands of more militant leaders. Two techniques of boycott and terrorism were to be applied to make their mission successful. Consequently the younger generation, who were unwittingly drawn into politics, adopted terrorist methods by using firearms, pistols and bombs indiscriminately. The agitation soon took a turn towards anarchy and disorder. Several assassinations were committed and attempts were made on the lives of officials including Sir andrew fraser. The terrorist movement soon became an integral part of the Swadeshi agitation. Bengal terrorism reached its peak from 1908 through 1910, as did the severity of official repression and the number of 'preventive detention' arrests. The new militant spirit was reflected in the columns of the nationalist newspapers, notably the Bande Mataram, Sandhya and Jugantar. The press assisted a great deal to disseminate revolutionary ideas. In 1907, the Indian National Congress at its annual session in Surat split into two groups-one being moderate, liberal, and evolutionary; and the other extremist, militant and revolutionary. The young militants of Bal Gangadhar Tilak's extremist party supported the 'cult of the bomb and the gun' while the moderate leaders like Gopal Krishna Gokhale and Surendranath Banerjea cautioned against such extremist actions fearing it might lead to anarchy and uncontrollable violence. Surendranath Banerjea, though one of the front-rank leaders of the anti-Partition agitation, was not in favour of terrorist activities.

When the proposal for partition was first published in 1903 there was expression of Muslim oppcsition to the scheme. The moslem chronicle, the central national Muhamedan association, chowdhury kazemuddin ahmad siddiky and Delwar Hossain Ahmed condemned the proposed measure. Even Nawab salimullah termed the suggestion as 'beastly' at the initial stage. In the beginning the main criticism from the Muslim side was against any part of an enlightened and advanced province of Bengal passing under the rule of a chief commissioner. They felt that thereby, their educational, social and other interests would suffer, and there is no doubt that the Muslims also felt that the proposed measure would threaten Bengali solidarity. The Muslim intelligentsia, however, criticised the ideas of extremist militant nationalism as being against the spirit of Islam. The Muslim press urged its educated co-religionists to remain faithful to the government. On the whole the Swadeshi preachers were not able to influence and arouse the predominantly Muslim masses in east Bengal. The anti-partition trend in the thought process of the Muslims did not continue for long. When the wider scheme of a self contained separate the educated section of the Muslims knew province they soon changed their views. They realised that the partition would be a boon to them and that their special difficulties would receive greater attention from the new administration.

The Muslims accorded a warm welcome to the new Lieutenant-Governor bampfylde fuller. Even the Moslem Chronicle soon changed its attitude in favour of partition. Some Muslims in Calcutta also welcomed the creation of the new province. The Mohammedan literary society brought out a manifesto in 1905 signed by seven leading Muslim personalities. The manifesto was circulated to the different Muslim societies of both west and east Bengal and urged the Muslims to give their unqualified support to the partition measure. The creation of the new province provided an incentive to the Muslims to unite into a compact body and form an association to voice their own views and aspiration relating to social and political matters. On 16 October 1905 the Mohammedan Provincial Union was founded. All the existing organisations and societies were invited to affiliate themselves with it and Salimullah was unanimously chosen as its patron.

Even then there was a group of educated liberal Muslims who came forward and tendered support to the anti-partition agitation and the Swadeshi Movement. Though their number was insignificant, yet their role added a new dimension in the thought process of the Muslims. This broad-minded group supported the Indian National Congress and opposed the partition. The most prominent among this section of the Muslims was Khwaza atiqullah. At the Calcutta session of the Congress (1906), he moved a resolution denouncing the partition of Bengal. Abdur Rasul, Khan Bahadur Muhammad Yusuf (a pleader and a member of the Management Committee of the Central National Muhamedan Association), Mujibur Rahman, AH Abdul Halim Ghaznavi, Ismail Hossain Shiraji, Muhammad Gholam Hossain (a writer and a promoter of Hindu-Muslim unity), Maulvi Liaqat Hussain (a liberal Muslim who vehemently opposed the 'Divide and Rule' policy of the British), Syed Hafizur Rahman Chowdhury of Bogra and Abul Kasem of Burdwan inspired Muslims to join the anti-Partition agitation. There were even a few Muslim preachers of Swadeshi ideas, like Din Muhammad of Mymensingh and Abdul Gaffar of Chittagong. It needs to be mentioned that some of the liberal nationalist Muslims like AH Ghaznavi and Khan Bahadur Muhammad Yusuf supported the Swadeshi Movement but not the Boycott agitation.

A section of the Muslim press tried to promote harmonious relations between the Hindus and the Muslims. Ak Fazlul Huq and Nibaran Chandra Das preached non-communal ideas through their weekly Balaka (1901, Barisal) and monthly Bharat Suhrd (1901, Barisal). Only a small section of Muslim intellectuals could rise above their sectarian outlook and join with the Congress in the anti-partition agitation and constitutional politics.

The general trend of thoughts in the Muslim minds was in favour of partition. The All India Muslim league, founded in 1906, supported the partition. In the meeting of the Imperial Council in 1910 Shamsul Huda of Bengal and Mazhar-ul-Huq from Bihar spoke in favour of the partition.

The traditional and reformist Muslim groups-the Faraizi, Wahabi and Taiyuni-supported the partition. Consequently an orthodox trend was visible in the political attitude of the Muslims. The Bengali Muslim press in general lent support to the partition. The Islam Pracharak described Swadeshi as a Hindu movement and expressed grave concern saying that it would bring hardship to the common people. The Muslim intelligentsia in general felt concerned about the suffering of their co-religionists caused by it. They particularly disliked the movement as it was tied to the anti-partition agitation. Reputed litterateurs like Mir Mosharraf Hossain were virulent critics of the Swadeshi Movement. The greater body of Muslims at all levels remained opposed to the Swadeshi Movement since it was used as a weapon against the partition and a religious tone was added to it.

The economic aspect of the movement was partly responsible for encouraging separatist forces within the Muslim society. The superiority of the Hindus in the sphere of trade and industry alarmed the Muslims. Fear of socioeconomic domination by the Hindus made them alert to safeguard their own interests. These apprehensions brought about a rift in Hindu-Muslims relations. In order to avoid economic exploitation by the Hindus, some wealthy Muslim entrepreneurs came forward to launch new commercial ventures. One good attempt was the founding of steamer companies operating between Chittagong and Rangoon in 1906. In the context of the partition the pattern of the land system in Bengal played a major role to influence the Muslim mind. The absentee Hindu zamindars made no attempt to improve the lot of the raiyats who were mostly Muslims. The agrarian disputes (between landlords and tenants) already in existence in the province also appeared to take a communal colour. It was alleged that the Hindu landlords had been attempting to enforce Swadeshi ideas on the tenants and induce them to join the anti-partition movement.

In 1906, the Muslims organised an Islamic conference at Keraniganj in Dhaka as a move to emphasise their separate identity as a community. The Swadeshi Movement with its Hindu religious flavour fomented aggressive reaction from the other community. A red pamphlet of a highly inflammatory nature was circulated among the Muslim masses of Eastern Bengal and Assam urging them completely to dissociate from the Hindus. It was published under the auspices of the Anjuman-I-Mufidul Islam under the editorship of a certain Ibrahim Khan. Moreover, such irritating moves as the adoption of the Bande Mataram as the song of inspiration or introduction of the cult of Shivaji as a national hero, and reports of communal violence alienated the Muslims. One inevitable result of such preaching was the riot that broke out at Comilla in March 1907, followed by similar riots in Jamalpur in April of that year. These communal disturbances became a familiar feature in Eastern Bengal and Assam and followed a pattern that was repeated elsewhere. The 1907 riots represent a watershed in the history of modern Bengal.

While Hindu-Muslims relations deteriorated, political changes of great magnitude were taking place in the Government of India's policies, and simultaneously in the relations of Bengali Muslim leaders with their non-Bengali counterparts. Both developments had major repercussions on communal relations in eastern Bengal. The decision to introduce constitutional reforms culminating in the morley-minto reforms of 1909 introducing separate representation for the Muslims marked a turning point in Hindu-Muslim relations.

The early administrators of the new province from the lieutenant governor down to the junior-most officials in general were enthusiastic in carrying out the development works. The anti-Partition movement leaders as being extremely partial to Muslims accused Bampfylde Fuller. He, because of a difference with the Government of India, resigned in August 1906. His resignation and its prompt acceptance were considered by the Muslims to be a solid political victory for the Hindus. The general Muslim feeling was that in yielding to the pressure of the anti-Partition agitators the government had revealed its weakness and had overlooked the loyal adherence of the Muslims to the government.

Consequently, the antagonism between the Hindus and Muslims became very acute in the new province. The Muslim leaders, now more conscious of their separate communal identity, directed their attention in uniting the different sections of their community to the creation of a counter movement against that of the Hindus. They keenly felt the need for unity and believed that the Hindu agitation against the Partition was in fact a communal movement and as such a threat to the Muslims as a separate community. They decided to faithfully follow the directions of leaders like Salimullah and Nawab Ali Chowdhury and formed organisations like the Mohammedan Provincial Union.

Though communalism had reached its peak in the new province by 1907, there is evidence of a sensible and sincere desire among some of the educated and upper class Muslims and Hindus to put an end to these religious antagonisms. A group of prominent members of both communities met the Viceroy Lord Minto on 15 March 1907 with suggestions to put an end to communal violence and promote religious harmony between the two communities.

The landlord-tenant relationship in the new province had deteriorated and took a communal turn. The Hindu landlords felt alarmed at the acts of terrorism committed by the anti-partition agitators. To prove their unswerving loyalty to the government and give evidence of their negative attitude towards the agitation, they offered their hands of friendship and cooperation to their Muslim counterparts to the effect that they would take a non-communal stand and work unitedly against the anti-government revolutionary movements.

In the meantime the All-India Muslim League had come into being at Dacca on 30 December 1906. Though several factors were responsible for the formation of such an organisation, the Partition of Bengal and the threat to it was, perhaps, the most important factor that hastened its birth. At its very first sitting at Dacca the Muslim League, in one of its resolutions, said: 'That this meeting in view of the clear interest of the Mohammedans of Eastern Bengal consider that Partition is sure to prove beneficial to the Muhammadan community which constitute the vast majority of the populations of the new province and that all such methods of agitation such as boycotting should be strongly condemned and discouraged'.

To assuage the resentment of the assertive Bengali Hindus, the British government decided to annul the Partition of Bengal. As regards the Muslims of Eastern Bengal the government stated that in the new province the Muslims were in an overwhelming majority in point of population, under the new arrangement also they would still be in a position of approximate numerical equality or possibly of small superiority over the Hindus. The interests of the Muslims would be safeguarded by special representation in the Legislative Councils and the local bodies.

Lord hardinge succeeded Minto and on 25 August 1911. In a secret despatch the government of India recommended certain changes in the administration of India. According to the suggestion of the Governor-General-in-Council, King George V at his Coronation Darbar in Delhi in December 1911 announced the revocation of the Partition of Bengal and of certain changes in the administration of India. Firstly, the Government of India should have its seat at Delhi instead of Calcutta. By shifting the capital to the site of past Muslim glory, the British hoped to placate Bengal's Muslim community now aggrieved at the loss of provincial power and privilege in eastern Bengal. Secondly, the five Bengali speaking Divisions viz The Presidency, Burdwan, Dacca, Rajshahi and Chittagong were to be united and formed into a Presidency to be administered by a Governor-in-Council. The area of this province would be approximately 70,000 sq. miles with a population of 42 million. Thirdly, a Lieutenant-Governor-in-Council with Legislative Council was to govern the province comprising of Bihar, Chhota Nagpur and Orissa. Fourthly, Assam was to revert back to the rule of a Chief Commissioner. The date chosen for the formal ending of the partition and reunification of Bengal was I April 1912.

Reunification of Bengal indeed served somewhat to soothe the feeling of the Bengali Hindus, but the down grading of Calcutta from imperial to mere provincial status was simultaneously a blow to 'Bhadralok' egos and to Calcutta real estate values. To deprive Calcutta of its prime position as the nerve centre of political activity necessarily weakened the influence of the Bengali Hindus. The government felt that the main advantage, which could be derived from the move, was that it would remove the seat of the government of India from the agitated atmosphere of Bengal.

Lord Carmichael, a man of liberal sympathies, was chosen as the first Governor of reunified Bengal. The Partition of Bengal and the agitation against it had far-reaching effects on Indian history and national life. The twin weapons of Swadeshi and Boycott adopted by the Bengalis became a creed with the Indian National Congress and were used more effectively in future conflicts. They formed the basis of Gandhi's Non-Cooperation, Satyagraha and Khadi movements. They also learned that organised political agitation and critical public opinion could force the government to accede to public demands.

The annulment of the partition as a result of the agitation against it had a negative effect on the Muslims. The majority of the Muslims did not like the Congress support to the anti-partition agitation. The politically conscious Muslims felt that the Congress had supported a Hindu agitation against the creation of a Muslim majority province. It reinforced their belief that their interests were not safe in the hands of the Congress. Thus they became more anxious to emphasise their separate communal identity and leaned towards the Muslim League to safeguard their interest against the dominance of the Hindu majority in undivided India. To placate Bengali Muslim feelings Lord Hardinge promised a new University at Dacca on 31 January 1912 to a Muslim deputation led by Salimullah.

The Partition of Bengal of 1905 left a profound impact on the political history of India. From a political angle the measure accentuated Hindu-Muslim differences in the region. One point of view is that by giving the Muslim's a separate territorial identity in 1905 and a communal electorate through the Morley-Minto Reforms of 1909 the British Government in a subtle manner tried to neutralise the possibility of major Muslim participation in the Indian National Congress.

The Partition of Bengal indeed marks a turning point in the history of nationalism in India. It may be said that it was out of the travails of Bengal that Indian nationalism was born. By the same token the agitation against the partition and the terrorism that it generated was one of the main factors, which gave birth to Muslim nationalism and encouraged them to engage in separatist politics. The birth of the Muslim League in 1906 at Dacca (Dhaka) bears testimony to this. The annulment of the partition sorely disappointed not only the Bengali Muslims but also the Muslims of the whole of India. They felt that loyalty did not pay but agitation does. Thereafter, the dejected Muslims gradually took an anti-British stance.

7

Garam Dal

Garam Dal, (literally translated as *Hot Faction*) was the extremist faction of Indian National Congress which was formed and led by Bal Gangadhar Tilak in the year 1907.

Tilak disagreed with the modernist views of mainstream Indian National Congress members, under the leadership of Gopal Krishna Gokhale, which was content with self governance instead of complete independence. On receiving support from same minded folks like Bipin Chandra Pal and Lala Lajpat Rai the Garam Dal was formed. It was the year of 1907, when Indian National Congress was effectively split even into two factons Garam Dal (*Extremists*) and Naram Dal (*Moderists*).

Bal Gangadhar Tilak

Bal Gangadhar Tilak 23 July 1856(1856-07-23)–1 August 1920 (aged 64), was an Indian nationalist, teacher, social reformer and independence fighter who was the first popular leader of the Indian Independence Movement. The British colonial authorities infamously and derogatorily called the great leader as "Father of the Indian unrest". He was also conferred upon the honorary title of Lokmanya, which literally means "Accepted by the people (as their leader)". Tilak was one of the first and strongest advocates of "Swaraj" (self-rule) in Indian consciousness. His famous quote, *"Swaraj is my birthright, and I shall have it !"* is well-remembered in India even today.

Early Life

Tilak was born in *Madhali Alee* (Middle Lane) in Ratnagiri, Maharashtra, into a middle class Chitpavan Brahmin family. His father was a famous schoolteacher and a scholar of Sanskrit. He died when Tilak was sixteen. His brilliance rubbed off on young Tilak, who graduated from Deccan College, Pune in 1877. Tilak was among one of the first generation of Indians to receive a college education.

Tilak was expected, as was the tradition then, to actively participate in public affairs. He believed that "Religion and practical life are not different. To take to Samnyasa (renunciation) is not to abandon life. The real spirit is to make the country your family instead of working only for your own. The step beyond is to serve humanity and the next step is to serve God." This dedication to humanity would be a fundamental element in the Indian Nationalist movement.

After graduating, Tilak began teaching mathematics in a private school in Pune. Later due to some philosophical differences with the colleagues in the New School, he decided to withdraw from that activity. In that time frame he became a journalist. He was a strong critic of the Western education system, feeling it demeaned the Indian students and disrespected India's heritage. He organized the Deccan Education Society with a few of his college friends, including Gopal Ganesh Agarkar, Mahadev Ballal Namjoshi and Vishnu Krishna Chiplunkar whose goal was to improve the quality of education for India's youth. The Deccan Education Society was set up to create a new system that taught young Indians nationalist ideas through an emphasis on Indian culture. Tilak began a mass movement towards independence that was camouflaged by an emphasis on a religious and cultural revival. He taught Mathematics at Fergusson College.

Political Career

Journalism: Tilak co-founded two newspapers with Gopal Ganesh Agarkar, Vishnushastri Chiplunakar and other colleagues: Kesari, which means "Lion" in Sanskrit and was a Marathi newspaper, and 'The Maratha', an English newspaper in 1881. In just two years 'Kesari' attracted more readers than any other language newspaper in India. The editorials were generally about the people's sufferings under the British. These newspapers called upon every Indian to fight for his or her rights. Tilak used to say to his colleagues: "You are not writing for the university students. Imagine you are talking to a villager. Be sure of your facts. Let your words be clear as daylight." Tilak strongly criticized the government for its brutality in suppressing free expression, especially in face of protests against the division of Bengal in 1905, and for denigrating India's culture, its people and heritage. He demanded that the British immediately give Indians the right to self-government.

Indian National Congress

Tilak joined the Indian National Congress in the 1890. He opposed its moderate attitude, especially towards the fight for self government.

In 1891 Tilak opposed the Age of Consent bill. The act raised the age at which a girl could get married from 10 to 12. The Congress and other liberals supported it, but Tilak was set against it, terming it an interference with Hinduism. However, he personally opposed child marriage, and his own daughters married at 16.

Plague epidemic spread from Mumbai to Pune in late 1896, and by January 1897, it reached epidemic proportions. In order to suppress the epidemic and prevent its spread, it was decided to take drastic action, accordingly a Special Plague Committee, with jurisdiction over Pune city, its suburbs and Pune cantonment was appointed under the Chairmanship of W. C. Rand, I. C. S, Assistant Collector of Pune by way of a government order dated 8 March 1897. On 12 March 1897, 893 officers and men both British and native, under command of a Major Paget of the Durham Light Infantry were placed on plague duty. By the end of May the epidemic had ebbed and the military action was gradually ended. In his report on the administration of the Pune plague, Rand wrote, "*It is a matter of great satisfaction to the members of the Plague Committee that no credible complaint that the modesty of a woman had been intentionally insulted was made either to themselves or to the officers under whom the troops worked*". He also writes that closest watch was kept on the troops employed on plague duty and utmost consideration was shown for the customs and traditions of the people. Indian sources however report that Rand used tyrannical methods and harassed the people.

An account based on local Indian sources writes that the appointment of military officers introduced an element of severity and coercion in the house searches, the high handedness of the government provoked the people of Pune and some soldiers were beaten in Re-establish locality. It quotes Kelkar on the conduct of British soldiers, "Either, through ignorance or impudence, they would mock, indulge in monkey tricks, talk foolishly, intimidate, touch innocent people, shove them, enter any place without justification, pocket valuable items, etc.."

Tilak took up the people's cause by publishing inflammatory articles in his paper *Kesari,* quoting the Hindu scripture, the Bhagavad Gita, to say that no blame could be attached to anyone who killed an oppressor without any thought of reward. Following this, on 22 June, Rand and another British officer Lt. Ayerst were shot and killed by the Chapekar brothers and their other associates. Tilak was charged with incitement to murder and sentenced to 18 months' imprisonment. When he emerged from prison, he was revered as a martyr and a national hero and adopted a new slogan, "Swaraj (Self-Rule) is my birth right and I will have it."

Following the partition of Bengal in 1905, which was a strategy set out by Lord Curzon to weaken the nationalist movement, Tilak encouraged a boycott, regarded as the Swadeshi movement.

Tilak opposed the moderate views of Gopal Krishna Gokhale, and was supported by fellow Indian nationalists Bipin Chandra Pal in Bengal and Lala Lajpat Rai in Punjab. They were referred to as the Lal-Bal-Pal triumvirate. In 1907, the annual session of the Congress Party was held at Surat (Gujarat). Trouble broke out between the moderate and the extremist factions of the party over the selection of the new president of the Congress. The party split into the "Jahal matavadi" ("Hot Faction," or extremists), led by Tilak, Pal and Lajpat Rai, and the "Maval matavadi" ("Soft Faction," or moderates).

Arrest

On 30 April 1908 two Bengali youths, Prafulla Chaki and Kudiram Bose, threw a bomb on a carriage at Muzzafurpur in order to kill a District Judge Douglass Kenford but erroneously killed some women travelling in it. While Chaki committed suicide when caught, Bose was tried and hanged. Tilak in his paper Kesari defended the revolutionaries and called for immediate Swaraj or Self-rule. The Government swiftly arrested him for sedition. He asked a young Muhammad Ali Jinnah to represent him. But the British judge convicted him and he was imprisoned from 1908 to

1914 in the Mandalay Prison, Burma. While imprisoned, he continued to read and write, further developing his ideas on the Indian Nationalist movement.

Much has been said of his trial of 1908, it being the most historic trial. His last words on the verdict of the Jury were such: *"In spite of the verdict of the Jury, I maintain that I am innocent. There are higher powers that rule the destiny of men and nations and it may be the will of providence that the cause which I represent may prosper more by my suffering than my remaining free"*. These words now can be seen imprinted on the wall of Room. No. 46 at Bombay High Court.

Life After Prison

Tilak had mellowed after his release in June 1914. When World war I started in August, Tilak, cabled the King-Emperor in Britain of his support and turned his oratory to find new recruits for war efforts. He welcomed The Indian Councils Act, popularly known as Minto-Morley Reforms which had been passed by British parliament in May 1909 terming it as 'a marked increase of confidence between the Rulers and the Ruled'. Acts of violence actually retarded than hastened the pace of political reforms, he felt. He was eager for reconciliation with Congress and had abandoned his demand for direct action and settled for agitations 'strictly by constitutional means'-a line advocated his rival Gopal Krishna Gokhale since beginning

All India Home Rule League

Later, Tilak re-united with his fellow nationalists and re-joined the Indian National Congress in 1916. He also helped found the All India Home Rule League in 1916-18 with Joseph Baptista, Annie Besant, G. S. Khaparde and Muhammad Ali Jinnah. After years of trying to reunite the moderate and radical factions, he gave up and focused on the Home Rule League, which sought self-rule. Tilak travelled from village to village trying to conjure up support from farmers and locals to join the movement towards self-rule. Tilak was impressed by the Russian Revolution, and expressed his admiration for Lenin.

Tilak, who started his political life as a Maratha protagonist, during his later part of life progressed into a prominent nationalist after his close association with Indian nationalists following the partition of Bengal. When asked in Calcutta whether he envisioned a Maratha type of government for Free India, Tilak replied that the Maratha dominated Governments of 17th and 18th centuries were outmoded in 20th century and he wanted a genuine federal system for Free India where every religion and race were equal partners. He added that only such a form of Government would be able to safeguard India's freedom. He was the first Congress leader to suggest that Hindi written in the Devanagari script, should be accepted as the sole national language of India.

Social Contribution

In 1894, Tilak transformed household worshipping of Ganesha into Sarvajanik Ganeshotsav and he also made Shiva jayanthi as a social festival. It is touted to be an effective demonstration of festival procession. Gopal Ganesh Agarkar was the first editor of Kesari, a prominent Marathi weekly in his days which was started by Lokmanya Tilak in 1880-81. Gopal Ganesh Agarkar subsequently left Kesari out of ideological differences with Bal Gangadhar Tilak concerning the primacy of political reforms versus social reforms, and Gopal Ganesh Agarkar started his own periodical Sudharak.

Later Years and Legacy

After Tilak's death on August 1, 1920, on the first day of Gandhi's first non-cooperation campaign, Gandhi paid his respects at his cremation in Mumbai, along with 20,000,000 people. Gandhi called Tilak "The Maker of Modern India". The court which convicted Tilak bears a plaque that says, "The actions of Tilak has been justified as the right of every individual to fight for his country. Those two convictions have gone into oblivion — oblivion reserved by history for all unworthy deeds".

Books

In 1903, he wrote the book The Arctic Home in the Vedas. In it he argued that the Vedas could only have been composed in the Arctics, and the Aryan bards brought them south after the onset of the last Ice age. He proposed the radically new way to determine the exact time of Vedas. Up to that time, antiquity of Vedas was mostly decided by the form of the language used in it. He tried to calculate the time of Vedas by using the position of different Nakshatras. Positions of Nakshtras were described in different Vedas. Knowing the motion of Nakshtras and there positions (at the time of Vedas and current) we can calculate the time of Vedas. Sri Tilak found that the vedas were written around 4500 B.C., when the Vernal equinox was in the constellation of M[iga or Orion during the period of the Vedic hymns, and that it had receded to the constellation of the Kittikas, or the Pleiades (about 2500 B.C.) in the days of the Brahmanas. This was his basic idea. This idea was criticized by some scholars, praised by some others. But originality and charm of this new way of looking towards this problem was largely accepted. Tilak also authored 'Shrimadbhagwadgeetarahasya'- the analysis of 'Karmayoga' in the Bhagavadgita, which is known to be gist of the Vedas and the Upanishads.

Satish Chandra Mukherjee

Satish Chandra Mukherjee (June 5, 1865-April 18, 1948) was a pioneer in establishing a system of national education in India, along with Sri Aurobindo.

The Positivist Background

Satish Chandra was born at Banipur in the Hooghly district, near Kolkata (Calcutta). His father, Krishnanath Mukherjee, had been a childhood friend and classmate of Justice Dvarkanath Mitra, who appointed him as a translator of official documents in the Calcutta High Court. Mitra was a leading believer in the Religion of Humanity as founded by the Positivist Auguste Comte. Adept of this faith, an atheist servant of Man and of society, Krishnanath impressed this ideology on his sons, Tinkori and Satish. Bankim Chandra Chattopadhay himself was not only one of the first in India to write on Comte and his philosophy but, also, he had zealous Positivist friends like Yogendrachandra Ghose and Rajkrishna Mukherjee; in 1874, Bankim published the latter's article on Positivism in his *Bangadarshan*, which began with the sentence, "Among the successfully educated classes of our country, there is a great deal of animation concerning the philosophy of Comte." While writing on psychological purification, Bankim wrote: "He who has been psychologically purified is the best Hindu, the best Christian, the best Buddhist, the best Muslim, the best Positivist."

In 1884, in the preface of his novel *Devi Chaudhurani*, Bankim quoted from the *Catechism of Positive Religion*: "The general law of Man's progress (...) consists in this that Man becomes more and more religious."

Early Life

As a student of the South Suburban School in Bhowanipore in Kolkata, Satish Chandra received inspiration from Ishwar Chandra Vidyasagar and would have a wide range of acquaintances like Ashvinikumar Datta, Sivanath Shastri, Bipin Chandra Pal, Brojendranath Seal, Ashutosh Mukherjee (his class-friend), Rabindranath Tagore, Sri Aurobindo, Raja Subodh Mullick. With his classmate Narendra Datta (Swami Vivekananda) and his friend Kaliprasad Chandra (Swami Abhedananda), he attended the lectures by Pandit Sashadhar Tarka Chudamani on the *shad-darshana* ("six schools of Hindu philosophy") at the Albert Hall, presided over by Bankim Chandra Chattopadhay.

"Alive to the necessity and the usefulness of all other systems, secular or religious, Eastern or Western," Satish Chandra's intense religious temperament laid emphasis on the study of Hindu life, thought and faith. He joined the Presidency College to obtained his M.A. in 1886 and B.L. in 1890, and enrolled himself as a pleader of the Calcutta High Court. In 1887, he was appointed a Lecturer in history and economics in the Berhampore College. In 1895 he founded the Bhagavat Chatuspathi, a first attempt to an alternate system of higher studies.

The Dawn Society

Founder-editor of the *Dawn* magazine (1897-1913), an organ of Indian Nationalism, in 1902 he organised the "Dawn Society" of culture, to protest against the Report of the Indian Universities Commission, representing the inadequate university education imposed by the Government to fabricate clerks for the merchant offices. "The cry for thorough overhauling of the whole system of University education was in the air."

Dawn occupied an apartment on the first floor of the present Vidyasagar College (formerly known as the Metropolitan Institution: its Principal, Nagendranath Ghosh was the President, and Satish its General Secretary). The Dawn Society was "functioning (...) as a training ground of youths and a nursery of patriotism, became in 1905 one of the most active centres for the propagation of Boycott-Swadeshi ideologies..."

In tune with the programme of a new pedagogy introduced by Sri Aurobindo, the Society's object was to draw the attention of the students to the needs of the country, to love Mother India, to cultivate their moral character, to inspire original thinking. It had a weekly session for a "general training course". One of the members, Benoy Kumar Sarkar, considering having lived significantly thanks to Satish Chandra's influence, would remember his ardent message of patriotism and philanthropy rousing the youth to dedicated service; he would also write about the method of Pandit Nilakantha Goswami's explaining the *Bhagavad Gita*, impressing on the listeners' mind the futility of life and death, the insignificance of the body: the sole thing that counts is Duty, the right Action.

Among active members of the "Dawn" were Sister Nivedita, Bagha Jatin (Jatin Mukherjee), Rajendra Prasad (first President of India), Haran Chakladar, Radhakumud Mukherjee, Kishorimohan Gupta (principal, Daulatpur College), Atulya Chatterjee, Rabindra Narayan Ghosh, Benoykumar Sarkar, all future celebrities. One day, Satish Chandra heard an inner voice uttering firmly: "God exists."

The National College

The Positivist awaited further light from within. In September, a friend of his, follower of the saint Bejoykrishna Goswami, told him that the Master wanted him to come. After receiving initiation in September 1893, he learnt from the saint that on completing his present activities, Satish was to leave for Varanasi (Benares) for his spiritual pursuit.

By the side of Subodh Chandra Mullick, in 1906, Satish took a leading part in forming the Council of National Education and became a lecturer in the Bengal National College. In 1907, after Sri Aurobindo's resignation on 2 August 1907 (fearing "that he might be spirited away to prison at any moment, and his association with the National College might cause great damage to the institution"), Satish Chandra succeeded him as principal, and a contributor to the daily *Bande Mataram*. Four years after Sri Aurobindo's retiring to Pondicherry, Satish left for Varanasi in 1914, settled there till his death. Prominent among the regular visitors who consulted him for guidance, there was Malani, Professor of English at the Hindu University, who took profuse notes while listening to Satish Chandra. There were also Madan Mohan Malaviya, Narendra Deva, Jadunath Sarkar.

Satish Chandra and Gandhi

Another professor of the same university, Jivatram Kripalani, introduced him to Mohandas Karamchand Gandhi, who held Satish Chandra so high that whenever Gandhi went to Varanasi, he spent some time with Satish Chandra.

At a juncture, it seems Gandhi even approached him for receiving initiation; but Satish Chandra did not feel that Gandhi needed it. Both of them were seekers of God. Gandhi strove to solve the problem of suffering in man's daily life and look for the Truth; Satish Chandra sought after spiritual deliverance.

Following Gandhi's arrest in 1922, he spent two months at the Sabarmati Ashram helping in the management and publication of *Young India.* Those were years when Gandhi had been moving all over India, without caring for his failing health.

One day Satish Chandra was asked by his Guru Bejoykrishna to send Gandhi one hundred rupees every month for his personal use. Gratefully Gandhi accepted this gift. In 1924, hospitalized for appendicitis, whereas Gandhi was flooded with messages of solicitude, he wondered about Satish Chandra's silence and wanted his son Devdas to enquire. The only reply that came was that Satish Chandra knew that Gandhi was going to recover soon.

The Concluding Message

In the habit of exchanging letters regularly, the last time Satish Chandra wrote to Gandhi was on 24 January 1947, explaining how to repeat the name of Rama with a breath control; happy with that instruction, on 1 February, Gandhi thanked Satish Chandra for "Your lovely letter" : on 30 January 1948, Gandhi breathed his last by repeating *He Rama.*

Ashutosh Mukherjee

Sir Ashutosh Mookerjee, CIE 1864-1924 was an Indian educator and Vice Chancellor of the University of Calcutta from 1906 to 1924.

He was responsible for the foundation of the Bengal Technical Institute in 1906 and the Calcutta University College of Science in 1914. The Calcutta Mathematical Society was also founded by Sir Ashutosh Mookerjee in 1908 and he served as the founder president of the Society during 1908 to 1923.

Early Life

Asutosh Mukherjee's father was the well known doctor Ganga Prasad Mookerjee, who was also the founder of South Suburban School in Calcutta. He was born in the Bowbazar area of Calcutta and showed an early aptitude for mathematics. In 1883 he came first in the BA examination at Calcutta University and was awarded the Premchand-Roychand scholarship to complete a postgraduate degree in mathematics. Two years later he also acquired an MA in physics, making him the first student to be awarded a dual degree from Calcutta University. However, he turned down an offer of a job in the Department of Public Instruction in favour of completing his Bachelor of Law degree. Nevertheless, he continued to publish scholarly papers on issues in mathematics and physics, and was elected to the Senate of Calcutta University in 1889.

Career in Law

Mookerjee dabbled in politics while practicing law, but gave it up when he was appointed as a judge of the Bengal High Court in 1904. He approached different people to raise funds for the establishment of the Calcutta University College of Science, which became the foremost institute of scientific education and research in the country. In 1906 he was appointed Vice Chancellor of Calcutta University

Contribution to Education

Ashutosh Mookerjee had a vision of the kind of education he wanted young people to have, and he had the acumen and courage to extract it from his colonial masters. He set up several new academic graduate programmes: comparative literature, anthropology, applied psychology, industrial chemistry, ancient Indian history and culture and Islamic culture. He also made arrangements for postgraduate teaching and research in Bengali, Hindi, and Sanskrit. The diverse range of subjects offered by Calcutta University is largely a result of his labour. Scholars from all over India, irrespective of race, caste, and gender, came to study and teach there. He even persuaded European scholars to teach at his university. He was one of the first persons to recognize the worth of Srinivasa Ramanujan.

Lord Curzon's education mission in 1902 identified the universities, and Calcutta University especially, as centres of sedition where young people formed networks of resistance to colonial domination. The cause of this was thought to be the unwise granting of autonomy to these universities in the nineteenth century. Thus in the period 1905 to 1935 the colonial administration tried to reinstate government control of education. In 1923, when Lord Lytton tried to impose conditions on his reappointment as Vice Chancellor, Mookerji indignantly refused the post. For his intransigence and academic integrity he was known as the *Tiger of Bengal.*

Other Positions Held

Mookerji was a member of the 1917-1919 Sadler Commission, presided over by Michael Ernest Sadler, which inquired into the state of Indian education. He was three times president of the Asiatic Society, and in 1910 of the Imperial (now National) Library Council. He donated his entire personal collection of 80,000 books to the Library and it is arranged in a separate section. He was the president of the inaugural session of the Indian Science Congress in 1914. He was learned in Pali, French and Russian, and was awarded the titles of Saraswati and Shastravachaspati by the pandits of Bengal for his service to Indian education. Mookerjee was knighted in 1911.

The epitaph beneath his marble bust at the Ashutosh Museum of Arts at the University of Calcutta reads:

"His noblest achievement, surest of them all/ "A place for his mother tongue — in stepmother's hall".

Rabindranath Tagore

Rabindranath Tagore (7 May 1861 – 7 August 1941), sobriquet Gurudev, was a Bengali polymath. As a poet, novelist, musician, and playwright, he reshaped Bengali literature and music in the late 19th and early 20th centuries. As author of *Gitanjali* and its "profoundly sensitive, fresh and beautiful verse", being the first non-European to win the 1913 Nobel Prize in Literature, Tagore was perhaps the most important literary figure of Bengali literature and a mesmerising representative of the Indian culture whose influence and popularity internationally perhaps could only be compared to that of Gandhi whom Tagore named 'Mahatma' out of his deep admiration for him. A Pirali Brahmin from Calcutta, Tagore wrote poems at age eight. At age sixteen, he published his first substantial poetry under the pseudonym *Bhanushingho* ("Sun Lion") and wrote his first short stories and dramas in 1877. Tagore denounced the British Raj and supported independence. His efforts endure in his vast canon and in the institution he founded, Visva-Bharati University.

Tagore modernised Bengali art by spurning rigid classical forms. His novels, stories, songs, dance-dramas, and essays spoke to political and personal topics. *Gitanjali* (*Song Offerings*), *Gora* (*Fair-Faced*), and *Ghare-Baire* (*The Home and the World*) are his best-known works, and his verse, short stories, and novels were acclaimed for their lyricism, colloquialism, naturalism, and contemplation. Tagore was perhaps the only litterateur who penned anthems of two countries: Bangladesh and India: *Amar Shonar Bangla* and *Jana Gana Mana.*

Early Life (1861–1901)

The youngest of thirteen surviving children, Tagore was born in the Jorasanko mansion in Kolkata of parents Debendranath Tagore (1817–1905) and Sarada Devi (1830–1875). Tagore family patriarchs were the Brahmo founding fathers of the Adi Dharm faith. He was largely raised by servants, as his mother had died in his early childhood; his father travelled extensively. Tagore largely declined classroom schooling, preferring to roam the mansion or nearby idylls: Bolpur, Panihati, and others. Upon his *upanayan* initiation at age eleven, Tagore left Kolkata on 14 February 1873 to tour India with his father for several months. They visited his father's Santiniketan estate and stopped in Amritsar before reaching the Himalayan hill station of Dalhousie. There, young "Rabi" read biographies and was home-educated in history, astronomy, modern science, and Sanskrit, and examined the poetry of Klidsa. He set major works in 1877, one a long poem of the Maithili style pioneered by Vidyapati. Published pseudonymously, experts accepted them as the lost works of Bhanusimha, a newly discovered 17th-century Vaisnava poet. He wrote "Bhikharini" (1877; "The Beggar Woman"—the Bengali language's first short story) and *Sandhya Sangit* (1882)—including the famous poem "Nirjharer Swàpnabhanga" ("The Rousing of the Waterfall").

A prospective barrister, Tagore enrolled at a public school in Brighton, East Sussex, England in 1878. He read law at University College London, but left school to explore Shakespeare and more:

Religio Medici, Coriolanus, and *Antony and Cleopatra;* he returned degreeless to Bengal in 1880. On 9 December 1883 he married Mrinalini Devi (born Bhabatarini, 1873–1900); they had five children, two of whom died before reaching adulthood. In 1890, Tagore began managing his family's vast estates in Shilaidaha, a region now in Bangladesh; he was joined by his wife and children in 1898. In 1890, Tagore released his *Manast* poems, among his best-known work. As "Zamindar Babu", Tagore crisscrossed the holdings while living out of the family's luxurious barge, the *Padma,* to collect (mostly token) rents and bless villagers, who held feasts in his honour. These years—1891–1895: Tagore's *Sadhana* period, after one of Tagore's magazines—were his most fecund. During this period, more than half the stories of the three-volume and eighty-four-story *Galpaguchchha* were written. With irony and gravity, they depicted a wide range of Bengali lifestyles, particularly village life.

Santiniketan (1901–1932)

In 1901, Tagore left Shilaidaha and moved to Santiniketan to found an *ashram* which grew to include a marble-floored prayer hall ("The *Mandir*"), an experimental school, groves of trees, gardens, and a library. There, Tagore's wife and two of his children died. His father died on 19 January 1905, and he received monthly payments as part of his inheritance.

He received additional income from the Maharaja of Tripura, sales of his family's jewellery, his seaside bungalow in Puri, and mediocre royalties (Rs. 2,000) from his works. By now, his work was gaining him a large following among Bengali and foreign readers alike, and he published such works as *Naivedya* (1901) and *Kheya* (1906) while translating his poems into free verse. On 14 November 1913, Tagore learned that he had won the 1913 Nobel Prize in Literature, becoming the first Asian Nobel laureate. The Swedish Academy appreciated the idealistic and—for Western readers—accessible nature of a small body of his translated material, including the 1912 *Gitanjali: Song Offerings.* In 1915, Tagore was knighted by the British Crown.

In 1921, Tagore and agricultural economist Leonard Elmhirst set up the Institute for Rural Reconstruction, later renamed Shriniketan—"Abode of Peace"—in Surul, a village near the ashram at Santiniketan. Through it, Tagore bypassed Gandhi's symbolic

Swaraj protests, which he despised. He sought aid from donors, officials, and scholars worldwide to "free village[s] from the shackles of helplessness and ignorance" by "vitalis[ing] knowledge". In the early 1930s, he targeted India's "abnormal caste consciousness" and untouchability. Lecturing against these, he penned untouchable heroes for his poems and dramas and campaigned—successfully—to open Guruvayoor Temple to Dalits.

Twilight Years (1932–1941)

To the end, Tagore scrutinized orthodoxy. He upbraided Gandhi for declaring that a massive 15 January 1934 earthquake in Bihar—leaving thousands dead—was divine retribution brought on by the oppression of Dalits. He mourned the endemic poverty of Calcutta and the accelerating socioeconomic decline of Bengal, which he detailed in an unrhymed hundred-line poem whose technique of searing double-vision would foreshadow Satyajit Ray's film *Apur Sansar*.

Fifteen new volumes of Tagore writings appeared, among them the prose-poems works *Punashcha* (1932), *Shes Saptak* (1935), and *Patraput* (1936). Experimentation continued: he developed prose-songs and dance-dramas, including *Chitrangada* (1914), *Shyama* (1939), and *Chandalika* (1938), and wrote the novels *Dui Bon* (1933), *Malancha* (1934), and *Char Adhyay* (1934). Tagore took an interest in science in his last years, writing *Visva-Parichay* (a collection of essays) in 1937. His exploration of biology, physics, and astronomy impacted his poetry, which often contained extensive naturalism that underscored his respect for scientific laws. He also wove the process of science, including narratives of scientists, into many stories contained in such volumes as *Se* (1937), *Tin Sangi* (1940), and *Galpasalpa* (1941).

Tagore's last four years were marked by chronic pain and two long periods of illness. These began when Tagore lost consciousness in late 1937; he remained comatose and near death for an extended period. This was followed three years later in late 1940 by a similar spell, from which he never recovered. The poetry Tagore wrote in these years is among his finest, and is distinctive for its preoccupation with death. After extended suffering, Tagore died on 7 August 1941 (22 Shravan 1348) in an upstairs room of the Jorasanko mansion in which he was raised; his death anniversary is mourned across the Bengali-speaking world.

Travels

Between 1878 and 1932, Tagore visited more than thirty countries on five continents; many of these trips were crucial in familiarising non-Indian audiences to his works and spreading his political ideas. In 1912, he took a sheaf of his translated works to England, where they impressed missionary and Gandhi protege Charles F. Andrews, Anglo-Irish poet William Butler Yeats, Ezra Pound, Robert Bridges, Ernest Rhys, Thomas Sturge Moore, and others. Indeed, Yeats wrote the preface to the English translation of Gitanjali, while Andrews joined Tagore at Santiniketan. On 10 November 1912, Tagore began touring the United States and the United Kingdom, staying in Butterton, Staffordshire with Andrews' clergymen friends. From 3 May 1916 until April 1917, Tagore went on lecturing circuits in Japan and the United States and denounced nationalism. His essay "Nationalism in India" was scorned and praised, this latter by pacifists, including Romain Rolland.

Shortly after returning to India, the 63-year-old Tagore accepted the Peruvian government's invitation to visit. He then travelled to Mexico. Each government pledged US$100,000 to the school at Shantiniketan (Visva-Bharati) in commemoration of his visits. A week after his 6 November 1924 arrival in Buenos Aires, Argentina, an ill Tagore moved into the Villa Miralrio at the behest of Victoria Ocampo. He left for India in January 1925. On 30 May 1926, Tagore reached Naples, Italy; he met Benito Mussolini in Rome the next day. A warm rapport ended when Tagore criticised Mussolini on 20 July 1926.

On 14 July 1927, Tagore and two companions began a four-month tour of Southeast Asia, visiting Bali, Java, Kuala Lumpur, Malacca, Penang, Siam, and Singapore. Tagore's travelogues from the tour were collected into the work "Jatri". In early 1930 he left Bengal for a nearly year-long tour of Europe and the United States. Once he returned to the UK, while his paintings were being exhibited in Paris and London, he stayed at a Friends settlement in Birmingham. There he wrote his Oxford Hibbert Lectures and spoke at London's annual Quaker gathering. There (addressing relations between the British and Indians, a topic he would grapple with over the next two years), Tagore spoke of a "dark chasm of aloofness". He visited Aga Khan III, stayed at Dartington Hall, and toured Denmark, Switzerland, and Germany from June to mid-September 1930, then the Soviet Union. Lastly, in April 1932,

Tagore—who was acquainted with the legends and works of the Persian mystic Hafez—was hosted by Reza Shah Pahlavi of Iran. Such extensive travels allowed Tagore to interact with many notable contemporaries, including Henri Bergson, Albert Einstein, Robert Frost, Thomas Mann, George Bernard Shaw, H.G. Wells and Romain Rolland. Tagore's last travels abroad, including visits to Persia and Iraq (in 1932) and Ceylon in 1933, only sharpened his opinions regarding human divisions and nationalism.

Works

Tagore's Bengali-language initials are worked into this "Ra-Tha" wooden seal, which bears close stylistic similarity to designs used in traditional Haida carvings. Tagore often embellished his manuscripts with such art.

Though known mostly for his poetry, Tagore also wrote novels, essays, short stories, travelogues, dramas, and thousands of songs. Of Tagore's prose, his short stories are perhaps most highly regarded; indeed, he is credited with originating the Bengali-language version of the genre. His works are frequently noted for their rhythmic, optimistic, and lyrical nature. Such stories mostly borrow from deceptively simple subject matter: common people.

Novels and Non-fiction

Tagore wrote eight novels and four novellas, among them *Chaturanga, Shesher Kobita, Char Odhay,* and *Noukadubi. Ghare Baire* (*The Home and the World*)—through the lens of the idealistic *zamindar* protagonist Nikhil—excoriates rising Indian nationalism, terrorism, and religious zeal in the *Swadeshi* movement; a frank expression of Tagore's conflicted sentiments, it emerged out of a 1914 bout of depression. The novel ends in Hindu-Muslim violence and Nikhil's (likely mortal) wounding. *Gora* raises controversial questions regarding the Indian identity. As with *Ghore Baire,* matters of self-identity (*jati*), personal freedom, and religion are developed in the context of a family story and love triangle.

In *Jogajog* (*Relationships*), the heroine Kumudini—bound by the ideals of *Shiva-Sati,* exemplified by Dakshayani—is torn between her pity for the sinking fortunes of her progressive and compassionate elder brother and his foil: her exploitative, rakish, and patriarchical husband. In it, Tagore demonstrates his feminist leanings, using *pathos* to depict the plight and ultimate demise of

Bengali women trapped by pregnancy, duty, and family honour; simultaneously, he treats the decline of Bengal's landed oligarchy.

Others were uplifting: *Shesher Kobita* (translated twice as *Last Poem* and *Farewell Song*) is his most lyrical novel, with poems and rhythmic passages written by the main character, a poet. It also contains elements of satire and postmodernism; stock characters gleefully attack the reputation of an old, outmoded, oppressively renowned poet who, incidentally, goes by the name of Rabindranath Tagore. Though his novels remain among the least-appreciated of his works, they have been given renewed attention via film adaptations by Satyajit Ray and others: *Chokher Bali* and *Ghare Baire* are exemplary. Their soundtracks often feature *rabindrasangit*. Tagore wrote many non-fiction books, writing on topics ranging from Indian history to linguistics. Aside from autobiographical works, his travelogues, essays, and lectures were compiled into several volumes, including *Europe Jatrir Patro* (*Letters from Europe*) and *Manusher Dhormo* (*The Religion of Man*).

Music and Art

Tagore composed roughly 2,230 songs and was a prolific painter. His songs comprise *rabindrasangit*, an integral part of Bengali culture. Tagore's music is inseparable from his literature, most of which—poems or parts of novels, stories, or plays alike—became lyrics for his songs. Influenced by the *thumri* style of Hindustani music, they ran the entire gamut of human emotion, ranging from his early dirge-like Brahmo devotional hymns to quasi-erotic compositions. They emulated the tonal colour of classical *ragas* to varying extents. Though at times his songs mimicked a given raga's melody and rhythm faithfully, he also blended elements of different ragas to create innovative works.

For Bengalis, their appeal, stemming from the combination of emotive strength and beauty described as surpassing even Tagore's poetry, was such that the *Modern Review* observed that "[t]here is in Bengal no cultured home where Rabindranath's songs are not sung or at least attempted to be sung... Even illiterate villagers sing his songs". Arthur Strangways of *The Observer* introduced non-Bengalis to *rabindrasangeet* in *The Music of Hindostan,* calling it a "vehicle of a personality... [that] go behind this or that system of music to that beauty of sound which all systems put out their hands to seize." Among them are Bangladesh's national anthem

Amar Shonar Bangla and India's national anthem *Jana Gana Mana,* making Tagore unique in having scored two national anthems. He influenced the styles of such musicians as *sitar* maestro Vilayat Khan, and the *sarodiyas* Buddhadev Dasgupta and Amjad Ali Khan.

At age sixty, Tagore took up drawing and painting; successful exhibitions of his many works—which made a debut appearance in Paris upon encouragement by artists he met in the south of France —were held throughout Europe. Tagore—who likely exhibited protanopia ("colour blindness"), or partial lack of (red-green, in Tagore's case) colour discernment—painted in a style characterised by peculiarities in aesthetics and colouring schemes. Tagore emulated numerous styles, including craftwork from northern New Ireland, Haida carvings from the west coast of Canada (British Columbia), and woodcuts by Max Pechstein. Tagore also had an artist's eye for his own handwriting, embellishing the scribbles, cross-outs, and word layouts in his manuscripts with simple artistic leitmotifs, including simple rhythmic designs.

Theatre

At age sixteen, Tagore led his brother Jyotirindranath's adaptation of Moliere's *Le Bourgeois Gentilhomme.* At age twenty, he wrote his first drama-opera—*Valmiki Pratibha* (*The Genius of Valmiki*)—which describes how the bandit Valmiki reforms his ethos, is blessed by Saraswati, and composes the *Ramayana.* Through it, Tagore vigorously explores a wide range of dramatic styles and emotions, including usage of revamped *kirtans* and adaptation of traditional English and Irish folk melodies as drinking songs. Another notable play, *Dak Ghar* (*The Post Office*), describes how a child—striving to escape his stuffy confines—ultimately "fall[s] asleep" (which suggests his physical death). A story with worldwide appeal (it received rave reviews in Europe), *Dak Ghar* dealt with death as, in Tagore's words, "spiritual freedom" from "the world of hoarded wealth and certified creeds". During World War II, Polish doctor and educator Janusz Korczak selected "The Post Office" as the play the orphans in his care in the Warsaw Ghetto would perform. This occurred on 18 July 1942, less than three weeks before they were to be deported to the Treblinka extermination camp. According to his main English-language biographer, Betty Jean Lifton, in her book *The King of Children,* Dr. Korszak thought a great deal about whether one should be able to determine when and how to die. He may have been trying to find a way for the children in his orphanage to accept death.

His other works—emphasizing fusion of lyrical flow and emotional rhythm tightly focused on a core idea—were unlike previous Bengali dramas. His works sought to articulate, in Tagore's words, "the play of feeling and not of action". In 1890 he wrote *Visarjan* (*Sacrifice*), regarded as his finest drama. The Bengali-language originals included intricate subplots and extended monologues. Later, his dramas probed more philosophical and allegorical themes; these included *Dak Ghar*. Another is Tagore's *Chandalika* (*Untouchable Girl*), which was modelled on an ancient Buddhist legend describing how Ananda—the Gautama Buddha's disciple—asks water of an *Adivasi* ("untouchable") girl. Lastly, among his most famous dramas is *Raktakaravi* (*Red Oleanders*), which tells of a kleptocratic king who enriches himself by forcing his subjects to mine. The heroine, Nandini, eventually rallies the common people to destroy these symbols of subjugation. Tagore's other plays include *Chitrangada, Raja,* and *Mayar Khela*. Dance dramas based on Tagore's plays are commonly referred to as *rabindra nritya natyas*.

Stories

The "Sadhana" period, 1891–1895, was among Tagore's most fecund, yielding more than half the stories contained in the three-volume *Galpaguchchha*, itself a group of eighty-four stories. They reflect upon Tagore's surroundings, on modern and fashionable ideas, and on mind puzzles. Tagore associated his earliest stories, such as those of the "*Sadhana*" period, with an exuberance of vitality and spontaneity; these traits were cultivated by zamindar Tagore's life in villages such as Patisar, Shajadpur, and Shilaida. Seeing the common and the poor, he examined their lives with a depth and feeling singular in Indian literature up to that point.

In "The Fruitseller from Kabul", Tagore speaks in first person as a town-dweller and novelist who chances upon the Afghani seller. He channels the longing of those trapped in mundane, hardscrabble Indian urban life, giving play to dreams of a different existence in the distant and wild mountains: "There were autumn mornings, the time of year when kings of old went forth to conquest; and I, never stirring from my little corner in Calcutta, would let my mind wander over the whole world. At the very name of another country, my heart would go out to it... I would fall to weaving a network of dreams: the mountains, the glens, the forest.... ". Many of the other *Galpaguchchha* stories were written in Tagore's *Sabuj Patra* period (1914–1917; also named for one of Tagore's magazines).

Tagore's *Golpoguchchho* (*Bunch of Stories*) remains among Bengali literature's most popular fictional works, providing subject matter for many successful films and theatrical plays. Satyajit Ray's film *Charulata* was based upon Tagore's controversial novella, *Nastanirh* (*The Broken Nest*). In *Atithi* (also made into a film), the young Brahmin boy Tarapada shares a boat ride with a village *zamindar*. The boy reveals that he has run away from home, only to wander around ever since. Taking pity, the zamindar adopts him and ultimately arranges his marriage to the *zamindar's* own daughter. However, the night before the wedding, Tarapada runs off—again. *Strir Patra* (*The Letter from the Wife*) is among Bengali literature's earliest depictions of the bold emancipation of women. The heroine Mrinal, the wife of a typical patriarchical Bengali middle class man, writes a letter while she is travelling (which constitutes the whole story). It details the pettiness of her life and struggles; she finally declares that she will not return to her husband's home with the statement *Amio bachbo. Ei bachlum*: "And I shall live. Here, I live".

Haimanti assails Hindu marriage and the dismal lifelessness of married Bengali women, hypocrisies plaguing the Indian middle classes, and how Haimanti, a sensitive young woman, must—due to her sensitiveness and free spirit—sacrifice her life. In the last passage, Tagore directly attacks the Hindu custom of glorifying Sita's attempted self-immolation as a means of appeasing her husband Rama's doubts. *Musalmani Didi* examines Hindu-Muslim tensions and, in many ways, embodies the essence of Tagore's humanism. *Darpaharan* exhibits Tagore's self-consciousness, describing a fey young man harbouring literary ambitions. Though he loves his wife, he wishes to stifle her own literary career, deeming it unfeminine. Tagore himself, in his youth, seems to have harboured similar ideas about women. *Darpaharan* depicts the final humbling of the man as he acknowledges his wife's talents. As do many other Tagore stories, *Jibito o Mrito* equips Bengalis with a ubiquitous epigram: *Kadombini moriya proman korilo she more nai*—"Kadombini died, thereby proving that she hadn't".

Poetry

Tagore's poetry—which varied in style from classical formalism to the comic, visionary, and ecstatic—proceeds from a lineage established by 15th-and 16th-century Vaishnava poets. Tagore was awed by the mysticism of the *rishi*-authors who—including Vyasa—wrote the Upanishads, the Bhakti-Sufi mystic Kabir, and Ramprasad Sen. Yet Tagore's poetry became most innovative and mature after his exposure to rural Bengal's folk music, which included Baul ballads—especially those of bard Lalon. These—rediscovered and popularised by Tagore—resemble 19th-century Kartbhaj hymns that emphasize inward divinity and rebellion against religious and social orthodoxy. During his Shilaidaha years, his poems took on a lyrical quality, speaking via the *maner manus* (the Bauls' "man within the heart") or meditating upon the *jivan devata* ("living God within"). This figure thus sought connection with divinity through appeal to nature and the emotional interplay of human drama. Tagore used such techniques in his Bhanusimha poems (which chronicle the romance between Radha and Krishna), which he repeatedly revised over the course of seventy years.

Tagore responded to the mostly crude emergence of modernism and realism in Bengali literature by writing experimental works in the 1930s. Examples works include *Africa* and *Camalia*, which are among the better known of his latter poems. He occasionally wrote poems using *Shadhu Bhasha* (a Sanskritised dialect of Bengali); later, he began using *Cholti Bhasha* (a more popular dialect). Other notable works include *Manasi*, *Sonar Tori* (*Golden Boat*), *Balaka* (*Wild Geese*—the title being a metaphor for migrating souls), and *Purobi*. *Sonar Tori*'s most famous poem—dealing with the ephemeral nature of life and achievement—goes by the same name; hauntingly it ends: ("*Shunno nodir tire rohinu pori/Jaha chhilo loe gelo shonar tori*"—"all I had achieved was carried off on the golden boat—only I was left behind."). Internationally, *Gitanjali* is Tagore's best-known collection, winning him his Nobel Prize. Song VII of *Gitanjali*:

Tagore's poetry has been set to music by various composers, among them classical composer Arthur Shepherd's triptych for soprano and string quartet, as well as composer Garry Schyman's "Praan", an adaptation of Tagore's poem "Stream of Life" from Gitanjali. The latter was composed and recorded with vocals by Palbasha Siddique to accompany Internet celebrity Matt Harding's

2008 viral video.. In 1917 his words were translated adeptly and set to music by Richard Hageman (an Anglo-Dutch composer) to produce what is regarded as one of the finest art songs in the English language: Do not go my love (Ed.Schirmer NY 1917).

Political Views

Tagore's political thought was complex. He opposed imperialism and supported Indian nationalists. His views have their first poetic release in *Manast*, mostly composed in his twenties. Evidence produced during the Hindu-German Conspiracy trial and later accounts affirm his awareness of the Ghadarite conspiracy, and stated that he sought the support of Japanese Prime Minister Terauchi Masatake and former Premier Okuma Shigenobu. Yet he lampooned the Swadeshi movement, denouncing it in "The Cult of the Charka", an acrid 1925 essay. He emphasized self-help and intellectual uplift of the masses as an alternative, stating that British imperialism was a "political symptom of our social disease", urging Indians to accept that "there can be no question of blind revolution, but of steady and purposeful education".

Such views enraged many. He narrowly escaped assassination by Indian expatriates during his stay in a San Francisco hotel in late 1916. The plot failed only because the would-be assassins fell into argument. Yet Tagore wrote songs lionizing the Indian independence movement and renounced his knighthood in protest against the 1919 Jallianwala Bagh Massacre. Two of Tagore's more politically charged compositions, "Chitto Jetha Bhayshunyo" ("Where the Mind is Without Fear") and "Ekla Chalo Re" ("If They Answer Not to Thy Call, Walk Alone"), gained mass appeal, with the latter favoured by Gandhi. Despite his tumultuous relations with Gandhi, Tagore was key in resolving a Gandhi-Ambedkar dispute involving separate electorates for untouchables, ending Gandhi's fast "unto death".

Tagore lampooned rote schooling: in "The Parrot's Training", a bird is caged and force-fed pages torn from books until it dies. These views led Tagore, while visiting Santa Barbara on 11 October 1917, to conceive of a new type of university, desiring to "make Santiniketan the connecting thread between India and the world [and] a world centre for the study of humanity somewhere beyond the limits of nation and geography." The school, which he named Visva-Bharati had its foundation stone laid on 22 December 1918;

it was later inaugurated on 22 December 1921. Here, Tagore implemented a *Brahmacharya* pedagogical structure employing *gurus* to provide individualised guidance for pupils. Tagore worked hard to fundraise for and staff the school, even contributing all of his Nobel Prize monies. Tagore's duties as steward and mentor at Santiniketan kept him busy; he taught classes in mornings and wrote the students' textbooks in afternoons and evenings. Tagore also fundraised extensively for the school in Europe and the U.S. between 1919 and 1921.

Impact

Tagore's relevance can be gauged by festivals honouring him: *Kabipranam,* Tagore's birth anniversary; the annual Tagore Festival held in Urbana, Illinois, in the United States; *Rabindra Path Parikrama* walking pilgrimages from Calcutta to Shantiniketan; ceremonial recitals of Tagore's poetry held on important anniversaries; and others. This legacy is most palpable in Bengali culture, ranging from language and arts to history and politics. Nobel laureate Amartya Sen saw Tagore as a "towering figure", being a "deeply relevant and many-sided contemporary thinker". Tagore's Bengali-language writings—the 1939 *Rabindra Rachanvali*—is also canonised as one of Bengal's greatest cultural treasures. Tagore himself was proclaimed "the greatest poet India has produced".

Tagore was famed throughout much of Europe, North America, and East Asia. He co-founded Dartington Hall School, a progressive coeducational institution; in Japan, he influenced such figures as Nobel laureate Yasunari Kawabata. Tagore's works were widely translated into English, Dutch, German, Spanish, and other European languages by Czech indologist Vincenc Lesny, French Nobel laureate Andre Gide, Russian poet Anna Akhmatova, former Turkish Prime Minister Bulent Ecevit, and others. In the United States, Tagore's lecturing circuits, particularly those in 1916–1917, were widely attended and acclaimed. Yet, several controversies involving Tagore resulted in a decline in his popularity in Japan and North America after the late 1920s, concluding with his "near total eclipse" outside of Bengal.

Via translations, Tagore influenced Spanish literature: Chileans Pablo Neruda and Gabriela Mistral, Mexican writer Octavio Paz, and Spaniards Jose Ortega y Gasset, Zenobia Camprubi, and Juan Ramon Jimenez. Between 1914 and 1922, the Jimenez-Camprubi spouses translated twenty-two of Tagore's books from English into Spanish and extensively revised and adapted such works as Tagore's *The Crescent Moon*. In this time, Jimenez developed "naked poetry" (Spanish: «poesia desnuda»), a landmark innovation. Ortega y Gasset wrote that "Tagore's wide appeal [may stem from the fact that] he speaks of longings for perfection that we all have... Tagore awakens a dormant sense of childish wonder, and he saturates the air with all kinds of enchanting promises for the reader, who... pays little attention to the deeper import of Oriental mysticism". Tagore's works circulated in free editions around 1920 alongside those of Dante Alighieri, Miguel de Cervantes, Johann Wolfgang von Goethe, Plato, and Leo Tolstoy.

Tagore was deemed overrated by some Westerners. Graham Greene doubted that "anyone but Mr. Yeats can still take his poems very seriously." Modern remnants of a past Latin American reverence of Tagore were discovered, for example, by an astonished Salman Rushdie during a trip to Nicaragua.

Kazi Nazrul Islam

Kazi Nazrul Islam (26 May 1899–29 August 1976) was a Bengali poet, musician and revolutionary who pioneered poetic works espousing intense spiritual rebellion against fascism and oppression. His poetry and nationalist activism earned him the popular title of *Bidrohi Kobi* (Rebel Poet). Accomplishing a large body of acclaimed works through his life, Nazrul is officially recognised as the national poet of Bangladesh and commemorated in India.

Born into a poor Muslim family, Nazrul received religious education and worked as a muezzin at a local mosque. He learned of poetry, drama, and literature while working with theatrical groups. After serving in the British Indian Army, Nazrul established himself as a journalist in Kolkata (then Calcutta). He assailed the British Raj in India and preached revolution through his poetic works, such as "Bidrohi" ("The Rebel") and "Bhangar Gaan" ("The Song of Destruction"), as well as his publication "Dhumketu" ("The Comet"). His impassioned activism in the Indian independence movement often led to his imprisonment by British authorities. While in prison, Nazrul wrote the "Rajbandir Jabanbandi" ("Deposition of a Political Prisoner"). Exploring the life and conditions of the downtrodden masses of India, Nazrul worked for their emancipation. Nazrul's writings explore themes such as love, freedom, and revolution; he opposed all bigotry, including religious and gender. Throughout his career, Nazrul wrote short stories, novels, and essays but is best-known for his poems, in which he pioneered new forms such as Bengali ghazals. Nazrul wrote and composed music for his nearly 4,000 songs (including gramophone records), collectively known as Nazrul geeti (Nazrul songs), which are widely popular today. At the age of 43 (in 1942) he began suffering from an unknown disease, losing his voice and memory. Eventually diagnosed as Pick's disease, it caused Nazrul's health to decline steadily and forced him to live in isolation for many years. Invited by the Government of Bangladesh, Nazrul and his family moved to Dhaka in 1972, where he died four years later.

Early Life

Kazi Nazrul Islam was born in the village of Churulia in the Burdwan District of Bengal (now located in the Indian state of West Bengal). He was born in a Muslim family who is second of three sons and a daughter, Nazrul's father Kazi Fakeer Ahmed was the imam and caretaker of the local mosque and mausoleum. Nazrul's mother was Zaheda Khatun. Nazrul had two brothers, Kazi Shahebjan and Kazi Ali Hussain, and a sister, Umme Kulsum. Nicknamed *Dukhu Mia* (Sad Man), Nazrul began attending the *maktab* — the local religious school run by the mosque — where he studied the Qur'an and other scriptures, Islamic philosophy and theology. His family was devastated with the death of his father in 1908. At the young age of ten, Nazrul began working in his father's place as a caretaker to support his family, as well as assisting teachers in school. He later became the muezzin at the mosque, delivering the Athan and calling the people for prayer.

Attracted to folk theatre, Nazrul joined a *leto* (travelling theatrical group) run by his uncle Bazle Karim. Working and travelling with them, learning acting, as well as writing songs and poems for the plays and musicals. Through his work and experiences, Nazrul began learning Bengali and Sanskrit literature, as well as Hindu scriptures such as the Puranas. The young poet composed a number of folk plays for his group, which included "Chasar San" ("The story of a Farmer"), "Shakunibadh" ("The Killing of a Vulture"), "Raja Yudhisthirer San" ("The story of King

Yudhisthir"), "Data Karna" ("Philanthropic *Karna*"), "Akbar Badshah" ("Emperor *Akbar*"), "Kavi Kalidasa" ("Poet *Kalidasa*"), "Vidyabhutum" ("The Learned Owl"), "Rajputrer San" ("The story of a Prince").

In 1910, Nazrul left the troupe and enrolled at the Raniganj Searsole Raj School, and later transferred to the Mathrun High English School, studying under the headmaster and poet Kumudranjan Mallik. Unable to continue paying his school fees, Nazrul left the school and joined a group of kaviyals. Later he took jobs as a cook at the house of a Christian railway guard and at a bakery and tea stall in the town of Asansol. In 1914, Nazrul studied in the Darirampur School (now Jatiya Kabi Kazi Nazrul Islam University) in Trishal, Mymensingh District. Amongst other subjects, Nazrul studied Bengali, Sanskrit, Arabic, Persian literature and classical music under teachers who were impressed by his dedication and skill.

Studying up to Class X, Nazrul did not appear for the matriculation pretest examination, enlisting instead in the Indian Army in 1917 at the age of eighteen. He joined the British army mainly for two reasons: first, his youthful romantic inclination to respond to the unknown and, secondly, the call of politics. Attached to the 49th Bengal Regiment, he was posted to the cantonment in Karachi, where he wrote his first prose and poetry. Although he never saw active fighting, he rose in rank from corporal to *havildar*, and served as quartermaster for his battalion. During this period, Nazrul read extensively, and was deeply influenced by Rabindranath Tagore and Sarat Chandra Chattopadhay, as well as the Persian poets Hafez, Rumi and Omar Khayyam. He learnt Persian poetry from the regiment's Punjabi moulvi, practiced music and pursued his literary interests. His first prose work, "Baunduler Atmakahini" ("Life of a Vagabond") was published in May, 1919. His poem "Mukti" ("Freedom") was published by the "Bangla Mussalman Sahitya Patrika" ("Bengali Muslim Literary Journal") in July 1919.

Rebel Poet

Nazrul left the army in 1920 and settled in Calcutta, which was then the *Cultural capital of India* (it had ceased to be the political capital in 1911). He joined the staff of the "Bangiya Mussalman Sahitya Samiti" ("Bengali Muslim Literary Society") and roomed at 32 College Street with colleagues. He published his first novel "Bandhan-hara" ("Freedom from bondage") in 1920, which he kept working on over the next seven years. His first collection of poems included "Bodhan", "Shat-il-Arab", "Kheya-parer Tarani" and "Badal Prater Sharab" and received critical acclaim.

Working at the literary society, Nazrul grew close to other young Muslim writers including Mohammad Mozammel Haq, Afzalul Haq, Kazi Abdul Wadud and Muhammad Shahidullah. He was a regular at clubs for Calcutta's writers, poets and intellectuals like the Gajendar Adda and the Bharatiya Adda. In October 1921, Nazrul went to Santiniketan with Muhammad Shahidullah and met Rabindranath Tagore. Despite many differences, Nazrul looked to Tagore as a mentor and the two remained in close association. In 1921, Nazrul was engaged to be married to Nargis, the niece of a well-known Muslim publisher Ali Akbar Khan, in Daulatpur, Comilla. But on June 18, 1921—the day of the wedding—upon public insistence by Ali Akbar Khan that the term *"Nazrul must reside in Daulatpur after marriage"* be included in the marriage contract, Nazrul walked away from the ceremony.

Nazrul reached the peak of fame with the publication of "Bidrohi" in 1922, which remains his most famous work, winning admiration of India's literary classes by his description of the rebel whose impact is fierce and ruthless even as its spirit is deep:.

- I am the unutterable grief,
- I am the trembling first touch of the virgin,
- I am the throbbing tenderness of her first stolen kiss.
- I am the fleeting glance of the veiled beloved,
- I am her constant surreptitious gaze...
- I am the burning volcano in the bosom of the earth,
- I am the wild fire of the woods,
- I am Hell's mad terrific sea of wrath!
- I ride on the wings of lightning with joy and profundity,
- I scatter misery and fear all around,
- I bring earthquakes on this world! "(8th stanza)" I am the rebel eternal,
- I raise my head beyond this world,

- High, ever erect and alone! "(Last stanza)" (*English translation by Kabir Choudhary*).

Published in the "Bijli" (*Thunder*) magazine, the rebellious language and theme was popularly received, coinciding with the Non-cooperation movement — the first, mass nationalist campaign of civil disobedience against British rule.

Nazrul explores a synthesis of different forces in a rebel, destroyer and preserver, expressing rage as well as beauty and sensitivity. Nazrul followed up by writing "Pralayollas" ("Destructive Euphoria"), and his first anthology of poems, the "Agniveena" ("Lyre of Fire") in 1922, which enjoyed astounding and far-reaching success. He also published his first volume of short stories, the "Byather Dan" ("Gift of Sorrow") and "Yugbani", an anthology of essays.

Revolutionary

Nazrul started a bi-weekly magazine, publishing the first "Dhumketu" (*Comet*) on August 12, 1922. Earning the moniker of the "rebel poet", Nazrul also aroused the suspicion of British authorities. A political poem published in "Dhumketu" in September 1922 led to a police raid on the magazine's office. Arrested, Nazrul entered a lengthy plea before the judge in the court.

I have been accused of sedition. That is why I am now confined in the prison. On the one side is the crown, on the other the flames of the comet. One is the king, sceptre in hand; the other Truth worth the mace of justice. To plead for me, the king of all kings, the judge of all judges, the eternal truth the living God... His laws emerged out of the realization of a universal truth about mankind. They are for and by a sovereign God. The king is supported by an infinitesimal creature; I by its eternal and indivisible Creator. I am a poet; I have been sent by God to express the unexpressed, to portray the unportrayed. It is God who is heard through the voice of the poet... My voice is but a medium for Truth, the message of God... I am the instrument of that eternal self-evident truth, an instrument that voices forth the message of the ever-true. I am an instrument of God. The instrument is not unbreakable, but who is there to break God?

On April 14, 1923 he was transferred from the jail in Alipore to Hooghly in Kolkata, he began a 40-day fast to protest mistreatment by the British jail superintendent. Nazrul broke his fast more than a month later and was eventually released from prison in December 1923. Nazrul composed a large number of poems and songs during the period of imprisonment and many his works were banned in the 1920s by the British authorities.

Kazi Nazrul Islam became a critic of the Khilafat struggle, condemning it as hollow, religious fundamentalism. Nazrul's rebellious expression extended to rigid orthodoxy in the name of religion and politics. Nazrul also criticised the Indian National Congress for not embracing outright political independence from the British Empire. He became active in encouraging people to agitate against British rule, and joined the Bengal state unit of the Congress party. Nazrul also helped organise the Sramik Praja Swaraj Dal, a political party committed to national independence and the service of the peasant masses. On December 16, 1925 Nazrul started publishing the weekly "Langal", with himself as chief editor. The "Langal" was the mouthpiece of the Sramik Praja Swaraj Dal.

During his visit to Comilla in 1921, Nazrul met a young Hindu woman, Pramila Devi, with whom he fell in love and they married on April 25, 1924. Pramila belonged to the Brahmo Samaj, which criticised her marriage to a Muslim. Nazrul in turn was condemned by Muslim religious leaders and continued to face criticism for his personal life and professional works, which attacked social and religious dogma and intolerance. Despite controversy, Nazrul's popularity and reputation as the "rebel poet" rose significantly.

Weary of struggles, I, the great rebel,

Shall rest in quiet only when I find

The sky and the air free of the piteous groans of the oppressed.

Only when the battle fields are cleared of jingling bloody sabres

Shall I, weary of struggles, rest in quiet,

I the great rebel.

Mass Music

With his wife and young son Bulbul, Nazrul settled in Krishnanagar in 1926. His work began to transform as he wrote poetry and songs that articulated the aspirations of the downtrodden classes, a sphere of his work known as "mass music."

Nazrul assailed the socioeconomic norms and political system that had brought upon misery. From his poem *Daridro* (Pain or Poverty):

O poverty, thou hast made me great.
Thou hast made me honoured like Christ
With his crown of thorns. Thou hast given me
Courage to reveal all. To thee I owe
My insolent, naked eyes and sharp tongue.
Thy curse has turned my violin to a sword...
O proud saint, thy terrible fire
Has rendered my heaven barren.
O my child, my darling one
I could not give thee even a drop of milk
No right have I to rejoice.
Poverty weeps within my doors forever
As my spouse and my child.
Who will play the flute?

In what his contemporaries regarded as one of his greatest flairs of creativity, Nazrul began composing the very first ghazals in Bengali, transforming a form of poetry written mainly in Persian and Urdu. Nazrul for the first introduced Islam into the larger mainstream tradition of Bengali music. The first record of Islamic songs by Nazrul Islam was a commercial success and many gramophone companies showed interest in producing these. A significant impact of Nazrul was that it drew made Muslims more comfortable in the Bengali Arts, which used to be dominated by Hindus. Nazrul also composed a number of notable *Shamasangeet, Bhajan* and *Kirtan,* combining Hindu devotional music. Arousing controversy and passions in his readers, Nazrul's ideas attained great popularity across India. In 1928, Nazrul began working as a lyricist, composer and music director for His Master's Voice Gramophone Company. The songs written and music composed by him were broadcast on radio stations across the country. He was also enlisted/attached with the Indian Broadcasting Company.

Nazrul professed faith in the belief in the equality of women—a view his contemporaries considered revolutionary. From his poet *Nari* (Woman):

I don't see any difference
Between a man and woman
Whatever great or benevolent achievements
That are in this world
Half of that was by woman,
The other half by man. (Translated by Sajed Kamal)

His poetry retains long-standing notions of men and women in binary opposition to one another and does not affirm gender similarities and flexibility in the social structure:

Man has brought the burning, scorching heat of the sunny day;

Woman has brought peaceful night, soothing breeze and cloud.

Man comes with desert-thirst; woman provides the drink of honey.

Man ploughs the fertile land; woman sows crops in it turning it green.

Man ploughs, woman waters; that earth and water mixed together, brings about a harvest of golden paddy.

However, Nazrul's poems strongly emphasise the confluence of the roles of both sexes and their equal importance to life. He stunned society with his poem "Barangana" ("Prostitute"), in which he addresses a prostitute as "mother". Nazrul accepts the prostitute as a human being, reasoning that this person was breast-fed by a noble woman and belonging to the race of "mothers and sisters"; he assails society's negative notions of prostitutes.

Who calls you a prostitute, mother?
Who spits at you?
Perhaps you were suckled by someone
as chaste as Seeta.
And if the son of an unchaste mother is 'illegitimate',
so is the son of an unchaste father.
("Barangana" ("Prostitute") Translated by Sajed Kamal).

Nazrul was an advocate of the emancipation of women; both traditional and non-traditional women were portrayed by him with utmost sincerity. Nazrul's songs are collectively called as *Nazrul geeti.*

Exploring Religion

Nazrul's mother died in 1928, and his second son Bulbul died of smallpox the following year. His first son, Krishna Mohammad had died prematurely. His wife gave birth to two more sons – Savyasachi in 1928 and Aniruddha in 1931 – but Nazrul remained shaken and aggrieved for a long time.

His works changed significantly from rebellious expositions of society to deeper examination of religious themes. His works in these years led Islamic devotional songs into the mainstream of Bengali folk music, exploring the Islamic practices of *namaz* (prayer), *roza* (fasting), *hajj* (pilgrimage) and *zakat* (charity). This was regarded by his contemporaries as a significant achievement as Bengali Muslims had been strongly averse to devotional music. Nazrul's creativity diversified as he explored Hindu devotional music by composing *Shama Sangeet, bhajans* and *kirtans,* often merging Islamic and Hindu values. Nazrul's poetry and songs explored the philosophy of Islam and Hinduism.

Let people of all countries and all times come together. At one great union of humanity. Let them listen to the flute music of one great unity. Should a single person be hurt, all hearts should feel it equally. If one person is insulted; it is a shame to all mankind, an insult to all! Today is the grand uprising of the agony of universal man.

Nazrul's poetry imbibed the passion and creativity of Shakti, which is identified as the Brahman, the personification of primordial energy. He wrote and composed many *bhajans, shyamasangeet, agamanis* and *kirtans*. He also composed large number of songs on invocation to Lord Shiva, Goddesses Lakshmi and Saraswati and on the theme of love of Radha and Krishna.

Nazrul assailed fanaticism in religion, denouncing it as evil and inherently irreligious. He devoted many works to expound upon the principle of human equality, exploring the *Quran* and the life of Islam's prophet Muhammad.

Nazrul has been compared to William Butler Yeats for being the first Muslim poet to create imagery and symbolism of Muslim historical figures such as Qasim, Ali, Umar, Kamal Pasha, Anwar Pasha and the prophet Muhammad. His vigorous assault on extremism and mistreatment of women provoked condemnation from Muslim and Hindu fundamentalists.

In 1920, Nazrul expressed his vision of religious harmony in an editorial in *Yuga Bani,*

"Come brother Hindu! Come Musalman! Come Buddhist! Come Christian! Let us transcend all barriers, let us foresake forever all smallness, all lies, all selfishness and let us call brothers as brothers. We shall quarrel no more".

In another article entitled *Hindu Mussalman* published in *Ganabani* on September 2, 192 he wrote-

"I can tolerate Hinduism and Muslims but I cannot tolerate the Tikism (Tiki is a tuft of never cut hair kept on the head by certain Hindus to maitain personal Holiness) and beardism. Tiki is not Hinduism. It may be the sign of the pundit. Similarly beards is not Islam, it may be the sign of the pundit. Similarly beard is not Islam, it may be the sign of the mollah. All the hair-pulling have originated from those two tufts of hair. Todays fighting is alos between the Pundit and the Mollah: It is not between the Hindus and the Muslims. No prophet has said, "I have come for Hindus I have come for Muslims I have come for Christians." They have said, "I have come for the humanity for everyone, like light". But the devotees of Krishna says, "Krishna is for Hindus". The followers of Muhammad (Sm) says, "Muhammad (Sm) is for the Muslims". The Disciple of Christ is for Christian". Krishna-Muhammad-Christ have become national property. This property is the root of all trouble. Men do not quarrel for light but they quarrel over cattles."

Nazrul was an exponent of humanism. Although a Muslim, he named his sons with both Hindu and Muslim names: Krishna Mohammad, Arindam Khaled (bulbul), Kazi Sazbyasachi and Kazi Aniruddha.

Later Life and Illness

In 1933, Nazrul published a collection of essays titled "Modern World Literature", in which he analyses different styles and themes of literature. Between 1928 and 1935 he published 10 volumes containing 800 songs of which more than 600 were based on classical *ragas.* Almost 100 were folk tunes after *kirtans* and some 30 were patriotic songs. From the time of his return to Kolkata until he fell ill in 1941, Nazrul composed more than 2,600 songs, many of which have been lost. His songs based on *baul, jhumur,* Santhali folksongs, jhanpan or the folk songs of *snake charmers, bhatiali* and *bhaoaia* consist of tunes of folk-songs on the one hand and a refined lyric with poetic beauty on the other. Nazrul also wrote and published poems for children.

Nazrul's success soon brought him into Indian theatre and the then-nascent film industry. The first picture for which he worked was based on Girish Chandra Ghosh's story "Bhakta Dhruva" in 1934. Nazrul acted in the role of Narada and directed the film. He also composed songs for it, directed the music and served as a playback singer. The film "Vidyapati" ("Master of Knowledge") was produced based on his recorded play in 1936, and Nazrul served as the music director for the film adaptation of Tagore's novel *Gora*. Nazrul wrote songs and directed music for Sachin Sengupta's bioepic play "Siraj-ud-Daula". In 1939, Nazrul began working for Calcutta Radio, supervising the production and broadcasting of the station's musical programmes. He produced critical and analytic documentaries on music, such as "Haramoni" and "Navaraga-malika". Nazrul also wrote a large variety of songs inspired by the raga *Bhairav*. Nazrul sought to preserve his artistic integrity by condemning the adaptation of his songs to music composed by others and insisting on the use of tunes he composed himself.

Nazrul's wife Pramila Devi fell seriously ill in 1939 and was paralysed from waist down. To provide for his wife's medical treatment, he resorted to mortgaging the royalties of his gramophone records and literary works for 400 rupees. He returned to journalism in 1940 by working as chief editor for the daily newspaper "Nabayug" ("New Age"), founded by the eminent Bengali politician A. K. Fazlul Huq.

Nazrul also was shaken by the death of Rabindranath Tagore on August 8, 1941. He spontaneously composed two poems in Tagore's memory, one of which, "Rabihara" (loss of Rabi or without Rabi) was broadcast on the All India Radio. Within months, Nazrul himself fell seriously ill and gradually began losing his power of speech. His behaviour became erratic, and spending recklessly, he fell into financial difficulties. In spite of her own illness, his wife constantly cared for her husband. However, Nazrul's health seriously deteriorated and he grew increasingly depressed. He underwent medical treatment under homeopathy as well as Ayurveda, but little progress was achieved before mental dysfunction intensified and he was admitted to a mental asylum in 1942. Spending four months there without making progress, Nazrul and his family began living a silent life in India.

In 1952, he was transferred to a mental hospital in Ranchi. With the efforts of a large group of admirers who called themselves the "Nazrul Treatment Society" as well as prominent supporters such as the Indian politician Syama Prasad Mookerjee, the treatment society sent Nazrul and Promila to London, then to Vienna for treatment. Examining doctors said he had received poor care, and Dr. Hans Hoff, a leading neurosurgeon in Vienna, diagnosed that Nazrul was suffering from Pick's disease. His condition judged to be incurable, Nazrul returned to Calcutta on 15 December 1953. On June 30, 1962 his wife Pramila died and Nazrul remained in intensive medical care.

In 1972, the newly independent nation of Bangladesh obtained permission from the Government of India to bring Nazrul to live in Dhaka and accorded him honorary citizenship. Despite receiving treatment and attention, Nazrul's physical and mental health did not improve. In 1974, his youngest son, Kazi Aniruddha, an eminent guitarist died, and Nazrul soon succumbed to his long-standing ailments on August 29, 1976. In accordance with a wish he had expressed in one of his poems, he was buried beside a mosque on the campus of the University of Dhaka. Tens of thousands of people attended his funeral; Bangladesh observed two days of national mourning and the Indian Parliament observed a minute of silence in his honour.

Criticism and Legacy

Nazrul's poetry is characterised by an abundant use of rhetorical devices, which he employed to convey conviction and sensuousness. He often wrote without care for organisation or polish. His works have often been criticized for egotism, but his admirers counter that they carry more a sense of self-confidence than ego. They cite his ability to defy God yet maintain an inner, humble devotion to Him. Nazrul's poetry is regarded as rugged but unique in comparison to Tagore's sophisticated style. Nazrul's use of Persian vocabulary was controversial but it widened the scope of his work. Nazrul's works for children have won acclaim for his use of rich language, imagination, enthusiasm and an ability to fascinate young readers. Nazrul is regarded for his secularism. He was the first person to cite of Christians of Bengal in his novel Mrityukhudha. He was also the first user of folk terms in Bengali literature. He first printed the Sickle and Hammer in any Indian magazine. Nazrul pioneered new styles and expressed radical ideas and emotions in a large body of work. Scholars credit him for spearheading a cultural renaissance in Muslim-majority Bengal, "liberating" poetry and literature in Bengali from its medieval mould. Nazrul was awarded the Jagattarini Gold Medal in 1945 – the highest honour for work in Bengali literature by the University of Calcutta – and awarded the Padma Bhushan, one of India's highest civilian honours in 1960. The Government of Bangladesh conferred upon him the status of being the "national poet". He was awarded the Ekushey Padak by the Government of Bangladesh. He was awarded Honorary D.Litt. by the University of Dhaka. Many centres of learning and culture in India and Bangladesh have been founded and dedicated to his memory. The Nazrul Endowment is one of several scholarly institutions established to preserve and expound upon his thoughts and philosophy, as well as the preservation and analysis of the large and diverse collection of his works. The Bangladesh Nazrul Sena is a large public organization working for the education of children throughout the country.

Khudiram Bose

Khudiram Bose (3 December 1889-11 August 1908) was a Bengali revolutionary, one of the youngest revolutionaries early in the Indian independence movement.

Early Life

Bose was born on December 3, 1889 in the village Mohobony in Midnapore district of Bengal. His father Trailokyanath Basu was the revenue agent of the town of the Nadazol prince. His mother was Lakshmipriya Devi.

Revolutionary Activities

Bose was inspired by his teacher Satyendranath Bose and readings of the Bhagavad Gita, which helped him embrace revolutionary activities aimed at ending the British Raj. He was especially disillusioned with the British following the partition of Bengal conflagration in 1905. He joined Jugantar-the party of revolutionary activists. At the nascent age of sixteen, Bose was defying police after planting bombs near police stations and targeting government officials. He was arrested three years later on charges of conducting a series of bomb attacks. The specific bombing for which he was sentenced to death resulted in the deaths of 3 persons: a Mrs. Kennedy, her daughter and a servant.

The Muzaffarpur Killing

Khudiram and Prafulla Chaki were sent to Muzaffarpur, Bihar to assassinate Kingsford, the Calcutta Presidency Magistrate, and later, magistrate of Muzaffarpur, Bihar.

Khudiram and Prafulla watched the usual movements of Kingsford and prepared a plan to kill him. On the evening of April 30, 1908, the duo waited in front of the gate of the European Club for the carriage of Kingsford to come. When a vehicle came out of the gate, they threw bombs and blew up the carriage. However, the vehicle was not carrying Kingsford and instead two British ladies-Mrs. and Miss Kennedy (the wife and daughter of barrister Pringle Kennedy) were killed. The revolutionary duo fled. Prafulla committed suicide when cornered by police at the Samastipur Railway station. Khudiram was later arrested about 20 km from Samastipur at a distance of 12 km from Pusa Bazaar where Rajendra Agricultural University was first established. The railway station where Khudiram was arrested while having tea was earlier known as Pusa Road and recently has been renamed as Khudiram Pusa. He was the first youngest freedom fighter. The police learned about Anusheelan Samiti. They started arresting the member of this organization

Death

On this Muzaffarpur bombing and other charges of bombings carried out by him, a pretense of trial was carried out for two months. Although the leading Calcutta advocate Narendra Kumar Basu mounted a stout defence of Khudiram's actions in defence of his motherland (without charging any fees), Khudiram was sentenced to death. The sentence was carried out, and he was hanged on August 11, 1908. But the one thing that surprised everyone was that as he was hanged he was still smiling. And to this the Bengali poet Kazi Nazrul Islam wrote a poem to honour him.

Khudiram Bose

It was this hero who threw the first bomb on the British who were crushing India. Even while at school, he was attracted towards the sacred words Vande Mataram!' (I bow to Mother India!) and plunged into the war of independence. The boy of sixteen defied the police. At the age of nineteen, he became a martyr, with the holy book the Bhagavadgita (the Divine Song) in his hand and with the slogan Vande Mataram' on his lips. *Author-K.Shivashankar.*

It was February 1906. A grand exhibition had been arranged at Medinipur in Bengal. The intention was to hide the injustice of the British then ruling India. On exhibition were articles like pictures and puppets which could create the impression that the British rulers, though foreigners, were doing much to help the people of India. There were big crowds to see the exhibition.

'Take Care, Don't Touch My Body!'

Then appeared a boy of sixteen with a bundle of handbills; he was distributing them to the people. The handbill bore the title 'Sonar Bangla'. It carried the slogan Vande Mataram'. In addition, the true purpose of the British in putting up the exhibition was also exposed. The various forms of British injustice and tyranny were also explained.

Among the visitors to the exhibition, there were a few loyal to the King of England. They were opposed to the persons who exposed the injustice of the British. Words like Vande Mataram', 'Swatantrya' (freedom) and 'Swarajya' (self-rule) were like pins and needles to them. They tried to prevent the boy from distributing the handbills. Their eyes red with anger, they glared at the boy, rebuked him and frightened him. But ignoring them the boy calmly went on distributing the handbills. When some people tried to capture him, he smartly escaped.

At last a policeman caught hold of the boy's hand. He pulled at the bundle of handbills. But to catch the boy was not so easy. He jerked free his hand. Then he swung the arm and powerfully struck the nose of the policeman. Again he took possession of the handbills, and said, "Take care, don't touch my body! I will see how you can arrest me without a warrant."

The policeman who had received the blow rushed forward again; but the boy was not there. He had disappeared in the midst of the crowd.

As the people burst into cries Vande Mataram' the police and t loyal to the King were filled with wonder and also felt humiliated.

Later a case was filed against the boy; but the court set him on the ground of his tender age.

Swami Abhedananda

Swami Abhedananda (2 October 1866 – 8 September 1939) was a direct disciple of Sri Ramakrishna, who Swami Vivekananda sent to the West to head the Vedanta Society, New York in 1897, and spread the message of Vedanta, a theme on which he authored several books through his life, and subsequently founded the Ramakrishna Vedanta Math, in Calcutta (now Kolkata) and Darjeeling.

Biography

He was born on 2 October 1866 as *Kaliprasad Chandra* in North Calcutta His father was Rasiklal Chandra and his mother was Nayantara Devi. In 1884, at the age of 18, while studying for the school final examination, he went to Dakshineswar and met Sri Ramakrishna. Thereafter in April 1885, he left home to be with him, during his final illness, first at Shyampukur and then at Cossipur Garden-house near Calcutta.

After his Master's death in 1886, he plunged into intense sadhana (meditations), by shutting himself up in a room at the Baranagar Math, this gave his the name "Kali Tapaswi" amongst his fellow disciples. After the passing away of Sri Ramakrishna, he formally became a Sanyasi along with Swami Vivekananda and others, and came to be known as "Swami Abhedananda".

For the next ten years, of his life as a monk he travelled extensively throughout India, depending entirely on alms. During this time he met several famous sages like Pavhari Baba, Trailanga Swami and Swami Bhaskaranand. He went to the sources of the Ganga and the Yamuna, and meditated in the Himalayas. He was a forceful orator, prolific writer, yogi and intellectual with devotional fervour.

In 1896, Vivekananda was in London, when he asked Abhedananda to join him, and propagate the message of Vedanta in the West, which he did with great success. He went to USA in 1897, when Vivekananda asked him to take charge of the Vedanta Society in New York, here he preached messages of Vedanta and teachings of his Guru for about 25 years, travelling far and wide to United States, Canada, Mexico, Japan and Hong Kong. Finally, he returned to India in 1921, after attending the Pan-Pacific Education Conference at Honolulu.

In 1922, he crossed the Himalayas on foot and reached Tibet, where he studied Buddhistic philosophy and Lamaism. In Hemis Monastery, he discovered a manuscript on the Lost years of Jesus, which has been incorporated in the book *Swami Abhedananda's Journey Into Kashmir & Tibet* published by the 'Ramakrishna Vedanta Math', Kolkata.

He formed the 'Ramakrishna Vedanta Society' in Kolkata in 1923, which is now known as Ramakrishna Vedanta Math. In 1924, he established Ramakrishna Vedanta Math in Darjeeling in West Bengal. In 1927, he started publishing Visvavani, the monthly magazine from 'Ramakrishna Vedanta Society', which he edited from 1927 to 1938, the magazine is published today as well. In 1936, he presided over the Parliament of Religions at the Town Hall, Kolkata, as a part the Birth Centenary celebrations of Sri Ramakrishna.

He died on 8 September 1939 at Ramakrishna Vedanta Math, he had established at Darjeeling. At the time of his death he was last surviving direct disciple of Sri Ramakrishna.

Prafulla Chandra Roy

Prafulla Chandra Roy was a Bengali academician, a chemist and entrepreneur. He was born on August 2, 1861 in the village Raruli-Katipara in Khulna District (now in Bangladesh) and died on June 16, 1944. He was the founder of Bengal Chemicals & Pharmaceuticals, India's first pharmaceutical company. He is the author of *A History of Hindu Chemistry from the Earliest Times to the Sixteenth Century* (1902).

Early Life

His father Harish Chandra Ray was a land proprietor. Up to age of nine, Prafulla Chandra studied in a school in his village. Then his family migrated to Calcutta and there he studied in Hare School. While studying in Hare School, he suffered from a severe attack of dysentery, which hampered his health throughout his life. Later, he studied at Albert School, Calcutta.

In 1879 he passed the Entrance Examination of the Calcutta University and entered the Metropolitan Institution. P. C. Roy developed his interest in science after reading the autobiography of Benjamin Franklin and his famous 'kite experiment'. At that time the Metropolitan Institution had no science classes or laboratories and Prafulla Chandra attended lectures in physics and chemistry at the Presidency College, Calcutta. Here he was specially attracted by the chemistry courses of professor Alexander Pedler. It was Pedler who first awakened his interest in natural science. While taking the science course for the B.A. Degree, he was awarded in 1882 one of the two Gilchrist Prize Scholarships after an all-India competitive examination. Without completing the course for his degree, Prafulla Chandra proceeded to the United Kingdom for further study and entered the Edinburgh University. In Chemistry, he was a pupil of Professor Alexander Crum Brown, F.R.S., noted for his philosophical outlook and engaging personality. Alexander Smith and James Walker were his fellow students. He obtained the B.Sc. degree in 1886, and the D.Sc. degree in 1887. He was awarded the Hope Prize. While being a student of Edinburgh University, he was elected Vice-President of Edinburgh University Chemical Society in 1888.

Career

Prafulla Chandra returned to India in 1889 and joined Presidency College, Calcutta as Assistant Professor of Chemistry. Though at that time, the Chemistry department of Presidency College did not boast of any well-equipped world standard laboratory, but a lot of original chemical experimentation occurred there.

In 1896, he published a paper on preparation of a new stable chemical compound: Mercurous nitrite. This work made way for a large number of investigative papers on nitrites and hyponitrites of different metals, and on nitrites of ammonia and organic amines. He started a new Indian School of Chemistry in 1924.

Prafulla Chandra retired from the Presidency College in 1916, and joined the Calcutta University College of Science (now known as Rajabazar Science College) as its first Palit Professor of Chemistry, a chair named after Tarak Nath Palit. Here also he got a dedicated team and he started working on compounds of gold, platinum, iridium etc. with mercaptyl radicals and organic sulphides. A number of papers were published on this work in the Journal of the Indian Chemical Society. In 1936, at the age of 75, he retired from active service and became Professor Emeritus. Long before that, on the completion of his 60th year in 1921, he made a free gift of his entire salary to the Calcutta University from that date onward, to be spent for the furtherance of chemical research, and the development of the Department of Chemistry in the University College of Science. He had written 107 papers in all branches of Chemistry by 1920.

Entrepreneurship

He realized that advancement of Indian and its people can happen only by economic advancement through development of new industries on scientific lines. He showed the way by investing his own money into forming Bengal Chemical and Pharmaceutical Works in 1893. This company culminated into the pioneer of chemical industry in India. In 1902, it became a limited company and grew up under his guidance.

Literary Works and Interests

He contributed articles in Bengali to many monthly magazines, particularly on scientific topics. He published the first volume of his autobiography *Life and Experience of a Bengali Chemist* in 1932, and dedicated it to the youth of India. The second volume of this work was issued in 1935.

In 1902, he published the first volume of *A History of Hindu Chemistry from the Earliest Times to the Sixteenth Century*. The second volume was published in 1908. The work was result of many years' search through ancient Sanskrit manuscripts and through works of orientalists.

Social Service

In 1923, Northern Bengal suffered a flood which made caused millions of people homeless and hungry. Prafulla Chandra organized Bengal Relief Committee, which collected nearly 2.5 million rupees in cash and kind and distributed it in the affected area in an organized manner.

He donated money regularly towards welfare of Sadharan Brahmo Samaj, Brahmo Girls' School and Indian Chemical Society. In 1922, he donated money to establish Nagarjuna Prize to be awarded for the best work in chemistry. In 1937, another award, named after Ashutosh Mukherjee, to be awarded for the best work in zoology or botany, was established from his donation.

Recognition

He earned his Ph.D. at Calcutta University in 1908. He received an honorary D.Sc. degree from Durham University in 1912, and another from Dacca University in 1936. He was made a Companion of the Order of the Indian Empire in 1911 and received the Knighthood in 1917. He was Honorary Fellow of the Chemical Society and Deutsche Akademie, Munich. He was president of the 1920 session of the Indian Science Congress.

Life

He remained a bachelor throughout his life who took active participation in politics.

His family, in particular, his father Harish Chandra Roy, was strongly associated with Brahmo Samaj. Prafulla Chandra developed direct connections with the Samaj as he grew up; he used to attend Sunday evening sermons of Keshub Chandra Sen and was deeply influenced by Sen's *Sulabha Samachar*.

Prafulla Chandra Roy

Prafulla Chandra Roy is one of the famous scientists that India has ever produced. Considered as one of the components of the Bengal Renaissance, P. C. Roy was an eminent scientist, an exemplary entrepreneur, a patriot and a passionate teacher.

He was born on 2nd August, 1861 at Khulna in undivided Bengal. He had his education in Calcutta, studying in some well-known schools and colleges. He went to England as a Gilchrist scholar and earned the degrees of BSc. and Dsc. from Edinburgh University. He returned to Calcutta and joined as a lecturer of Chemistry in the Presidency College. He was a very inspiring teacher and dedicated his spare time in research. He published his works on Ayurveda-' The History of Hindu Chemistry'. He faced severe financial crunches but he never gave up. His persistence paid up when he became successful in the chemical synthesizing of Potassium Nitrate. In 1901, he single handedly established 'The Bengal Chemical and Pharmaceutical Works Limited', the first Indian Pharmaceutical company. This led to the employment generation of many unemployed Indians.

Acharya P. C. Roy was a great patriot and highly influenced by leaders like S. N. Banerjee and Mahatma Gandhi. He loved his fellow men and devoted himself to the relief works during the calamities. In 1916, he joined the Science College of the Calcutta University and he was elected the President of the Indian Science Congress in 1920. Acharya Prafulla Chandra Roy dedicated himself to the cause of spreading scientific knowledge among the mass. A rationalist and a great academician he is considered as the 'Father of the modern Indian chemical Industry'. He breathed his last on June 16th, 1944.

Swaraj in Education

The eighteenth-century European colonization and Christianization indicated the direction in which the wind of education was to blow in India. But this is not a 'thing' to celebrate. It is common knowledge that the westerly direction of that wind has remained unchanged well into the twentieth century. We do not know why the wind is so particularly strong, but we do know that there are other directions in space-time.

Among early colonialists, there were liberal-minded Europeans who felt the desirability of "preserving the ancient culture of India from the state of rapid decay into which it [had] fallen on account of the loss of royal patronage". They also saw the utility of the careful study of ancient Indian literature by Western scholars and the adoption of English as a medium of instruction for the Indian people. The missionaries and their friends, on the other hand, looked at Indian culture with utter contempt. They believed that Western 'light and knowledge' should take the place of Eastern culture and religion. The foremost among them was Charles Grant, the father of colonial education in India, who painted an exaggerated picture of the 'depraved' condition of Indian society. He analysed its cause and suggested a remedy: "The causes of the miserable condition of the Indian people were ignorance and want of a proper religion. The situation could only be improved if Indians were educated through the English language and finally converted to Christianity." Lord Macaulay, a torch-bearer in the path of colonial progress, also recommended the spread of Western learning through the medium of the English language. In his infamous minutes he wrote, "a single shelf of a good European library [was] worth the whole native literature of India and Arabia". He talked of creating "a class of persons who would be Indian in blood and colour but English in tastes, in opinions, and in intellects".

What flowed out of these two streams of thinking was a pattern of education with the ultimate objectives of:

(a) securing servants for public administration;

(b) diverting young men and women from the study of oriental to occidental literature; and

(c) arousing in young hearts a passion for Western knowledge and culture. The objectives were carried out by:

   (i) the creation of a government department of public instruction;

   (ii) the establishment of universities, colleges and graded schools;

   (iii) the training of teachers;

   (iv) the introduction of government grants-in-aid;

   (v) the maintenance of a few educational institutions under the direct control of the government and allowing private educational enterprise by missionaries and non-officials; and

   (vi) the recognition of educational institutions by the government department and universities.

At the culmination of the colonial process India inherited:

(a) employment-oriented education;

(b) Westernization of the content of education;

(c) public examinations so used as to impose uniform curricula and textbooks;

(d) a class of persons educated in a foreign language;

(e) neglect of indigenous systems of education; and

(f) the withdrawal of religious education through direct educational enterprise.

The Indian National Congress was formed in 1885. The Swadeshi movement brought about a great ferment of educational thought. It demanded Indian control of Indian educational policies, teaching love of the motherland, no servile imitation of England, and the removal of the domination of English. Unfortunately, hopes of educational reconstruction with a bolder and freer hand have not yet materialized.

India struggled for freedom, and it did achieve political independence. It asked for Indian control of Indian educational policies, and it got it. It wanted to teach love of the motherland, and it is doing so. But is independent India free from servile imitation of the West? Has the domination of English gone? Has the Western system of education enriched Indian culture? Has it added at all to its happiness? Does India need such education?

India debated Gandhi's great idea of education for nearly a century. It seems to be in earnest in its endeavour to educate people. More than 90 per cent of the country's rural areas now have schooling facilities within a radius of one kilometre. The national policy on education is revised periodically and the investment on education has now reached 6 per cent of the national income. Yet the picture is unclear.

The national policy aims at (a) promoting national progress; (b) creating a sense of common citizenship and culture; (c) strengthening national integration; and (d) giving greater attention to Western science and technology.

The national organization of education is formed by (a) sharing of responsibility between the governments at the centre and in the states; (b) administering at the national level, state level, district level, and local level; (c) establishing the Indian Educational Service as an all-India service to bring a national perspective to education; (d) forming education tribunals fashioned after administrative tribunals; and (e) giving shape to the national system of education through such institutions as the University Grants Commission, All-India Council for Technical Education, Indian Council of Agricultural Research, Indian Medical Council, National Council of Educational Research and Training, National Institute of Educational Planning and Administration, National Council of Teacher Education, National Council of Adult Education, etc.

It is not surprising that the results have been devastating. National policy has been influenced by the political expediency of conciliating the people and education has been politicized. There is greater and greater dependence on the government bureaucracy. Uniformity has been imposed through common education structure, common school system, common curricular framework, and universal literacy. Deculturation has come about through religious neutrality or secular education. Employment-oriented education has led to the privatization and commercialization of learning, and a colonialism of the English educated urban elites has come into being. Is there a way out of this slavish system? 'Where there is a will there is a way' is the old proverb. India's 'national policy' on education is at the moment geared to horizontal (westward) movement in time. If education is meant to provide an ever greater degree of moral and mental sophistication, it has to develop through vertical movement. Exploration of the vertical dimension with free will and accompanying intellectual responsibility implies a vertical movement from the past to the future. This essay is an invitation to appropriate for ourselves a vertical movement in education. To do that let us go to the sacred city of Kashi on the Ganga, the source from which India's wisdom tradition sprang.

Education in Kashi

Three cities, Rome, Mecca and Kashi (Varanasi or Banaras, as it is also known) need no introduction. So far as the continuity of the classical tradition is concerned, Kashi, the city of light surpasses all the civilizational centres of the world. And yet it is a puzzling city, a city which has an infinite capacity to absorb the most beauteous and bear the most repulsive things. It is like Shiva the Nilakantha, the supreme deity of the city.

Several centuries before Christ, Ajatsatru, the king of Kashi, defeated the Brahman Gargya in the shastrartha (debate on scriptural matters), and Gautam the Buddha turned here in Isipatan (modern Sarnath) the wheel of his dharma. In course of time Kashi grew into a great seat of learning, surpassing Takshashila and all other educational centres of India. Huien-Tsang was struck by the scholarship and devotion of the Brahman students and the Jain and Buddhist ascetics of Kashi in the seventh century. Earlier, in the fifth century, Fa-Hein noted that "here in this great city there were thirty monasteries and about three hundred Buddhist priests, and the Hindus had about one hundred temples with ten thousand sectaries and their principal God was Maheshwara whose copper image was a hundred feet high". The ancient travelogues also indicate that Brahman, Jain and Buddhist scholars lived in harmony while engaged in their pursuits of learning.

In later times Kashi gained a high reputation and attracted scholars from far and near. It became famous for the assembly of the pandits, which organized shastrartha on disputed matters of social importance. Any decision arrived at by the learned assembly of Kashi was accepted as the norm by the entire Hindu community. The chief source of the Banaras School of Law, one of the five recognized schools of Hindu law, was Vijnaneshvara, the author of the Mitakshara of the twelfth century. Bernier described in detail the methods of study of the pandits of Kashi in 1667. When Ward visited Kashi in 1917 he found forty-eight teachers instructing 893 in the Vedas alone, and seventeen teaching 218 disciples the mysteries of Panini's grammar.

The lamp of Sanskrit learning was kept alive in Kashi for a long time, particularly by the Maharashtra and Kannada Brahman families who migrated to the city at the beginning of the sixteenth century. These families remained at the helm of Sanskrit scholarship for no less than three centuries; later the pandits of Mithila and Bengal came to their support.

Besides being the leading centre for the study of religion, philosophy, medical sciences and astrology, Kashi enjoyed a reputation for its handicrafts and commerce even during the pre-Buddhist period. Banarasi silk fabrics were exported to all parts of India. It was famous for perfumes, scented oil, ivory works, and sculpture. Its contributions to Indian vocal music are the melodious thumri, dadra and tappa.

Education in ancient Kashi, as elsewhere in the India of that time, was a self-organizing system. Generally speaking, the schools had no buildings of their own.

Temples, private buildings donated by pious men, the houses of teachers, and even the ghats on the Ganga, were the glorious centres of learning. Of the teachers, the majority were Brahmans who taught more through a sense of righteousness rather than by consideration of economic gains. The pupils did not race through examinations to pick up lucrative jobs. As the outcome of a humanistic aspiration, education was considered at that time a life-long pursuit. Freedom in academic life was so firm that even the strongest ruler could not tamper with education. Education in the arts was largely informal and orally transmitted within hereditary, non-competitive, monopolistic, endogamous groups. However, this self-organizing system declined during the long period of changing political patterns.

The medieval rulers remained indifferent to India's integrated religious and metaphysical system of education. In the beginning, like their pandit brethren, the ulemas also enjoyed intellectual freedom. But as Islam's earlier democracy was replaced by authoritarianism, Muslim education became dogmatic and inward-looking. Hindus and Muslims built separate centres of learning. However, as Persian became the official language of administration and justice, many Hindus had to learn Persian by force of circumstance.

And yet Kashi provided sufficient incentives to all those who made it their home: artists, craftsmen, philosophers, traders and ordinary persons, regardless of their creed and caste. It did not permit a sectarian outlook to prevail upon the cultivation of excellence. Or else Babu Miyan, a Muslim, would not have been a specialist in the Hindu shilpashastra; Samsuddin, another Muslim, would not have been a pandit in Hindu astrology; Ulfatbai, a Muslim lady, would not have made an endowment for the playing of the shahanai by Muslim musicians in the temple of Vishwanath; and Muslim weavers would not have made auspicious wedding garments for Hindu ladies.

Kashi holds people by generating a deep sense of attachment, which is not restricted to Hindus alone. The illustrious Iranian poet Sheikh Ali Hazeen did not like to leave Kashi for anything, and wanted that even after his death his body should lie in this holy city of light where every scholar is treated like gods Rama and Lakshmana:

az banaras na ravam, mabadi-am ast een ja;

har barahman-pisaraya lachhaman-o-ram asta een ja.

The Sheikh further noted: "The people of Banaras admired and respected me and my talents in the like manner and that is what I longed for during all these roamings from Ispahan, my native place, to Banaras. Hence I feel satisfied to remain in Banaras till death". He died in 1180 and was buried in the Fatman of Banaras, as desired by him.

European colonization initiated the final death blow to the self-organizing system of Kashi's intellectual tradition. With the establishment of the Kashi Raj in 1725 and the control of the East India Company in 1757, a new educational system began to grow. Initially the British Company was reluctant to take responsibility for education. But later, in 1813, it felt that "it must educate the sons of influential Indians for higher posts under the government and thereby win the confidence of the upper classes and consolidate its rule in India".

The Banaras Government Sanskrit College owed its establishment to this political consideration. It was founded in 1791 by Jonathan Duncan, Resident of Banaras. In 1813, a Persian class was started in this Sanskrit college to teach those students of Hindu law who wished to be appointed pandits in the British courts; but not a single pandit ever availed of this opportunity. So in 1833 the Persian class was temporarily suspended. In 1841 it was begun again under the orders of the Governor-General; but the situation remained the same, and in 1844 the Persian class was finally removed to the English College, which had been started in 1830 under the title of the Banaras English Seminary or the Banaras Government School. Jayanarain Ghosal, a native Bengali, established here the first English school in 1817, and opened the door for English education. Christian missionaries began to operate through educational programmes with a view to capturing the intelligentsia of Kashi. This led to the establishment of the Church Missionary Society in 1888.

From enslavement and dispossession sprang a new consciousness, supported by large-hearted Europeans. In 1897, Mrs. Annie Besant founded the Hindu College and established the Theosophical Society to "revitalize the faith in Upanisadic Hinduism among those who were enamoured of English education and Western culture". While Sanskrit education in the Government College was christianizing and transforming and the British administration was patronizing the pandits, a number of scholars became interested in the development of Hindi. The Nagri Pracharani Sabha was founded in 1893.

Towards the powerful wave of Gandhi's freedom movement the intellectuals of Kashi were divided into two groups. Most pandits opposed Gandhi's attitude towards Brahmanic orthodoxy; others wholeheartedly supported his liberalism and nationalism. The establishment of the Bharat Dharma Mahamandal in 1902 and the foundation of the Syadbad Mahavidyala in 1905 were due to the response of the orthodox tradition. Mahamana Pandit Madan Mohan Malaviya, a liberal Brahman who wanted to instil the spirit of nationalism among the youth of the country through modern educational system, established the Banaras Hindu University in 1909. Further, the Mahamana wanted students to be firmly entrenched in the glorious tradition of this country, which obviously meant to him the Sanatani Varnashrama Dharma — the eternal order of human life visualized in the Hindu tradition. The nationalists, who did not approve of his attitude toward the Varnashrama order, established yet another educational institution. In 1920 the Kashi Vidyapeetha was founded by Mahatma Gandhi and began to operate as a national school for revolutionaries and freedom-fighters. Those who joined the Vidyapeetha were largely anti-Brahmans. The clash of ideologies came to the fore when the nationalists enrolled members of non-Brahman castes and Muslims for a course leading to a diploma called 'Shastri', a title derived from the Sanskrit system of learning, traditionally held by Brahmans. In imitation of the modern university system, the Vidyapeetha, having given up the title of 'Shastri', now awards bachelor's and master's degrees.

Although Kashi today is an important city enjoying all the benefits of modernization that are normally available to any other city of this size and resources in India, it has a unique way of modernizing its tradition. This is reflected in the formation and functioning of its three universities and three temples of Vishwanath — the presiding God of this sacred city — each symbolizing a cultural type. The Varanaseya Sanskrit University and the new Vishwanath temple, founded by Swami Karptrijee, represent the orthodox Brahmanic tradition; the Kashi Vidyapeetha and the golden temple of Vishwanath, managed by the state government, represent the liberal tradition; and the Banaras Hindu University with its magnificent temple of God Vishwanath and teaching of modern science and technology, represents the most modern view of tradition. However, the common factor which binds all these three cultural types together is the unshakable trust in tradition.

The experience of an experiment may perhaps be best expressed through the analogy of drama. As previously indicated, the context of education presents itself at the most magnificent theatre of Kashi; its text draws upon a humanistic appreciation of tradition having a universal significance; its melodies and notes produce a new life and freedom; and its joys proceed from truth and goodness.

8

The Sutradhar of an Experiment

On 1 November 1972 a Foundation was formed in Kashi in memory of Professor Nirmal Kumar Bose, the famous Gandhian anthropologist who had the fortune of serving Gandhi for several months in Noakhali in 1946-47 as his Bengali interpreter and private secretary. The Bose Foundation started with the objectives of promoting and propagating such elements of cultural tradition as are helpful to the development of Indian society in particular and to the cultivation and progress of a peaceful and loving coexistence of human societies in general, carrying on both applied and fundamental research in cultural anthropology, evolving an appropriate methodology for the studies of complex societies, and training researchers in the field of cultural anthropology. To begin with, the Foundation devoted considerable effort to examining the various elements of Kashi's cultural tradition, namely ascetics, pandits, temples, rituals and pilgrimage. This was followed by applied anthropological research on the status of widows and the problem of indebtedness among the scavengers of Kashi.

In October 1978 the Bose Foundation was made responsible for the Annapurna Shikshalaya, a social welfare trust located in Kashi at Gauriganj. The person who entrusted the Foundation with this responsibility was the late Professor Asit Bhattacharya, a student of Nirmal Bose and a great-grandson of Sarojini Devi who had founded the Shikshalaya. The Foundation felt that this good fortune of having been invited to perform a certain role in social work would not have come without the grace of guru and God. Nirmal Bose, in whose memory it was formed, was always concerned with making human beings. He was an ally in the struggle for freedom and his true terms of reference were the poor. In 1930 he organized a Khadi Sangha in a slum at the outskirts of Bolpur town located about 2 km away from Rabindranath Tagore's Shantiniketan and Visva Bharati. He set up there Shikhagar, a night school for adults of the poor 'untouchables' — the Muchi, Hadi and Bauri castes. Following Bose's ideology and experiment in social reconstruction, the Foundation found it fit to accept the new responsibility.

When the Annapurna Shikshalaya was handed over to the Foundation, it was in a moribund state with two widows, a lifeless primary school for children, and a loom for weaving carpets from tattered clothes. To streamline its activities, the Foundation reorganized itself into three departments. The old school was named Sarojini Vidyakendra after the name of the founder of the Shikshalaya, and the craft centre was called Kuntala Shilpakendra, after Kuntala Devi, the eldest grand-daughter of Sarojini Devi and the mother of Asit Bhattacharya. The school and the craft centre were placed under the charge of Shiva Shankar Dube and Ram Lakhan Maurya, two men of glorious light, the sutradhars who were earlier involved in the study of widows and scavengers of Kashi. The Bose Research Centre continued its academic activities as before.

The Theatre

In its early enterprise the Foundation had opened the whole panorama of Kashi. With the eye of a team of researchers it had seen a light within Kashi: a city of cultural pluralism, a city of bhoga and moksha — materiality and spirituality — a city of affluence and grinding poverty, a city with two major religions and three cultures, and a city where the sacred was in tune with the secular. The studies of widows and scavengers let it traverse the area of darkness. The Foundation was now called upon to rekindle a 'power for better things'.

Gauriganj is a magnificent complex of multiple cultures, sheltering at least thirty-seven Hindu castes and fifteen Muslim endogamous groups. Besides the first three varnas — Brahman, Kshatriya and Vaishya — there are castes of silk weavers, dyers of clothes, potters, ironsmiths, goldsmiths, tinkers and braziers, barbers, grocers, fowlers and hunters, palanquin-bearers, milkmen, washermen, cultivators and sellers of green vegetables, tavern-keepers and wine-merchants, manufacturers of salt, cobblers, shahanai players, and those who prepare and sell cups made of leaves. Most of these caste groups have now given up their traditional callings. There are only a few wealthy individuals; all others live in abject poverty.

The 'hub' of Gauriganj, a riot-prone area, is surrounded by a number of culturally significant shrines such as the cremation ghat, where in the Age of Truth (satayuga) the truthful king Harishchandra had to serve the master of the crematorium; the Shivala Imambara, where Muharram, a Muslim occasion of sorrow, is observed; the Assi ghat, where the lilas of Rama and Krishna are performed; the Tulasi ghat, where the great saint Tulasidas composed his celebrated Ramacharitamanas; the Durgakunda, where fairs are held in honour of the Mother Goddess; the Krimikunda, the pond of the worms, where healing and fertility rites are performed; the Lolarkakunda, where the 'Trembling Sun' is worshipped, and several other springs associated with legends and myths of therapeutical value. Here are located countless shrines of gods, the birthplace of the Jain tirthankaras, Sikh gurudwaras, mosques and tombs, cathedrals and missions, and a very large number of mathas and akharas of ascetics.

This southern sector of the city, according to the Padma Purana, is Kedara Khanda, the third segment of Kashikshetra. In the popular oral tradition the southern zone is called Shiva Kashi. In the human domain it is a meeting ground for Hindus and Muslims, north Indians and south Indians, ascetics and pandits, rich and poor, rural and urban, traditional and modern, and so on. This is the area where, for the first time, modern educational institutions were founded — the first English school, the first Hindu college, the first modern university, the first theological school for Jainism, and the first Arabic university. It is also the breeding ground for indigenous pathashalas, madarassahs and private modern schools.

Making an experiment in education in such a magnificent theatre of culture was a test of intellectual powers and patience. We had both advantages and disadvantages. The greatest advantage was easy access to the visual text of a living cultural tradition with its constant newness. The disadvantage was of facing iconoclasts of the Indian tradition who dogmatically affirm Western education. Though in thought this kind of challenge may appear destructive, in reality it is constructive. It makes differences between normal and abnormal conditions in education explainable; it provides for enduring contemplation; and it ultimately leads all activities to the carried end.

It is with this urge that the old school at the Annapurna Shikshalaya was directed to a new life and new rhyme. The new venture was envisioned as a 'lab school' alive with the ideas of making experiments with swaraj in education, developing aesthetic sensibility and cross-cultural understanding, evolving new perspectives and new methods in primary education, and making the school a self-organizing, self-supporting, non-commercial, non-governmental institution.

The Text

Equally important is the text of the drama, which its activities follow. Preparation of the text developed sequentially, designing new styles within the circle of a tradition. Five questions, all of which call for explanation, were raised to review the grounds of education.

From the depth of Kashi's cultural consciousness arose the first fundamental question. What is education? In traditional words, education is vinaya, the virtue of humility, which is the gateway to all other virtues; vinaya is the attribute of a perfect person; education is the light of the soul which is other than the body; a place where that light does not shine is not an educational institution; 'interior education' is real, complete in itself; 'exterior education' is illusory, incomplete, though useful in worldly life.

From the structural framework of the theatre arose the next question. Are these non-literate weavers, potters, ironsmiths, musicians and all the rest, uneducated? Knowing that their works of art and feelings of humanity are genuine and overwhelming, they cannot be called uneducated. Five hundred years ago Kabir, a weaver of Kashi's spirituality, had struck at book learning:

The Opening Scene

The sutradhar's movement in time began with chaos and despair. Within a few days of taking over the Shikshalaya opposition came from the two inmates. A group of Bengali women staged an angry protest. Not so surprisingly, the woman who used to clean the premises led the demonstration. In the midst of utter confusion the new management began its mission — 'the education of heart'. However, much of what happened in the beginning ultimately served as a shock absorber.

All the teachers of the old school were Bengali. They were retained but were told that no amount of dry discipline would do the children much good. In those days Muslim and Harijan children were not allowed to use the toilet, which was meant exclusively for the inmates and teachers. This was changed forthwith. Muslim girls above eight years used to attend the school in burkah (veils). They were asked to give up the veils within the school premises. The response was encouraging. After a few months no one came with the burkah. The attendant of the school was an old lady who had been given a low position. The headmistress of the school, a suchibai (purity-pollution maniac), treated her as an untouchable even though she was a Bengali Brahman. When the school attendant was invited to inaugurate the Independence Day celebration everybody present was shocked. This kind of radical change subsequently caused a silent stir inside the Shikshalaya.

A few months later there was a theft in the premises. What the thieves left behind was more dreadful than the loss of property: the footprints of a child followed by larger ones. After some time, another theft occurred. The drunkards, the gamblers and the goondas began to play their role of villain. At this stage a suggestion came from one of the members of the Bose Foundation that reformative measures should be initiated first to better the people of the locality whose children were to be educated in the new school. The sutradhar responded that the results of the reform would be seen only after two decades, when the children of the school were grown.

The next year, the old teachers left the school en masse without notice. By that time the number of students had sharply declined, and people got the impression that the school was going to be closed down. A wealthy trader in silk fabric came out with the suggestion of opening a madarassah-type school for which a suitable endowment and some two hundred children would be made available to the Foundation. The benevolent proposer was told that the Foundation would be happy to teach Urdu, Arabic or Persian and would also impart religious education in Islam, provided that the children received instructions in the arts, elementary science, mathematics, Hindi and English. This was unacceptable to him. Later he offered the Foundation a plot of land (double the present space) some 4 to 5 km away, a new building, and five lakh rupees as compensation for the campus. He was told that his pious resolution had no value because the objective of the Foundation School was to make education self-organizing and self-supporting and to develop aesthetic sensibility and cross-cultural understanding among both Hindu and Muslim children. He was assured that as soon as the school was firmly directed towards its goal and the neighbouring community became strongly inclined to take up the responsibility of running it without government aid, the Foundation would withdraw and would repeat the experiment in another area of the city.

The Foundation was prepared to brave the worst.

A Kashmiri pandit was staying at the Foundation as a guest scholar. He was working on Kalhana's Rajatarangini. A Persian teacher used to call on him frequently. Their relationship appeared to be normal. But a stage came when the teacher began terrorizing his student because he refused to be converted to Islam and married to a widow. The seventy-year-old pandit had no courage to face death in the present crisis. He left the Foundation in fright.

The air of the city was poisoned by communal bitterness and rancour following the court's verdict on the temple-mosque issue in Ayodhya, politicized by sections of Hindus and Muslims. All educational institutions were ordered to close down. When the Foundation School reopened after a few days, the Muslim children came with black strips on their arms. They did not know why their parents made them wear this colour of sorrow. For these innocents it was a mere fun and fashion. The school was sunk in shame and sorrow. Not a word was uttered on this subject. The bell rang for the prayer meeting. The usual duration of silence was prolonged. In silence the sutradhar and teachers prayed for purging all hearts of communal hatred and ill will. Within no time the Hindu and Muslim children rolled into one and the black strips disappeared completely unnoticed, as the darkness of night is dispelled by the sun.

The Melodies

From chaos and despair emerged new thoughts and activities like melodies in a concert. At the Foundation School swaraj, swadeshi and sarvodaya — the three arts of life and education —

began sounding together in harmony. Swaraj in education means "the self-rule in the management and administration of an educational institution". Most people today feel utterly unable to run a school without a government grant-in-aid. Alternatively they turn the school into a commercial enterprise. If the desire to establish swaraj is genuine the problem will have to be faced boldly, not replacing government rule by the rule of merchants. The teachers who came to the Bose Foundation School merely to earn a living without the spirit of service found it trying.

Many of them left within a few months; many insisted upon applying for a government grant-in-aid; many wanted expansion of classes or grades with a view to increasing income through pupil's fees; others suggested conducting special tutorial classes on extra payment. Nothing of this kind was conceded. The failure of their attempts caused many experienced teachers to leave the Foundation School. Happily, in course of time it was found that some youths from middle-class families developed a fascination for the School, despite the fact that they were barely paid a living wage. The Foundation is proud of having teachers like Rama Lahiri and Rajesh Iyer, who have served it lovingly for more than six years. Freedom, friendship and trust are the strongest bonding factors that give the workers at the Foundation School amazing courage to face collectively the music of life. Looking back, it can be said that the Foundation today demonstrates the ancient idea of teachers teaching for the love of it and receiving the barest maintenance.

The Foundation School has no corpus fund, no annual grant, not even irregular grants from any source. It is run on school fees and royalties on the books published by and for the Foundation. It is not a profit-making venture; it has learnt to live in holy poverty. The fact that it has managed in this manner for over sixteen years strengthens the Foundation's conviction that primary or elementary schools must necessarily be self-organizing and self-supporting. Community and religious trusts could provide a corpus fund for the life of the school. If education means the awakening of consciousness, if the children have the freedom to grow into fine human beings, and if cultural diversities are to be respected, then all primary schools must be managed by those whose children are to be educated. No centralized nation-wide system should operate at this level of education.

Swaraj in education means swadeshi in spirit. In the domain of education swadeshi implies that it is a virtue to remain firmly grounded in the perennial wisdom tradition of one's own culture. Education is essentially a cultural process of making human life efficient and complete. Hence indigenous institutions are the best to impart education at the early stage in life. As Gandhi said, "Swadeshi is not a cult of hatred". Swadeshi spirit in education means the spirit of expansion, not by driving out ideas but by absorbing new ideas without suffering cultural identity crises.

As a research centre, the Foundation receives distinguished scholars — specially anthropologists, sociologists, linguists, philosophers, historians of religion — both Indian and foreign. Their presence has contributed immeasurably to the awakening of the children. For several years the students of the Wisconsin College Year in India Program were affiliated with the Foundation. Their first step on entering into the Foundation was to interact with the children of the School. They practised Hindi on the children and in return widened the perceptions of those who had never seen the world beyond the physical space of Kashi. In this interchange, friendships developed. The children invited them to their homes. Most of the students of the Wisconsin Program studied various aspects of Kashi's cultural traditions. One of them studied the children's traditional games, another worked on the riddles known to the children. Joyce Hubert wrote in 1983 a dissertation based on an anthropological study of the Bose Foundation School. Some of them taught English to the children of classes IV and V. For the last six years the Foundation School has been a training-cum-study centre of the University of Karlstad (Sweden) for its teachers in education. Inger Wiklund, the co-ordinator of this scheme, has been a Visiting Teacher at the Foundation School since 1991. Indian scholars, Gandhian social workers, and religious personalities are frequent visitors to the School. This constant exposure affords a highly refined sense of perception that brings great confidence to the children and ultimately purity in cultural order. It is this way of education that enables the children of the Foundation School to live with the swadeshi spirit in the extraordinary world of ideas.

Swaraj in education aims at sarvodaya — education for all. A votary of true education cannot subscribe to the utilitarian formula of the greatest good of the greatest number. He must strive for the greatest good of all. Every child must be educated enough to observe morality and to attain mastery over its mind and its passions. The Foundation School brings transformation from within tradition; it maintains a high standard of teaching and tries its very best to serve the desire of parents, who demand instruction analogous to that of the modern mission schools or the commercialized public schools. But it does try in its own way to suit the capacity of poor parents. Life at the school is simple. The neighbourhood is poor. The school stands by what is implied in the Gandhian phrases 'Sarvodaya' and 'Antyodaya' – Unto This Last.

The Swadeshi Movement

The Swadeshi and Boycott movements which started with a view to ending the partition of Bengal of 1905, soon became powerful weapons of the struggle for freedom.

Swadeshi means 'of one's own country.

Everyone pledged to boycott the foreign clothes and adopt Swadeshi clothes in their place.

Thus, the movement against the partition of Bengal soon became a Swadeshi movement.

Wearing yellow turbans and red shirts, people marched out of Government schools, colleges and offices in thousands, shouting Vande Mataram, singing national songs, picketing shops or selling Swadeshi goods.

In Calcutta, most of the offices were kept closed and a strike was observed in some jute mills, ironworks and railway workshops. The port of Calcutta was paralyzed for some time.

The movements of Swadeshi and Boycott brought in participation by the common people in the anti-British political activities.

Thus, the partition of Bengal had consequences quite contrary to the ones that the government had expected.

During the struggle for freedom, it meant that people should used goods produced within the country. This would help promote Indian industries and strengthen the nation.

The promotion of Swadeshi was accompanied by the advocacy of Boycott. People were asked to boycott foreign goods.

It was also an effective method of developing patriotism.

It was stressed that the boycott of foreign goods, which were mostly British, would hurt Britain's economic interests and the British government would be forced to accept Indian demands.

The ideas of Swadeshi and boycott, born of the popular feelings in 1905, were not new.

The Americans, the Irish and the Chinese had adopted them before.

Swadeshi, as a purely economic measure for the development of Indian industry, had been preached much earlier by Gopalrao Deshmukh, G V Joshi and M G Ranade of Maharashtra and Rajnarain Bose, Nabagopal Mitra and the Tagore Family of Bengal.

Similarly, Bholanath Chandra had recommended boycott in the 1870's to bring economic pressure on the British public. Tilak had led a full-fledged boycott campaign in 1896.

It was realized that Swadeshi and boycott were complementary.

One would not succeed without the other.

These old concepts got a new impetus from the anti-partition movement.

The seeds of Swadeshi had been sown in Bengal by Ashvinikumar Dutta and Rabindranath Tagore.

Ashwini Kumar Dutt founded the Barisal Swadesh Bandhav, a voluntary organization.

The spirit of Swadeshi wanted the people to educate themselves on national lines.

The scheme of national education had been formulated by Satish Chandra Mukerjee, the editor of the Dawn in 1898.

Rabindranath Tagore repeatedly called for 'Atma Shakti' i.e. self-strength through Swadeshi and national education.

Self-reliance in various fields meant the re-asserting of national dignity, honour and confidence. Further, self-help and constructive work at the village level was envisaged as a means of bringing about the social and economic regeneration of the villages and of reaching the rural masses.

In actual terms this meant social reform and campaigns against evils such as caste oppression, early marriage, the dowry system, consumption of alcohol, etc. Rabindranath Tagore made suggestions for mass contact through Melas and Yatras, and the use of mother tongue in education and political work. Through his Shanti Niketan Ashram, he experimented with new forms of education.

Taking a clue from Tagore's Shantiniketan, the Bengal National College was setup in the vernacular medium with Aurobindo Ghosh as its Principal.

For technical education, the Bengal Technical Institute was set up and An association was established in March 1904 by Jogendra Chandra Ghosh to raise funds for sending students abroad (usually to Japan) to get technical training.

In August 1906, the National Council of Education was established. It consisted of virtually all the distinguished persons of the country at the time.

Its objective was to organize a system of Education Literary, Scientific and Technical-on National lines and under National control from primary to university level.

The chief medium of instruction was to be the vernacular to enable the widest possible reach.

The message of Swadeshi and the boycott of foreign goods soon spread to the rest of the country: Lokamanya Tilak took the movement to different parts of India, especially Poona and Bombay; Ajit Singh and Lala Lajpat Rai spread the Swadeshi message in Punjab and other parts of northern India; Syed Haidar Raza led the movement in Delhi; Rawalpindi, Kangra, Jammu, Multan and Hardwar witnessed active participation in the Swadeshi Movement; Chidambaram Pillai took the movement to the Madras presidency, which was also galvanized by Bipin Chandra Pal's extensive lecture tour.

The Extremists used the methods of Swadeshi and Boycott as the weapons against the Partition of Bengal.

The call for boycott of foreign goods and use of Swadeshi was given at thousands of public meetings all over Bengal and in most of the major cities and towns of India.

Harkishan Lal and Arya -Samajists (College faction) were active in Swadeshi enterprises from the 1890s.

Swadeshi literally means 'of one's own country'.

It implied that people should use goods produced within India itself, as this would promote Indian enterprise and industry and generate patriotism, thus strengthening the nation. B.G. Tilak declared, "Our motto is self reliance not mendicancy".

The Extremists established Samitis or Corps of national volunteers for mass contact.

These Samitis were engaged in a number of activities like physical and moral training of members, social work during famines, epidemics, or religious festivals, preaching the Swadeshi message through journals, pamphlets, speeches, patriotic songs, plays, use of folk media like Jatras, etc.

They also took up the organization of festivals and Melas, of crafts, schools, arbitration courts, and village societies and implementation of the techniques of passive resistance.

The Passive resistance Movement was to mean not only boycott of British goods and schools but of law-courts, municipalities and Legislative Councils; in short, all association with the Government.

By striking at the root of British prestige, its enchantment was to be dispelled. Administration was to be made impossible by an organized refusal to help British commerce to exploit and British bureaucracy to oppress the Indian people.

These twin techniques led to heightening of political activities all over India.

British cloth, sugar, and other goods were boycotted.

Shops selling foreign goods were picketed.

In many places, public burning of foreign cloth took place, which revealed the intensity of popular feelings over the partition issue.

School and college students played an important part in this movement.

The traditionally home-centred women of the urban middle class too joined in processions and picketing.

Women refused to use foreign bangles and glass utensils, students refused to use foreign papers, all classes refused to use foreign cloth, and so on.

Bonfires of British goods were made at different places.

Extremists wanted to extend the Swadeshi and the Boycott Movement from Bengal to the rest of the country. They also wanted to gradually extend the boycott from foreign goods to every form of association or cooperation with the colonial Government. The Moderates wanted to confine the boycott part of the movement to Bengal and were totally opposed to its extension to the Government.

The Bombay Moderates were against the idea of boycott as a general political weapon, though they welcomed Swadeshi.

Gokhale would leave alone the word 'boycott' which implied 'a vindictive desire to injure another' and 'which created unnecessary ill-will against ourselves'. Surendranath Banerjea considered boycott a special measure for fighting an immediate injustice.

He hoped that it would cease to be used when the partition was annulled.

Lajpat Rai was more radical.

The attention of the British, he said, would only be forced to the grievances of Indians by directly threatening their pockets.

To Tilak, Pal and Aurobindo boycott had many implications.

It was an economic pressure on Manchester, a weapon of political agitation against imperialism and a training in self-sufficiency for the attainment of Swaraj.

There was a significant revival of handlooms, silk-weaving and other traditional artisan crafts.

There were fairly successful ventures in porcelain, chrome tanning, matches, and cigarettes.

A number of attempts were made to promote modern industries.

Swadeshi textile mills, match and soap factories, potteries and tanneries sprouted up everywhere.

Acharya P C Ray set up his Bengal Chemicals Factory, which became famous in a very short time.

Over Rs. 1,800,000 were raised and the old cotton mill at Serampur was purchased, extended and renamed as the Banga Lakshmi Cotton Mills in August 1906.

A swadeshi Weaving Company was formed at Poona.

Chidambaran Pillai started the 'Swadeshi Steam Navigation Company' at Tuticorin on the east coast of the Madras Province in 19.

The 'Tata Iron and Steel Company' was founded in 1907.

The entire capital of this Company, which had refused all Government and foreign help, was subscribed by Indians within three months.

Tilak and Tagore helped to setup Swadeshi Cooperative Stores.

Many Zamindars and merchants joined hands with political leaders to found banks, insurance companies and shops.

For example, The Bengal National Bank was started to finance Indian enterprise.

The contribution of the Swadeshi movement was most marked in the cultural sphere.

A new type of nationalist poetry, prose and journalism, surcharged with passion and filled with idealism, was born.

The patriotic songs composed at that time by Rabindra Nath Tagore, Rajani Kant Sen, Durjendralal Ray, Mukunda Das, Syed Abu Muhammad, and others later became the moving spirit for nationalists of all views-revolutionary, Gandhian, or Communists- and are still popular.

Tagore's Amar Sonar Bangla later inspired the liberation struggle of Bangladesh and was adopted as its National anthem in 1971.

Political journalism, which resulted from the Swadeshi and national movements produced some classic testaments on freedom, liberty and Self-reliance.

Jagadish Chandra Bose

Sir Jagadish Chandra Bose CSI CIE FRS (November 30, 1858 – November 23, 1937) born in a Bengali Hindu Kayasth family was a polymath: a physicist, biologist, botanist, archaeologist, and writer of science fiction. He pioneered the investigation of radio and microwave optics, made very significant contributions to plant science, and laid the foundations of experimental science in the Indian subcontinent. He is considered one of the fathers of radio science, and is also considered the father of Bengali science fiction. He was the first person from the Indian subcontinent to get a US patent, in 1904.

Born during the British Raj, Bose graduated from St. Xavier's College, Calcutta. He then went to the University of London to study medicine, but could not complete his studies due to health problems. He returned to India and joined the Presidency College of University of Calcutta as a Professor of Physics. There, despite racial discrimination and a lack of funding and equipment, Bose carried on his scientific research. He made remarkable progress in his research of remote wireless signalling and was the first to use semiconductor junctions to detect radio signals. However, instead of trying to gain commercial benefit from this invention Bose made his inventions public in order to allow others to develop on his research. Subsequently, he made some pioneering discoveries in plant physiology. He used his own invention, the crescograph, to measure plant response to various stimuli, and thereby scientifically proved parallelism between animal and plant tissues. Although Bose filed for a patent for one of his inventions due to peer pressure, his reluctance to any form of patenting was well known. He is being recognised for many of his contributions to modern science.

Early Life and Education

Bose was born in Munshiganj District in Bengal (now in Bangladesh) on November 30, 1858. His father, Bhagawan Chandra Bose, was a Brahmo and leader of the Brahmo Samaj and worked as a deputy magistrate/assistant commissioner in Faridpur, Bardhaman and other places. His family hailed from the village Rarikhal, Bikrampur, in the current day Munshiganj District of Bangladesh.

Bose's education started in a vernacular school, because his father believed that one must know one's own mother tongue before beginning English, and that one should know also one's own people. Speaking at the Bikrampur Conference in 1915, Bose said:

"At that time, sending children to English schools was an aristocratic status symbol. In the vernacular school, to which I was sent, the son of the Muslim attendant of my father sat on my right side, and the son of a fisherman sat on my left. They were my playmates. I listened spellbound to their stories of birds, animals and aquatic creatures. Perhaps these stories created in my mind a keen interest in investigating the workings of Nature. When I returned home from school accompanied by my school fellows, my mother welcomed and fed all of us without discrimination.

Although she was an orthodox old fashioned lady, she never considered herself guilty of impiety by treating these 'untouchables' as her own children. It was because of my childhood friendship with them that I could never feel that there were 'creatures' who might be labelled 'low-caste'. I never realised that there existed a 'problem' common to the two communities, Hindus and Muslims."

Bose joined the Hare School in 1869 and then St. Xavier's School at Kolkata. In 1875, he passed the Entrance Examination (equivalent to school graduation) of University of Calcutta and was admitted to St. Xavier's College, Calcutta. At St. Xavier's, Bose came in contact with Jesuit Father Eugene Lafont, who played a significant role in developing his interest to natural science. He received a bachelor's degree from University of Calcutta in 1879.

Bose wanted to go to England to compete for the Indian Civil Service. However, his father, a civil servant himself, cancelled the plan. He wished his son to be a scholar, who would "rule nobody but himself." Bose went to England to study Medicine at the University of London. However, he had to quit because of ill health. The odour in the dissection rooms is also said to have exacerbated his illness.

Through the recommendation of Anand Mohan, his brother-in-law (sister's husband) and the first Indian wrangler, he secured admission in Christ's College, Cambridge to study Natural Science. He received the Natural Science Tripos from the University of Cambridge and a BSc from the University of London in 1884.

Among Bose's teachers at Cambridge were Lord Rayleigh, Michael Foster, James Dewar, Francis Darwin, Francis Balfour, and Sidney Vines. At the time when Bose was a student at Cambridge, Prafulla Chandra Roy was a student at Edinburgh. They met in London and became intimate friends.

On the second day of a two-day seminar held on the occasion of 150th anniversary of Jagadish Chandra Bose on 28-29th July at The Asiatic Society, Kolkata Professor Shibaji Raha, Director of the Bose Institute, Kolkata told in his valedictory address that he had personally checked the register of the Cambridge University to confirm the fact that in addition to Tripos he received an M.A. as well from it in 1884.

Joining Presidency College

Bose returned to India in 1885, carrying a letter from Fawcett, the economist to Lord Ripon, Viceroy of India. On Lord Ripon's request Sir Alfred Croft, the Director of Public Instruction, appointed Bose officiating professor of physics in Presidency College. The principal, C. H. Tawney, protested against the appointment but had to accept it.

Bose was not provided with facilities for research. On the contrary, he was a 'victim of racialism' with regard to his salary. In those days, an Indian professor was paid Rs. 200 per month, while his European counterpart received Rs. 300 per month. Since Bose was officiating, he was offered a salary of only Rs. 100 per month. With remarkable sense of self respect and national pride he decided on a new form of protest. Bose refused to accept the salary cheque. In fact, he continued his teaching assignment for three years without accepting any salary. Finally both the Director of Public Instruction and the Principal of the Presidency College fully realised the value of Bose's skill in teaching and also his lofty character. As a result his appointment was made permanent with retrospective effect. He was given the full salary for the previous three years in a lump sum. Presidency College lacked a proper laboratory. Bose had to conduct his research in a small 24 square foot room. He devised equipment for the research with the help of one untrained tinsmith. Sister Nivedita wrote, "I was horrified to find the way in which a great worker could be subjected to continuous annoyance and petty difficulties ... The college routine was made as arduous as possible for him, so that he could not have the time he needed for investigation." After his daily grind, which he of course performed with great conscientiousness, he carried out his research far into the night, in a small room in his college.

Moreover, the policy of the British government for its colonies was not conducive to attempts at original research. Bose spent his hard-earned money for making experimental equipment. Within a decade of his joining Presidency College, he emerged a pioneer in the incipient research field of wireless waves.

Abanindranath Tagore

Abanindranath Tagore (August 7, 1871-December 5, 1951), was the principal artist of the Bengal school and the first major exponent of swadeshi values in Indian art. He was also a noted writer. Tagore sought to modernize Mughal and Rajput styles in order to counter the influence of Western models of art, as taught in Art Schools under the British Raj. Such was the success of Tagore's work that it was eventually accepted and promoted as a national Indian style within British art institutions.

Abanindranath Tagore was born in Jorasanko, Kolkata to Gunendranath Tagore. His grandfather was Girindranath Tagore,the second son of "Prince' Dwarkanath Tagore. He is a member of the distinguished Tagore family, and a nephew of the poet Rabindranath Tagore. His grandfather and his elder brother Gaganendranath Tagore were also artists.

Tagore learned art when studying at Sanskrit college in the 1880s. In 1889 he married Suhasini Devi, daughter of Bhujagendra Bhusan Chatterjee, a descendant of Prasanna Coomar Tagore. At this time he left the Sanskrit College after nine years of study and studied English as a special student at St. Xavier's College, which he attended for about a year and a half.

He had a sister Sunayani Devi. His great granddaughter is actress, Sharmila Tagore.

Painting Career

In the early 1890s several illustrations were published in Sadhana magazine, and in Chitrangada, and other works by Rabindranath Tagore. He also illustrated his own books. About the year 1897 he took lessons from the Vice-Principal of the Calcutta Government School of Art, studying in the traditional European academic manner, learning the full range of techniques, but with a particular interest in watercolour. At this time he began to come under the influence of Mughal art, making a number of works based on the life of Krishna in a Mughal-influenced style. After meeting E.B. Havell, Tagore worked with him to revitalise and redefine art teaching at the Calcutta School of art, a project also supported by his brother Gaganendranath, who set up the Indian Society of Oriental Art.

Later Career

Abanindranath Tagore believed that Western art was "materialistic" in character, and that India needed to return to its own traditions in order to recover spiritual values. Despite its Indocentric nationalism, this view was already commonplace within British art of the time, stemming from the ideas of the Pre-Raphaelites. Tagore's work also shows the influence of Whistler's Aestheticism. Partly for this reason many British arts administrators were sympathetic to such ideas, especially as Hindu philosophy was becoming increasingly influential in the West following the spread of the Theosophy movement. Tagore believed that Indian traditions could be adapted to express these new values, and to promote a progressive Indian national culture.

With the success of Tagore's ideas, he came into contact with other Asian artists whose work was comparable to his own. In his later work, he began to incorporate elements of Chinese and Japanese calligraphic traditions into his art, seeking to construct a model for a modern pan-Asian artistic tradition which would merge the common aspects of Eastern spiritual and artistic culture.

His close students included Nandalal Bose, Surendranath Ganguly, Asit Kumar Haldar, Sarada Ukil, Kshitindranath Majumdar, Samarendranath Gupta, Mukul Dey, K. Venkatappa, Jamini Roy, Ranada Ukil and Kalipada Ghoshal.

For Abanindranath, the house he grew up in (5 Dwarakanath Tagore Lane) and its companion house (6 Dwarakanath Tagore Lane) connected two cultural worlds — 'white town' (where the British colonisers lived) and 'black town' (where the natives lived). According to architectural historian Swati Chattopadhay, Abanindranath "used the Bengali meaning of the word, Jorasanko — 'double bridge' to develop this idea in the form of a mythical map of the city. The map is, indeed, not of Calcutta, but an imaginary city, Halisahar, and is the central guide in a children's story Putur Boi (Putu's Book). The nineteenth-century place names of Calcutta, however, appear on this map, thus suggesting we read this imaginary city with the colonial city as a frame of reference. The map uses the structure of a board game—golokdham—and shows a city divided along a main artery; on one side a lion-gate leads to the Lal-Dighi in the middle of which is the 'white island.'

The publication of Rabanindrath Tagore's Gitanjali in English brought the Tagore family international renown, which helped to make Abanindranath's artistic projects better known in the west.

He contributed significantly to the Bengali literature beside his devotion towards painting. He was also a great teacher. He taught painting in his own style.

Nandalal Bose

Nandalal Bose (December 3, 1883 – April 16, 1966) was a noted Indian painter of Bengal school of art.

A foremost pupil of Abanindranath Tagore, a pioneer of the school, he started with "Indian style" of painting, before blazing off a alternative style at the Kala Bhawan, Shanti Niketan, eventually becoming its principal in 1922. He was influenced by the Tagore family and the murals of Ajanta, his classic works include paintings of scenes from Indian mythologies, women, and village life.

Today, his paintings are considered among India's best modern paintings by many critics..

In 1976, the Archaeological Survey of India, Department of Culture, Govt. of India declared his works of amongst the "nine artists", whose work "not being antiquities, were to be hence forth considered to be 'art treasures'.

Early Life

Nandalal Bose was born in Bihar, India.

Career

Nandalal Bose as a young artist was deeply influenced by the murals of Ajanta, already part of a circle of artists and writers who sought to revive classical Indian culture.

To mark the 1930 occasion of Gandhi's arrest for protesting the British tax on salt, Bose created a black on white linocut print of Gandhi walking with a staff. It became the iconic image for the nonviolent movement.

He was also famously asked by Jawaharlal Nehru to sketch the emblems for the Government of India's awards, including the Bharat Ratna and the Padmashri.

His genius and original style were recognized by famous artists and art critics like Gaganendranath Tagore, Ananda Coomaraswamy and O.C.Ganguli. These lovers of art felt that objective criticism was necessary for the development of painting and founded the Indian Society of Oriental Art.

He became principal of the Kala Bhavan (Art Department) at Santiniketan in 1922.

He died on April, the 16th 1966, in Calcutta.

Students

Some of his illustrious students are Pratima Thakur, Benode Behari Mukherjee, Ramkinkar Baiz, Jahar Dasgupta and Sabita Thakur.

Honours and Awards

In 1954, Nandalal Bose himself received the award of 'Padma Vibhushan'. Nandalal Bose was awarded a prize of Rs. 500 at the first art exhibition organized by it in 1908 CE for his painting *Shiva-Sati*. In 1956 CE, he became the second artist to be elected Fellow of the Lalit Kala Akademi, India's National Academy of Art.

Several universities conferred honorary Doctorates on him. Vishvabharati University honoured him by conferring on him the title of 'Deshikottama'. The Academy of Fine Arts in Calcutta honoured Nandalal with the Silver Jubilee Medal. The Tagore Birth Centenary Medal was awarded to Nandalal Bose in 1965 CE by the Asiatic Society of Bengal.

Dakshinaranjan Mitra Majumder

Dakshinaranjan Mitra Majumdar (1877-1957) was a celebrated Indian writer in Bengali of fairy tales and children's literature. He was born at Ulail in Dhaka district of Bengal province in British India (now Manikganj District of Bangladesh). His major contribution to Bengali literature was the collection and compilation of Bengali folk and fairy tales in four volumes-*Thakurmar Jhuli* (Grandmother's Bag of Tales), *Thakurdadar Jhuli* (Grandfather's Bag of Tales), *Thandidir Thale* (Maternal-Grandmother's Bag of Tales) and *Dadamashayer Thale* (Maternal-Grandfather's Bag of Tales).

V. O. Chidambaram Pillai

V. O. Chidambaram Pillai, popularly known by his initials, V.O.C. (spelt Vaa. Oo.Ce in Tamil), was an Indian freedom fighter born on 5 September 1872 in Ottapidaram, Tuticorin district of Tamil Nadu State of India. He was a prominent lawyer, and a trade union leader. He gets credit for launching *the first indigenous Indian shipping service* between Tuticorin and Colombo with the Swadeshi Steam Navigation Company, competing against British ships. He was an Indian National Congress (INC) member, later charged with sedition by the British government and sentenced to life imprisonment; his barrister license was stripped.

Early days

Vulaganathan Ottapidaaram Chidambaram Pillai or else V.O.C. was born on 5 September 1872 to an eminent lawyer Vulaganathan Pillai and Paramyee in Ottapidaram, Tuticorin district of Tamil Nadu State in India. After completing schooling in Ottapidaram and Tirunelveli, he worked for a few years in the Ottapidaram district administrative office. Later following his fathers footsteps he completed law.

Days as a Lawyer

As a lawyer he often pleaded for the poor, at times appearing against his father, who appeared for the affluent. Among his notable cases, he proved corruption charges on three sub-magistrates. In the Kulasekaranallur Asari case he proved innocence for the accused.

Entry into Politics

Background

In the 1890s and 1900s India's independence movement and the Swadeshi movement, initiated by Bal Gangadhar Tilak and Lala Lajpat Rai of Indian National Congress (INC), were at their peak. Mahatma Gandhi was yet to land in India. They were against the British Imperial coercion of trade, which was damaging traditional Indian industries and the communities dependent on them. This is the essence of the Swadeshi movement. In Madras Presidency the Independence movement was championed by the likes of Subramanya Siva, the poet Subramanya Bharathi, and Aurobindo Gosh later to be joined by V.O.C. He entered politics in 1905 following the partition of Bengal, joining the Indian National Congress and taking a hardliner stand. He also presided at the Salem District Congress session.

Shipping Company

V.O.C., drawing inspiration from Ramakrishnananda, a disciple of Sri Ramakrishna, resorted to Swadeshi work. Following requests by local citizens, he initiated steps to break the monopoly of British shipping in the coastal trade with Ceylon.

On 12 November 1906, V.O.C. formed the Swadeshi Steam Navigation Company, by purchasing two steamships 'S.S.Gaelia' and 'S.S.Lawoe', thanks to the assistance and support of Lokamanya Bal Gangadhar Tilak and Aurobindo Ghose. The ships commenced regular service between Tuticorin and Colombo (Srilanka), against the opposition of the British traders and the Imperial Government. V.O.C. was thus laying the foundation for a comprehensive shipping industry in the country, more than just a commercial venture.

Until then the commerce between Tuticorin and Colombo was a monopoly enjoyed by the British India Steam Navigation Company (BISN). This was later to be merged with P&O Lines and its Tuticorin agents, A.& F. Harvey.

The British had assumed the Indian venture would collapse like a house of cards, but soon found the Indian company to be a formidable challenge. To thwart the new Indian company they resorted to the monopolistic trade practice of reducing the fare per trip to Re.1 (16 annas) per head. Swadeshi company responded by offering a fare of Re.0.5 (8 Annas). The British company went further by offering a free trip to the passengers plus a free umbrella, which had 'S.S.Gaelia' and 'S.S.Lawoe' running nearly empty. By 1909 the company was heading towards bankruptcy.

Conflict with the British

To widen the swadeshi base and to create awareness of British Imperialism V.O.C. became instrumental in mobilising the workers of Coral Mills (also managed by A. & F. Harvey) (now part of Madura Coats) in Tirunelveli. This brought him into increasing conflict with the British Raj. On 12 March 1908, he was arrested on charges of sedition and for two days, Tirunelveli and Tuticorin witnessed unprecedented violence, quelled only by shooting four people to death (a Muslim, a Dalit, a baker and a Hindu temple priest). Punitive police forces were brought in from neighbouring districts.

The Press

But newspapers had taken note of V.O.C. Sri Aurobindo's nationalist Bengali newspaper *Bande Mataram* (spelt and pronounced as Bonde Matorom in the Bengali language) acclaimed him (March 27, 1908) with "Well Done, Chidambaram". Apart from the Madras press, Anand Bazaar Patrika from Kolkata

(Calcutta) carried reports of his prosecution every day. Funds were raised for his defence not only in India but also by the Indians in South Africa.

Trial

Poet Subramanya Bharathi and Subramanya Siva too appeared in the court for questioning for the case instituted against V.O.C. He was charged with sedition and a sentence of two life imprisonments (in effect 40 years) was imposed. He was confined in the Central Prison, Coimbatore (from 9 July 1908 to 1 December 1910). Court sentence may be seen as a reflection of the fear the British had of V.O.C. and their need to contain the rebellion and be sure that others would not follow in Chidambaram Pillai's footsteps.

Confinement in Prison

It is to be noted that Chidambaram Pillai was not treated as a 'political prisoner', nor was the sentence 'simple imprisonment', he was rather treated as a convict sentenced to life imprisonment and required to do hard labour. V.O.C. was in fact subjected to inhumane torture, which took a heavy toll on his health. The noted historian and Tamil scholar, R. A. Padmanabhan, would later note in his works "yoked (in place of Bulls) to the oil press like an animal and made to work it in the cruel hot sun...." Even from prison VOC continued a clandestine correspondence, maintaining a steady stream of petitions going into legal niceties. Later the High Court would reduce his sentence and he was finally released on December 12, 1912.

After his Release

The huge crowds present during his arrest were obviously absent, reminding him of Aurobindo's similar fate upon his release from Uttarpara in 1909 and his famous remark "When I went to jail the whole country was alive with the cry of Bande Mataram... when I came out of jail I listened for that cry, but there was instead a silence... a hush had fallen on the country and men seemed bewildered".

Upon V.O.C.'s release he was not permitted to return to his Tirunelveli district. With his bar license stripped from him he moved to Chennai with his wife and two young sons. To his dismay, the Swadeshi Steam Navigation Company had already been liquidated in 1911, and the ships auctioned to their competitors. V.O.C and his family had lost all their wealth and property in his legal defence. In Madras, almost broke, he continued organising labour welfare organisations. V.O.C. attended the Calcutta Indian National Congress in 1920. He later would quit, but rejoined later.

V.O.C. and Mahatma Gandhi

M.K. Gandhi in 1910s was yet to be known as Mahatma, and V.O.C. carried on a steady stream of correspondence between them (1915-16). They would even once meet in Chennai, but sadly none of their correspondence was published in the 100-volume *Collected Works of Mahatma Gandhi.* In one of the letters Gandhi enquires whether he received the money which he had collected for V.O.C. in South Africa. In another letter V.O.C. expresses unease over an early morning appointment to meet Gandhi, as he explains the unavailability of Tram service at that hour.

Last Days

On hearing V.O.C.'s destitute condition Justice Wallace, the judge who sentenced V.O.C. later being Chief Justice of Madras Presidency, restored his bar license. But V.O.C. spent his last years (1930s) in Kovilpatti heavily in debt, even selling all of his law books for daily survival. V.O.C died on the 18 November 1936 in the Indian National Congress Office at Tuticorin as was his last wish.

Family then and Now

V.O.C. married Valliammai in 1895, who died in 1901 due to complications in delivery. Later he married Meenakshi Ammiar. The couple would have four sons and four daughters. The eldest son Ulaganathan died in childhood. The second son, Arumugam Pillai, contested Ottapidaram in the 1967 Tamil Nadu assembly elections, but lost (as did many other Congress members, including K. Kamaraj). V.O.C.'s third son, Subramaniam, worked for many years in Dinamani (Indian Express group), later in the American Embassy in Chennai. His fourth son, Walleswaren, (referring to the Englishman E.H. Wallace, who first committed his case to the session's court but was instrumental in getting his sanad back) retired working from the Labour welfare department and settled in Dindigul Now settled in Madurai(2009) still alive. All of his daughters were married and several of his descendants live around various places in Chennai.

Scholarly Works

Apart from the above, V.O.C. was an erudite scholar. The autobiography in Tamil verse which he started in prison was completed upon his release in 1912. He also wrote a commentary on the Thirukural and compiled ancient works of Tamil grammar, Tolkappiam. He showed ingenuity in his works of "Meyyaram" and "Meyyarivu", praised for spontaneous style, and earned an indisputable reputation for translations of James Allen's books. He authored a few novels, as well.

Impact Today

V.O.C. was one of the colourful figures in Indian political life. V.O.C. showed the way for organized effort and sacrifice. He finished his major political work by 1908, but died in late 1936, the passion for freedom still raging in his mind till the last moment. He was an erudite scholar in Tamil, a prolific writer, a fiery speaker, a trade union leader of unique calibre and a dauntless freedom fighter.

His life is a story of resistance, strife, struggle, suffering and sacrifice for the cause to which he was committed.

Post Independence Honours

Today his name among people in Tamil Nadu evokes his sufferings in jail and his shipping company. He is aptly called as "Kappal' ottiya Thamizlan ' —the Tamil who drove the ship, and as "Chekkiluththa Chemmal" — a great man who pulled the oil press in jail for the sake of his people.

The Indian Posts & Telegraphs department of India issued a special postage stamp on 5 September 1972, on the occasion of his birth centenary.

A college in Tuticorin is named after V.O.C.

Sivaji Ganesan played the lead role in the 1961 Tamil movie "Kappal' ottiya Thamizlan '. The Public park and the meeting grounds of Coimbatore is named V.O.C. Park (Vaa. Vu.Ce Poonga) and V.O.C. Grounds (Vaa. Vu.Ce Thidal).

The Central Prison in Coimbatore has built a commemorative monument, preserving his Yoke and Oil Grinding stone.

The Bridge connecting Tirunelveli and Palayamkottai over the river Tamaraparani is named V.O.C. Bridge.

The Swadeshi Movement

The partition of Bengal in 1905 had far reaching repercussion and accelerated the pace of freedom movement in India. The event led to the launch of swadeshi movement and boycott of British goods. It also resulted in the split of the Indian National Congress into two factions, the moderates and the extremists and gave birth to revolutionaries clubs and Muslim League. The Partition of Bengal: The province of Bengal consisted of Bengal proper, Bihar and Orissa, with a population of 78 million people. In East Bengal, Muslims were in a majority while Hindus predominated in West Bengal as well as in Bihar and Orissa. Way back in 1896, William Ward, an official had prepared a scheme of partition of Bengal for administrative convenience. But due to financial constraints it was abandoned. The scheme attracted the attention of Viceroy Curzon and he decided to implement it. In February 1904, Curzon toured East Bengal and roped in Nawab Salimullah Khan of Dacca by promising him a loan at nominal interest and the latter succeeded in assembling a huge gathering of Muslims to cheer the Viceroy's plan for a Muslim province. But the Bengali intelligentsia and the Indian nationalists opposed the partition on the ground that it undermined the traditions, history and language of the Bengalis and divide them on the basis of religion. Curzon had admitted during his tour of East Bengal that one object of the partition proposal was to create a Mohammedan province where Islam could be predominate.

The Boycott Movement

The new province of East Bengal was inaugurated on 16th October 1905. The leaders of the anti-partition movement made a public declaration that the day of inauguration would be observed as a day of national mourning. A detailed programme was drawn up for the day. Food would not be cooked, except for the sick and invalid; business would be suspended and people would walk barefoot and bathe in the Ganga in the morning to purify themselves. To symbolise the unity among the Bengalis, the programme of tying a red band round the wrists of the people was undertaken. Streets was echoed with the cry 'Vande Mataram' and a national fund for carrying on the agitation was started and in a few hours Rs. 10,000 was collected through subscriptions. Earlier in a public meeting held at Ripon College in Calcutta under the leadership of S.N.Banerjee on 17th July 1905, a resolution asking the people to boycott all British goods till partition was undone had been passed. On the occasion of a religious festival in August 1905, about 50,000 people took a vow before goddess Kali not to buy foreign articles and not to employ foreigners for jobs for which suitable Indians are available. The boycott movement was not a new thing. Way back in 1849, Gopal Rao Deshmukh, better known as 'Lokahitawadi' of Bombay urged the use of indigenous goods. In 1873, Bholanath Chandra preached the establishment of indigenous Banks, Companies, Corporations, Mills and Factories and denounced the practice of preferring foreign goods to home made manufacturers. Swami Dayananda Saraswati also emphasized on swadeshi. Similarly the Tagore family also lent their full support to the use of swadeshi goods. Rabindranath Tagore started the 'Swadeshi Bhandar' in 1897 and 'Sarala Devi Lakshmi Bhandar' in 1903. During the anti-partition agitation, Swadeshi stores sold homemade goods in retail and student volunteers peddled them. In consonance with the boycott call, contents of the ships arriving with foreign goods were dumped; bags of Liverpool salt were pulled out of boats and thrown into the river. The priests refused to perform religious ceremonies with foreign articles. Those found wearing foreign clothes including Europeans were jeered at. So vehement was the public opinion that nobody would think of buying foreign clothes and those who went in for its cheapness would buy only at night. At an examination hall in Rippon College, students refused to touch answer papers of foreign make and country made sheets had to be substituted. A five-year old granddaughter of S.N.Banerjee returned a pair of shoes sent to her by a relative because they were made abroad. Similarly another girl aged six though suffering from fever refused to take any foreign medicine. If any foreign-made presents were given during marriages they were returned. Guests would refuse to participate in festivities in which foreign salt or sugar was used.

Karnataka and Swadeshi Movement

Karnataka enthusiastically responded to the call of swadeshi. On 5th May 1905 a public meeting presided by Gurunatha Rao Patak was held in the Victoria Theatre at Dharwad to protest against the partition of Bengal and to encourage swadeshi industries. The meeting resolved that everyone should vow not to use foreign cloth, except in unavoidable circumstances in order to encourage Indian artisans and trade in Indian goods. To spread the message of swadeshi and boycott, Tilak toured North Karnataka in 1905-06. Alur Venkata Rao, Sakkari Balachar, Krishna Rao Mudvedkar, Anantha Rao Dabade and others undertook extensive tours and delivered speeches on Swarajya, Swadeshi, Boycott and National Education. Swadeshi industries arose in many places. Vittal Rao Deshpande of Hebbal started a weaving factory at Kittur.

Another factory was built in Badami. Cloths made here were sent even to Bengal. Rama Rao Alagvadi opened a Match factory at Dharwad, while in Laxmeswar a Porcelain factory was established. Factories for manufacturing bangles, pencils and many other articles of common use arose in many places. A Karnataka Industrial Conference met at Dharwad in 1907 to chalk out plans to develop Swadeshi industries in Karnataka. New Banks were established to help these industries. Boycott of British goods: Apart from wide support to swadeshi movement, people of Karnataka wholeheartedly participated in the boycott of British goods. Ranibennur witnessed one of the biggest bonfires of foreign cloth. Textile dealers in Belgaum decided not to import foreign cloth and in Dharwad, grocers decided not to purchase Daboti and Johnson sugar. In Alnavar it was decided to smoke batti's instead of bidis and anyone found breaking the rule was fined. Hoteliers stopped the sale of tea and people poured kerosene into gutters and instead began to use indigenous oil for lighting. In one instance after it was noticed that a bangle seller had sold foreign bangles saying that it was Indian, the bangle seller was not only abused but also had to forego money.

In Belgaum, along with swadeshi movement, prohibition was also advocated and toddy contractors had to incur heavy loss. For picketing liquor shops in Belgaum nine persons were awarded one-week imprisonment and fined Rs. 680 in June 1908. Though a prominent person of Belgaum offered to pay the fine, the youths refused his help and preferred imprisonment. On 8th August 1908 a public meeting was held in Bagalkot, which was addressed by Jayarao Nargund, Jainapur, Yalagurdrao, Dharwadkar and others. It was proposed to establish a Swadeshi Vyaparottejak Samshtha in Bagalkot. The movement also saw the establishment of National

Schools in various parts of Karnataka. Alur Venkata Rao started the Nutana Vidyalaya at Dharwad with arts and crafts also as subjects in the curriculum. Another national school arose at Navalgund by the efforts of Dundopanth Sahasrabuddhe. In Belgaum Kaka Kalelkar established the Ganesh Vidyalaya, while Jaya Rao Nargund started another at Bagalkot. Similar schools were established at Hanagal, Agadi and other places. The government however saw that these schools close down one by one. In South Kanara district, Ammembala Srinivasa Pai was the moving spirit in the boycott of foreign goods and the spread of swadeshi. Men like K.P.Rao and Panje Mangesha Rao assisted him, while Kolachalam Venkata Rao and Sabhapathi Mudaliar were the leaders of the freedom movement in Bellary.

The Revolutionary Activities

The youth of Bengal had greatly contributed to the success of the anti-partition movement. They organized meetings, arranged demonstrations, roused enthusiasm, and provided volunteers for Swadeshi-Boycott propaganda and for picketing. Many were fined, expelled, beaten and flogged. But the harsher their treatment the more rebellious became their mood. The restriction on their public activities compelled them to form secret societies to achieve their aims. Moreover the Englishmen in the past had taunted the Bengalis that they were a race of weaklings, cowardly and lacking in manly virtues. By forming revolutionary clubs called 'Samitis', the Bengali youth proved that they did not lack courage. Newspapers like 'Jugnatara', 'Bhawani Mandir', 'Bande Mataram' and 'Sandhya' were launched to preach the cult of revolutionary violence. Some youths of Karnataka like Dr.Handoor, Baburao Gani and Bheema Rao Bevoor kept up a close correspondence with the revolutionaries of Bengal.

Seeds of Separatism Sown

Inspired by Muslim revolutionary activities in Egypt, Iran and Turkey, Abul Kalam Azad came into contact with Shyamsunder Chakravarthi of the Bande Mataram, met Aurobindo and joined one of the revolutionary bodies. He not only dissipated the anti-Muslim suspicious of the revolutionaries but helped in extending their activities outside Bengal and Bihar. The above development made Lawrence, the private secretary to Curzon and journalist like Valentine Chirol and Sidney Low to warn the then Viceroy

Minto of the danger of the Hindu-Muslim accord. Theodore Morrison, the former principal of the Aligarh College warned the government against the possibility of Muslim sympathies going over to the Congress party.

Colonel Dunlop Smith, the Private Secretary to Viceroy Minto wrote to William Archbold the then principal of Aligarh College that the Viceroy would be happy to receive a Muslim deputation. The principal asked Nawab Mohsinul Mulk, the secretary of the college to act quickly and to press for introducing the system of nomination or granting representation on religious lines. On 1st October 1906 a deputation led by Aga Khan met Viceroy Minto at Shimla and demanded that seats in the Central Legislative Assembly be reserved for the Muslim community not only on the basis of their population but on the basis of their political importance and their services in the defence of the Empire. Minto readily accepted the demand for according them separate electorates. After their successful deputation, the Muslim leaders mooted the idea of forming an association to look exclusively after the interests of the Muslim community. On 30th December 1906 the All India Muslim League was formed to promote the political and other rights of Indian Muslims and to promote among Indian Muslims the feeling of loyalty towards the British government. The true political ideas of the Muslim League became apparent from Nawab Waqar-ul-Mulk's speech delivered at Aligarh.

He said "God forbid, if the British rule disappears from India, Hindus will lord over it and there will be constant danger to our life, property and honour. The only way for the Muslims to escape this danger is to help in the continuance of the British rule. If the Muslims are heartily with the British, then that rule is bound to endure. Let the Muslims consider themselves as a British army ready to shed blood and sacrifice their lives for the British Crown". The League achieved its first success when the British government introduced separate electorates for Muslims in the 1909 Act.

Muslim Participation in Swadeshi Movement

Three months before the Partition of Bengal came into effect, two leaflets began to circulate in the province. Both appealed to Bengali Muslims to rise alongside Hindus in defence of the mother country. The first entitled, ?Who is our King?? exhorted: ?Brother Hindus, in the name of Kali, Durga, Mahadev, Sri Krishna; brother

Mohammedans, in the name of Khudatala, circulate from village to village, that we Hindus and Mohammedans jointly worship the feet of the mother native country? We shall give life and take life. We shall not use foreign articles? We must run our own country.?

The second leaflet, ?Golden Bengal,? believed in government circles to be the handiwork of Bipan Chandra Pal, also called for Hindu-Muslim joint action against the British venture: ??We will form into bands and run in all directions, from village to village, field to field, market to market, town to town, taking with us those who are ready to die, and who know their mother, the golden Bengal, and being united, we will beat and drive away Sahibs of the town and govern our own country. We will do our duty somehow.

Mussalmans, Mother, entertain high hopes in you. Strong as you are, broad as your chests are? say once ?Din! Din! Allah ho Akbar,? and take possession of the towns by whatever means you find at hand? lathi or sword, sticks or guns, or anything? You Hindus, for thousands and thousands of years you have been talking high of your Arya Dharma. Show to the people of the world your self-sacrificing manners??

Beginning with the swadeshi movement of 1905, a predominant feature of the freedom struggle was its dogged determination to enlist Muslim participation. As the Karmayogin argued, though Indian nationalism was ?largely Hindu in its spirit and tradition,? it was? wide enough also to include the Moslem and his culture and tradition and absorb them into itself.?

But in 1905, and for the entire duration of the freedom struggle, Muslim cooperation proved difficult to ensure. Resentful at being cut off from the colonial capital, Calcutta, the Bengali Muslim elite briefly endorsed the swadeshi movement. However, in July 1905 itself, the Mohammedan Provincial Union was founded to champion Muslim interests, followed in 1906 with the Mohammedan Vigilance Association, to collect evidence of Muslim oppression by swadeshi agitators. In December the same year, came the All India Muslim League which hailed the Partition as beneficial to the Mussalmans of eastern Bengal and condemned the swadeshi movement as ?a Hindu agitation?.

In a calculated move to obstruct, indeed torpedo, the ?Hindu agitation,? an intra-class alliance was struck between the urban, educated Muslim elite and Muslim religious leaders operating in the East Bengal countryside. The Mullahs were in fact pivotal in arousing the Muslim peasantry against the swadeshi movement. For several decades prior to the Bengal Partition, beginning at least with Hajji Shariatullah, they had assiduously attempted to Islamise the lifestyle of Muslim peasants and purge it of customs and practices shared with Hindu neighbours. Shariatullah, on his return from pilgrimage to Mecca, endeavoured particularly to end the veneration of Hindu deities and the celebration of Hindu festivals by Bengali Muslims.

His son, Dadu Miyan, added to his agenda a virulent economic campaign against Hindu landlords. Muslim peasantry were instigated to abstain from paying taxes, on the plea that the money could be used for Hindu festivities. The attacks Dadu Miyan organised on Hindu temples and property were the first significant attempts to link Muslim identity to resistance against Hindu landlords.

The Mullahs also organised anjumans (associations) throughout rural Bengal to organise the Muslim community around religious discussions and landlord? tenant disputes. Together Mullahs and anjumans popularised religious reform and resistance through a literary genre known as puthis. A typical puthi, Krishak Bilap (Lament of the Peasant) described the key figures of rural society? zamindars, moneylenders, and the police? as Congress Party members and urged Muslims to remember their own community and religion, study Islam and not mix with other religions, and rally behind the Muslim League.

British official communiques of the period record the ?new consciousness? among Bengali Muslims and identify ?itinerant Mullahs? as the principal catalysts in stirring religious passions and mobilising rural Muslims to ?violence and communal politics?. On-the-spot verifications confirmed the extent of Mullah complicity. In his report on the Melanda hut riots, the sub-divisional officer of Jamalpur, Mr. Barneville, observed: ?It has been reported from various places that Mohammedan Mullahs are going about amongst illiterate Mohammedans and exhorting them to rise against the Hindus.?

H.W. Nevinson, a visiting journalist, noted the inflammatory role of Maulvis. ?Priestly Mullahs went through the country preaching the revival of Islam and proclaiming to the villagers that the British government was on the Mohammedan side, that the law courts had been specially suspended for three months, and no penalty would be exacted for violence done to Hindus, or for the loot of Hindu shops, or the abduction of Hindu widows. A Red Pamphlet was everywhere circulated, maintaining the same wild doctrines??.

The Red Pamphlet (Lal Ishtahar), first came to light at the time of the establishment of the Muslim League in Dacca. It circulated widely with government connivance. Written by one Ibrahim Khan of Mymensingh district, its objective was to dissuade Muslims from joining the swadeshi movement and to involve them in a swajati movement (to promote the interests of ones own race), a forerunner of the two-nation theory. In a strident note, it decreed: ?Ye Mussalmans arise, awake! Do not read in the same schools with Hindus. Do not buy anything from a Hindu shop. Do not touch any article manufactured by Hindu hands. Do not give any employment to a Hindu. Do not accept any degrading office under a Hindu? You form the majority of the population of this province. Among the cultivators also, you form the majority. It is agriculture that is the source of wealth. The Hindu has no wealth of his own and has made himself rich only by despoiling you of your wealth. If you become sufficiently enlightened, then the Hindus will starve and soon become Mohammedans?.

Thus, while heralding the commencement of the freedom struggle, the Bengal Partition also marked the beginning of modern communalism.

An assessment of Tilak's role in the Freedom Movement has often been hampered by charges of "communalism" and "Hindu Revivalism". But a closer and more balanced inspection of Tilak's record in public life reveals a rather different picture.

As early as 1888, Tilak had made a decisive break with his former cohort-Chiplunkar, unwilling to align with any narrow and sectarian agenda of chauvinist Hindu revivalism. This is not to say that Tilak was indifferent to Hindu traditions. Few leaders were. Many of the Muslim leaders were Maulanas, and Hindu leaders often had connections with the Arya Samaj or Brahmo Samaj. Tilak's interest in the Gita was neither exceptional, nor should it have brought any unduly unfavorable commentaries.

In fact, Tilak's interest in Hindu philosophy stemmed neither from conservatism nor from any tendency towards reactionary revivalism. Taken in the context of his vigorous contributions to the freedom movement, and the political clarity and directness of his message, it would be more appropriate to argue that his interest in his Hindu and Maratha heritage stemmed from the cultural vacuum that had been created by the alien and impersonal character of the British educational system. To find inspiration from ancient Indian texts, to find in the traditional Indian discourse, insights of contemporary value was for Tilak (and other leaders like him) not only something that contributed to developing self-awareness and self-esteem, it was as much an act of defiance towards the prevailing colonial-induced norms that ridiculed all things Indian, and valorized Western science and civilization to the exclusion of all else.

At a time when loyalist and "moderate" Indian politicians were enraptured by Western values and Western literature, discovering and connecting with Indian cultural traditions was not entirely without merit. In Tilak's case, it is especially important to note that he never counter-posed Indian tradition with Western scientific knowledge and technology. He was no xenophobe, and was all for India benefiting from the scientific and civilizational progress made in Europe. But unlike those that were utterly beholden to the colonial agenda, he saw no reason for educated Indians to eschew all interest in the Indian heritage either.

Tilak on the Gita

It is also important to note that his commentary on the Gita was critical of those who emphasized renunciation and retreat from the real world. His interpretation of the Gita was very much in the spirit of the times-focused towards enhancing participation in the freedom movement, and in many ways, his comments were far more insightful than those of Gandhi. Whereas Gandhi often veered towards excessive idealism and even mystical obscurantism, Tilak's approach was sharply practical, and always geared towards taking concrete action. His interest in Hindu spiritualism arose from a feeling that British rule was creating a society that was losing it's ethical moorings, that colonial exploitation was destroying people's sense of social-connectedness and duty towards community and nation. Unlike Gandhi who was inconsistent (and sometimes even seemed quite arbitrary) in his political practices, Tilak strived hard to practice what he preached, and to preach only what he himself could practice.

Whereas Gandhi feared the militant rising of the masses, and therefore advanced ideas that caused a blurring or obfuscation of seething social and ethical contradictions, Tilak faced no such compulsion for being obtuse. His uncompromising opposition to colonial exploitation permitted him to espouse a view of "dharma" or duty in a way that was more ethical and more suitable to fighting against the injustice of colonial rule.

In his early years, when he encouraged participation in Hindu festivals in Maharashtra, he was motivated by the desire to instill confidence amongst the people, so that the numbing effect of colonization could be counter-acted. That such activities might provoke hostility, resentment or sectarian feelings amongst Muslims never occurred to him, for he had no desire to cause any rift between the two communities, and wanted both communities to participate jointly in the festivals.

Importance of Hindu-Muslim Unity

As he matured as a national leader, he became all too aware of the importance of Hindu-Muslim unity in the freedom movement. As early as 1893, Tilak had become conscious of how conflicts between Hindus and Muslims came about at the instigation of Anglo-Indian officers in the colonial administration. He was not oblivious to the 'Divide and Rule' policy of the colonial administrators, and knew how detrimental that was to the cause of freedom.

Following his release from prison, seeing how the national movement had fallen apart during his years in jail, and how Hindu-Muslim divisions were a serious impediment to the advance of the national movement, Tilak (like many other secular leaders of the Congress) bent over backwards to disarm Muslim leaders in the freedom movement, and redoubled his efforts in trying to win over the Muslim League to the cause of *Swaraj*. Viewing the unity of India's Hindus and Muslims as paramount, Tilak helped seal the 1916 Congress-Muslim League pact that conceded virtually all the demands made by the League.

In a speech to the 31st Indian National Congress in Lucknow, Tilak could not have made his secular outlook any more explicit when he stated: *"It has been said by some that we Hindus have yielded too much to our Mohammedan brethren. I am sure I represent the sense of the Hindu community all over India when I say that we could not have yielded too much."* He went on to assert how he would rather see the British hand over the governance of India to Indian Muslims (or Indians of any caste) than see the British remain as India's paramount colonial authority.

Although such attempts to wean away the League from it's hostile posture towards the national movement eventually came to nought, there is little denying that during this period, Tilak and the Congress went a considerable distance to accommodate even unreasonable and undemocratic demands from the League.

Thus, Muslims who were Tilak's contemporaries regarded Tilak as a true "nationalist". Maulana Shaukat Ali and Maulana Hasrat Mohani, who were both staunch members of the Khilafat movement, and early supporters of the national movement (until they later joined the Muslim League) had been admirers of Tilak. Mazarul Haque, a Swarajist and a trusted follower of Deshbandhu Chittaranjan Das spoke well of Tilak, as did Dr. Ansari, (one of the former Presidents of the Congress) who avowed that Tilak's vision was not of Hindu dominance.

But once the League was committed on a path towards partition, pro-Pakistani agitators of the Muslim League such as Jinnah (who had earlier regarded Tilak with cordiality) began to malign Tilak, painting him as a Hindu revivalist and communalist.

Once the League had made a decisive turn towards partition, it was not surprising that the champions of Pakistan would turn sharply against Tilak (and any leader of significance in the national movement), and begin to contradict all that they had said of Tilak earlier. The compulsions of the two-nation theory required such heightened polemics, and Tilak, who had played such an invigorating role in the early years of the Indian Freedom Struggle came to be presented more and more through biased and distorted caricatures of his public record.

Although Jinnah was equally unsparing in his attacks on the Congress, (who he dismissed as a "Hindu" organization), his attacks on Tilak appeared to find a certain measure of resonance even amongst some Indian liberals. But as noted earlier, Tilak was hardly alone among national leaders in his interest in Hindu culture and philosophy. What is especially ironic is how his most strident critics were themselves seeped in religious sectarianism, and held quite reactionary and conservative views on how society ought to develop and mature in a free India. Indian critics of Tilak who now brand him as a "communal" untouchable are either seriously misguided or misinformed, but more likely have succumbed to a tendency where secularism has been turned into Hindu-phobia.

Tilak on Non-violence

In 1908, there were few leaders (Hindu, Muslim or Sikh) of comparable stature in the Indian freedom movement, and in several ways, Tilak's ideas remain far ahead of Gandhi's. Any lover of Indian freedom and progress would have to be cognizant of that. Tilak's writings on non-violence are especially revealing of an advanced intellect. Tilak was neither a gun-fetishist nor an idealist rejecter of violence. In 1908, he saw nonviolent resistance through mass civil disobedience as the preferred method of struggle only because he did not see the possibilities of winning an armed struggle against the British at that particular time. But neither did he reject the possibility that a time may come when the Indian masses would be able, ready and prepared for an armed struggle, if no other option of defeating the British seemed likely to succeed. For that reason, he was never prepared to condemn the armed revolutionaries, and defended each one as a legitimate fighter and martyr in the cause of Indian independence.

Combining strong elements of pragmatic realism with unflinching devotion to principle is what allowed the young Tilak to mature into a leader of great national significance. His public record not only indicates that he was far more frank and forthright with the Indian masses than his duplicitous and hypocritical critics, but that he had also grappled with issues of tactics and strategy to a much greater degree than any of his contemporaries. Not only did Tilak display a level of perseverance and dedication towards the national cause that exceeded that of his detractors, he did not hesitate to take his message to the Indian masses.

Although internment seriously weakened Tilak's spirit, in the early years, it was leaders such as Tilak that truly helped enervate the mass movement, and prepared the ground for the freedom movement

The Swadeshi

Bengali or Bangla is an Indo-Aryan language of the eastern Indian subcontinent, evolved from the Magadhi Prakrit and Sanskrit languages movement, part of the Indian independence movement.

Indian Independence Movement

The term Indian independence movement incorporates various national and regional campaigns, agitations and efforts of both nonviolent and militant philosophy. The term encompasses a wide spectrum of political organizations, philosophies, and movements which had the common aim of ending the British..., was a successful economic strategy to remove the British Empire from power and improve economic conditions in India through following principles of *swadeshi* (self-sufficiency). Strategies of the swadeshi movement involved boycotting British products and the revival of domestic-made products and production techniques.

Swadeshi Movement emanated from the partition of bengal, 1905 and continued up to 1908. It was the most successful of the pre-Gandhian movements. Chief architects were Aurobindo Ghosh, Veer Savarkar, Lokmanya Bal Gangadhar Tilak, and Lala Lajpat Rai.

The Swadeshi Jagaran Manch

Swadeshi Jagaran Manch

The Swadeshi Jagaran Manch is an Indian political organisation committed to the promotion of Swadeshi industries and culture. It is usually recognised as a part of the Sangh Parivar of Hindu nationalist organisations. SJM came into existence on November 22, 1991 at Nagpur...

Principles

Mohandas Karamchand Gandhi was the pre-eminent political and spiritual leader of India during the Indian independence movement...described Swadeshi as "a call to the consumer to be aware of the violence he is causing by supporting those industries that result in poverty and harm to workers and to humans and other creatures."

"Swadeshi is that spirit in us which requires us to serve our immediate neighbours before others, and to use things produced in our neighbourhood in preference to those more remote. So doing, we serve humanity to the best of our capacity. We cannot serve humanity by neglecting our neighbours".

Origins

The word *Swadeshi* derives from Sanskrit and is a *Sandhi* or conjunction of two Sanskrit words. *Swa* means "self" or "own" and *Desh* means country, so *Swadesh* would be "own country", and *Swadeshi*, the adjectival form, would mean "of one's own country". The Opposite of *Swadeshi* in Sanskrit is *Videshi* or "not of one's country". Another Example of *Sandhi* or Conjunction in Sanskrit is *Swaraj*. *Swa* is Self (related to Latin reflexive root "su-") and *Raj* is "rule" (related to English "rich", Latin "rex", and German "Reich").

Dhaka Anushilan Samiti

Dhaka Anushilan Samiti was a branch of the Anushilan Samiti founded in the city of Dhaka in November 1905. Initially a group of eighty under the leadership of Pulin Behari Das, it "spread like wildfire" throughout the province of East Bengal. More than 500 branches were opened, linked by a "close and detailed organization" to Pulin's headquarters at Dhaka. It absorbed smaller groups in the province and soon overshadowed its parent organisation in Calcutta. Branches of Dhaka Anushilan emerged in the towns of Jessore, Khulna, Faridpur, Rajnagar, Rajendrapur, Mohanpur, Barvali, Bakarganj and other places. Estimates of Dhaka Anushilan Samiti's reach show a membership of between 15,000 and 20,000 members. Within another two years, Dhaka Anushilan would devolve its aims from the Swadeshi to the dedicated aim of political terrorism. The *Dhaka Anushilan Samiti* embarked on a radical program of political terrorism. It broke with the *Jugantar group* due to differences with Aurobindo's approach of slowly building a base for a revolution with a mass base. The Dhaka group saw this as slow and insufficient, and sought immediate action and result. It was responsible for a number of political assassinations, most notably the murder of D.C. Allen. However, it reached a temporary halt after the arrest and deportation of Pulin Das and the Barisal Conspiracy Case in 1913. Dhaka Anushilan decided not to participate in the German plot of World War I. After the war, it continued in its violent movement, and some of its members went on to form the Neo-violence group.

9

Anushilan Samiti

Anushilan Samiti was an armed anti-British organisation in Bengal and the principal secret revolutionary organisation operating in the region in the opening years of the 20th century. This association, like its offshoot the Jugantar, operated under the guise of suburban fitness club. The members were committed towards the path of armed revolution for independence of India from British rule. Kolkata and, later, Dhaka were the two major strongholds of the association. However, the group succeeded in penetrating rural Bengal and had branches all over Bengal and also other parts of India.

Its activities included robbery, making of bombs, arms training and assassination of British officials and Indians who they viewed as "traitors".

Background

The growth of the Indian middle class during the 18th century, amidst competition among regional powers and the ascendancy of the British East India Company, led to a growing sense of "Indian" identity.

The refinement of this perspective fed a rising tide of nationalism in India in the last decades of the 1800s. Its speed was abetted by the creation of the Indian National Congress in India in 1885 by A.O. Hume. The Congress developed into a major platform for the demands of political liberalisation, increased autonomy and social reform. However, the nationalist movement became particularly strong, radical and violent in Bengal and, later, in Punjab. Notable, if smaller, movements also appeared in Maharashtra, Madras and other areas in the South.

Beginnings

Political terrorism began taking an organised form in Bengal at the beginning of the twentieth century. By 1902, Calcutta had three societies working under the umbrella of *Anushilan Samity*, a society earlier founded by a Calcutta barrister by the name of Pramatha Mitra. These included Mitra's own group, another led by a Bengali lady by the name of Sarala Devi, and a third one led by Aurobindo Ghosh-one of the strongest proponents of militant nationlism of the time. The Anushilan Samiti had Sri Aurobindo and Deshabandhu Chittaranjan Das as the vice-presidents, Suren Tagore the treasurer. Jatindra Nath Banerjee (Niralamba Swami), Jatindra Nath Mukherjee (Bagha Jatin), Bhupendra Nath Datta (Swami Vivekananda's brother), Barindra Ghosh were among other initial leaders. By 1905, the works of Aurobindo and his brother Barin Ghosh allowed *Anushilan Samity* to spread through Bengal. The controversial 1905 partition of Bengal had a widespread political impact: it stimulated radical nationalist sentiments in the *Bhadralok* community in Bengal, and helped *Anushilan* acquire a support base amongst of educated, politically conscious and disaffected young in local youth societies of Bengal. The Dhaka branch of the Anushilan Samiti was formed by Pulin Bihari Das, who was once a teacher in the Dhaka Government College and, later, a founding headmaster of 'National School' (Dhaka), along with his followers, in 1906. He, like Barindra Ghosh, believed in a highly centralised one-leader organisation. Under their leadership, respectively in Dhaka and elsewhere, in a spirit of a boastful showdown, Anushilan Samiti slowly adopted untimely terrorism programmes during the first decade of 20th century, with 1905 Partition of Bengal acting as a major catalyst. The Dhaka branch of *Anushilan* was led by Pulin Behari Das and spread branches through East Bengal and Assam. Aurobindo and Bipin Chandra Pal, a Bengali politician, began in 1907 the radical Bengali nationalist publication of *Jugantar* (Lit: Change), and its English counterpart *Bande Mataram*. Among the early recruits who emerged noted leaders where Rash Behari Bose, Jatindranath Mukherjee, and Jadugopal Mukherjee.

Revolutionary Acitivites

Anushilan, notably from early on, established links with foreign movements and Indian nationalism abroad. In 1907, Barin Ghosh arranged to send to Paris one of his associates by the name of Hem Chandra Kanungo (Hem Chandra Das), he was to learn the art of bomb making from Nicholas Safranski, a Russian revolutionary in exile in the French Capital. Paris was also home at the time Madam Cama who was amongst the leading figures of the Paris Indian Society and the India House in London. The bomb manual later found its way through V.D. Savarkar to the press at India House for mass printing. In the meantime, in December 1907 the Bengal revolutionary cell derailed the train carrying the Bengal Lieutenant Governor Sir Andrew Fraser. A few days later, on 23 December, they attempted to assassinate Mr. Allen, formerly District Magistrate of Dhaka. *Anushilan* also engaged at this time in a number of notable incidences of political assassinations and *dacoities* to obtain funds. This was, however, the crest for *Anushilan*.

Alipore Conspiracy Case

In April 1908, two young recruits, Khudiram Bose and Prafulla Chaki were sent on a mission to Muzaffarpur to assassinate the Chief Presidency Magistrate D.H. Kingford. The duo bombed a carriage they mistook as Kingsford's, killing two English women in it. In the aftermath of the murder, Khudiram Bose was arrested while attempting to flee, while Chaki took his own life. Narendra Nath Bhattacharya, then a member of the group, shot dead Nandalal Bannerjee, the officer who had arrested Kshudiram. Police investigations into the murders revealed the organisations quarters in Manicktala suburb of Calcutta and led to a number of arrests, opening the famous Alipore Conspiracy trial. Some of its leadership were executed or incarcerated, while others went underground. Aurobindo Ghosh himself retired from active politics after serving a prison sentence, his brother Barin was imprisoned for life.

The result of the trial was a division of the Anushilan Samiti. Two main groups that remained were the Jugantar itself and the Dhaka Anushilan Samiti, in the western and the eastern parts of the Bengal, respectively. The initial Anushilan disappeared. Jatindra Nath Mukherjee escaped arrest in the Alipore case, and took over the leadership of the secret society, to be known as the Jugantar Party. He revitalised the links between the central organisation in Calcutta and its several branches spread all over Bengal, Bihar, Orissa and several places in U.P., and opened hideouts in the Sunderbans for members who had gone underground The group slowly reorganised guided Mukherjee's efforts of aided by an emerging leadership which included Amarendra Chatterjee, Naren Bhattacharya and other younger leaders. Some of its younger members including Taraknath Das left India. Through the next two years, the organisation operated under the covers of two seemingly detached organisations, *Sramajeebi Samabaya* (The Labourer's cooperative) and Harry & Sons. At around this time, Jatin began attempts to establish contacts with the 10th Jat Regiment then garrisoned at Fort William in Calcutta. Narendra Nath carried out through this time a number of robberies to obtain funds. In the meantime, However, a second blow came in 1910 when Shamsul Alam, a Bengal Police officer then preparing a conspiracy case against the group, was assassinated by an associate of Jatindranath by the name of Biren Dutta Gupta. The assassination led to the arrests which ultimately precipitated the Howrah-Sibpur Conspiracy Case.

Further investigations led the police to a small scale bomb manufacturing unit in Maniktala of Kolkata. Barindra Ghosh and several other members of Anushilan Samiti and Jugantar were arrested and tried in the famous Alipore Bomb Conspiracy case. Many were deported for life to Port Blair in the Andaman Islands.

Buddhist economics is a set of economic principles partly inspired by Buddhist beliefs that individuals ought to do good work in order to ensure proper human development....

Bagha Jatin

Bagha Jatin (7 December 1879 – 10 September 1915) was a Bengali Indian revolutionary philosopher against British rule. He was the principal leader of the Yugantar party that was the central association of revolutionaries in Bengal. Having personally met the German Crown-Prince in Calcutta shortly before the World War I, he obtained the promise of arms and ammunition from Germany; as such, he was responsible for the planned German Plot during World War I. Another of his original contributions was the indoctrination of the Indian soldiers in various regiments in favour of an insurrection. [In 1925] Gandhi told Tegart that Jatin Mukherjee, generally referred to as "Bagha Jatin", was "a divine personality". Little did he know that Tegart had once told his colleagues that if Jatin were an Englishman, then the English people would have built his statue next to Nelson's at Trafalgar

Square. In his note to J.E. Francis of the India Office in 1926, he described Bengali revolutionaries as "the most selfless political workers in India".

Early Life

Jatin was born to Sharatshashi and Umeshchandra Mukherjee in Kayagram, a village in the Kushtia subdivision of Nadia district in what is now Bangladesh. He grew up in his ancestral home at Sadhuhati, P.S. Rishkhali Jhenaidah until his father's death when Jatin was five years old. Well versed in Brahmanic studies, his father liked horses and was respected for the strength of his character. Sharatshashi settled in her parents' home in Kayagram with her husband and his elder sister Benodebala (or Vinodebala). A gifted poet, she was affectionate and stern in her method of raising her children. Familiar with the essays by contemporary thought leaders like Bankimchandra Chatterjee and Yogendra Vidyabhushan, she was aware of the social and political transformations of her times. Her brother Basantakumar Chatterjee taught and practised law, and counted among his clients the poet Rabindranath Tagore. Since the age of 14, Tagore had claimed in meetings organised by his family members equal rights for Indian citizens inside railway carriages and in public places. As Jatin grew older, he gained a reputation for physical bravery and great strength; charitable and cheerful by nature, he was fond of caricature and enacting mythological plays, himself playing the roles of god-loving characters like Prahlad, Dhruva, Hanuman, Raja Harish Chandra. He not only encouraged several playwrights to produce patriotic pieces for the urban stage, but also engaged village bards to spread nationalist fervour in the countryside. Jatin had a natural respect for the human creature, heedless of class or caste or religions. He carried for an aged Muslim villager a heavy bundle of fodder and, on reaching her hut, he shared with her the only platter of rice she had, and sent her some money every month.

Student in Calcutta

After passing the Entrance examination in 1895, Jatin joined the Calcutta Central College (now Khudiram Bose College), to study Fine Arts. At the same time, he took lessons in steno typing with Mr. Atkinson: this is a new qualification opening possibilities of a coveted career. Soon he started visiting Swami Vivekananda, whose social thought, and especially his vision of a politically independent India-indispensable for the spiritual progress of humanity-had a great influence on Jatin. The Master taught him the art of conquering libido before raising a batch of young volunteers "with iron muscles and nerves of steel", to serve miserable compatriots during famines, epidemics and floods, and running clubs for "man-making" in the context of a nation under foreign domination. They soon assisted Sister Nivedita, the Swami's Irish disciple, in this venture. According to J. E. Armstrong, Superintendent of the colonial Police, Jatin "owed his preeminent position in revolutionary circles, not only to his qualities of leadership, but in great measure to his reputation of being a Brahmachari with no thought beyond the revolutionary cause." Noticing his ardent desire to die for a cause, Vivekananda sent Jatin to the Gymnasium of Ambu Guha where he himself had practised wrestling. Jatin met here, among others, Sachin Banerjee, son of Yogendra Vidyabhushan (a popular author of biographies like *Mazzini* and *Garibaldi*), who turned into Jatin's mentor. In 1900, his uncle Lalit Kumar married Vidyabhushan's daughter.

Fed up with the colonial system of education, Jatin left for Muzaffarpore in 1899, as secretary of barrister Pringle Kennedy, founder and editor of the *Trihoot Courrier*. He was impressed by this historian: through his editorials and from the Congress platform, he showed how urgent it was to have an Indian National Army and to react against the British squandering of Indian budget to safeguard their interests in China and elsewhere.

In 1900, Jatin married Indubala Banerjee of Kumarkhali *upazila* in Kushtia; they had four children: Atindra (1903–1906), Ashalata (1907–1976), Tejendra (1909–1989), and Birendra (1913–1991). Struck by Atindra's death, Jatin, with his wife and sister, set out on a pilgrimage and recovered their inner peace by receiving initiation from the saint Bholanand Giri of Hardwar. Aware of his disciple's revolutionary commitments, the holy man extended to him his full support. Upon returning to his native village Koya in March 1906, Jatin learned about the disturbing presence of a leopard in the vicinity; while reconnoitring in the nearby jungle, he came across a Royal Bengal tiger and foughthand-to-hand with it. Mortally wounded, he managed to strike with a Gorkha dagger (Khukuri) on the tiger's neck, killing it instantly. The famous surgeon of Calcutta, Lt-Colonel Suresh Sarbadhikari, "took upon himself the responsibility for curing the fatally wounded patient whose whole body had been poisoned by the tiger's nails." Impressed by Jatin's exemplary heroism, Dr. Sarbadhikari published an article about Jatin in the English press. The Government of Bengal awarded him a silver shield with the scene of him killing the tiger engraved on it.

Anushilan Samiti

Anushilan Samiti was an armed anti-British organisation in Bengal and the principal secret revolutionary organisation operating in the region in the opening years of the 20th century. This association, like its offshoot the Jugantar, operated under the guise of suburban fitness club. The members were committed towards the path of armed revolution for independence of India from British rule. Kolkata and, later, Dhaka were the two major strongholds of the association. However, the group succeeded in penetrating rural Bengal and had branches all over Bengal and also other parts of India.

Its activities included robbery, making of bombs, arms training and assassination of British officials and Indians who they viewed as "traitors".

Background

The growth of the Indian middle class during the 18th century, amidst competition among regional powers and the ascendancy of the British East India Company, led to a growing sense of "Indian" identity. The refinement of this perspective fed a rising tide of nationalism in India in the last decades of the 1800s. Its speed was abetted by the creation of the Indian National Congress in India in 1885 by A.O. Hume. The Congress developed into a major platform for the demands of political liberalisation, increased autonomy and social reform. However, the nationalist movement became particularly strong, radical and violent in Bengal and, later, in Punjab. Notable, if smaller, movements also appeared in Maharashtra, Madras and other areas in the South.

Beginnings

Political terrorism began taking an organised form in Bengal at the beginning of the twentieth century. By 1902, Calcutta had three societies working under the umbrella of Anushilan Samity, a society earlier founded by a Calcutta barrister by the name of

Pramatha Mitra. These included Mitra's own group, another led by a Bengali lady by the name of Sarala Devi, and a third one led by Aurobindo Ghosh-one of the strongest proponents of militant nationlism of the time. The Anushilan Samiti had Sri Aurobindo and Deshabandhu Chittaranjan Das as the vice-presidents, Suren Tagore the treasurer. Jatindra Nath Banerjee (Niralamba Swami), Jatindra Nath Mukherjee (Bagha Jatin), Bhupendra Nath Datta (Swami Vivekananda's brother), Barindra Ghosh were among other initial leaders. By 1905, the works of Aurobindo and his brother Barin Ghosh allowed Anushilan Samity to spread through Bengal. The controversial 1905 partition of Bengal had a widespread political impact: it stimulated radical nationalist sentiments in the Bhadralok community in Bengal, and helped Anushilan acquire a support base amongst of educated, politically conscious and disaffected young in local youth societies of Bengal. The Dhaka branch of the Anushilan Samiti was formed by Pulin Bihari Das, who was once a teacher in the Dhaka Government College and, later, a founding headmaster of 'National School' (Dhaka), along with his followers, in 1906. He, like Barindra Ghosh, believed in a highly centralised one-leader organisation. Under their leadership, respectively in Dhaka and elsewhere, in a spirit of a boastful showdown, Anushilan Samiti slowly adopted untimely terrorism programmes during the first decade of 20th century, with 1905 Partition of Bengal acting as a major catalyst. The Dhaka branch of Anushilan was led by Pulin Behari Das and spread branches through East Bengal and Assam. Aurobindo and Bipin Chandra Pal, a Bengali politician, began in 1907 the radical Bengali nationalist publication of Jugantar (Lit:Change), and its English counterpart Bande Mataram. Among the early recruits who emerged noted leaders where Rash Behari Bose, Jatindranath Mukherjee, and Jadugopal Mukherjee.

Revolutionary Acitivites

Anushilan, notably from early on, established links with foreign movements and Indian nationalism abroad. In 1907, Barin Ghosh arranged to send to Paris one of his associates by the name of Hem Chandra Kanungo (Hem Chandra Das), he was to learn the art of bomb making from Nicholas Safranski, a Russian revolutionary in exile in the French Capital. Paris was also home at the time Madam Cama who was amongst the leading figures of the Paris Indian Society and the India House in London. The bomb manual later found its way through V.D. Savarkar to the press at India House for mass printing. In the meantime, in December 1907 the Bengal revolutionary cell derailed the train carrying the Bengal Lieutenant Governor Sir Andrew Fraser. A few days later, on 23 December, they attempted to assassinate Mr. Allen, formerly District Magistrate of Dhaka. Anushilan also engaged at this time in a number of notable incidences of political assassinations and dacoities to obtain funds. This was, however, the crest for Anushilan.

Alipore Conspiracy Case

In April 1908, two young recruits, Khudiram Bose and Prafulla Chaki were sent on a mission to Muzaffarpur to assassinate the Chief Presidency Magistrate D.H. Kingford. The duo bombed a carriage they mistook as Kingsford's, killing two English women in it. In the aftermath of the murder, Khudiram Bose was arrested while attempting to flee, while Chaki took his own life. Narendra Nath Bhattacharya, then a member of the group, shot dead Nandalal Bannerjee, the officer who had arrested Kshudiram. Police investigations into the murders revealed the organisations quarters in Manicktala suburb of Calcutta and led to a number of arrests, opening the famous Alipore Conspiracy trial. Some of its leadership were executed or incarcerated, while others went underground. Aurobindo Ghosh himself retired from active politics after serving a prison sentence, his brother Barin was imprisoned for life.

The result of the trial was a division of the Anushilan Samiti. Two main groups that remained were the Jugantar itself and the Dhaka Anushilan Samiti, in the western and the eastern parts of the Bengal, respectively. The initial Anushilan disappeared. Jatindra Nath Mukherjee escaped arrest in the Alipore case, and took over the leadership of the secret society, to be known as the Jugantar Party. He revitalised the links between the central organisation in Calcutta and its several branches spread all over Bengal, Bihar, Orissa and several places in U.P., and opened hideouts in the Sunderbans for members who had gone underground The group slowly reorganised guided Mukherjee's efforts of aided by an emerging leadership which included Amarendra Chatterjee, Naren Bhattacharya and other younger leaders. Some of its younger members including Taraknath Das left India. Through the next two years, the organisation operated under the covers of two seemingly detached organisations, Sramajeebi Samabaya (The

Labourer's cooperative) and Harry & Sons. At around this time, Jatin began attempts to establish contacts with the 10th Jat Regiment then garrisoned at Fort William in Calcutta. Narendra Nath carried out through this time a number of robberies to obtain funds. In the meantime, However, a second blow came in 1910 when Shamsul Alam, a Bengal Police officer then preparing a conspiracy case against the group, was assassinated by an associate of Jatindranath by the name of Biren Dutta Gupta. The assassination led to the arrests which ultimately precipitated the Howrah-Sibpur Conspiracy Case.

Further investigations led the police to a small scale bomb manufacturing unit in Maniktala of Kolkata. Barindra Ghosh and several other members of Anushilan Samiti and Jugantar were arrested and tried in the famous Alipore Bomb Conspiracy case. Many were deported for life to Port Blair in the Andaman Islands.

Extrimisat and Moderat

This was a very very busy day. We had to make arrangements about our nationalist conference. Delegates kept pouring in all the morning. Bengal, Madras, Belgaum, Dharwad, Berar, C.P and nationalists all over the country have turned up very very strong & we number over six hundred. Babasaheb Khare of Nasik, Balasaheb Deshpande of Ahmednagar and very many others, have either arrived or are on their way. Arobind Babu, Suresh Babu, & many others are here. Talks of compromise are all in the air & our party without exception are in favour of an amicable settlement. The moderates would appear to be in uncertain temper. Some are for a compromise & others for holding out indefinitely. Our conference held in Ghee-Kanta Wadi was an unqualified success. All our nationalist delegates attended. We have made a separate camp for ourselves & that is a distinct advantage. The moderates are mostly gathered in the camp near the Pandal and are more or less dispersed. They are not very well off. Tilak made a very clear & forcible statement in our conference. Mr. Arobindo Babu presided. After the conference we went to our Tekda meeting. It was unprecedentedly large, over ten thousand being present and a number of speakers spoke from our platform; Tilak, Hyder Raiza, Sardar Ajitsing, Sangavi KKV [?]. It became so late that I did not speak though people called for me. We returned to our lodgings after 9 p.m. Our meeting was a tremendous success.

Compromise is more than ever talked of & not a man in our camp but has a suggestion to make.

25 December 1907

Mr. Tilak went out in the morning to bring about a compromise. I have & had my misgivings from the beginning. Sir P[herozeshah] M[ehta] is a very haughty & proud man. He will never yield. Gokhale has no backbone. Ambalal is showing no coolness & appears confused by the situation. Tilak is doing his best to bring about a compromise. I did not go out in the morning. There is great discipline in our party.

In the afternoon we had our Nationalist Conference. Arobinda Babu presided and Tilak made another masterly statement, clear & concise & yet full, such as he alone can make. Everybody praises it: Bhagat is here & came to see us. Lala Lajapatraya is here and paid us a visit in Ghee-Kanta Wadi. He was not prepared to sign the Nationalist declaration nor to hold himself bound by the resolutions of the Nationalist party. I sent him to see Tilak & Arobinda Babu at our lodging. Lala is also talking of a compromise. Moti Babu arrived from Calcutta this evening at 10 p.m. He agreed to put up with us for a night, and we sat talking for a very very long time. Practically I had no sleep. There was a movement to increase the number of our delegates & many visitors paid their money and enrolled themselves.

30 December 1907

The moderates and the self-constituted congress officials have published a press-note full of lies and misrepresentations. Tilak commenced a reply to it and a statement of our own this morning. His work was much interrupted by visits, and he was not able to finish it till late in the day. Towards evening Mr. Kulabhai's son came and wished me & Tilak to go and visit his father. We went after finishing the statement. There we met Shrijut Narendra Nath Sen, Mr. Ghoshal & others and sat talking about the events of the last few days. Sir Bhalchandra came there with his brother Vishnu but did not speak with us. He visited the ladies and went away. We returned on foot from Kulabhai's house. Mr. Thengadi & two others accompanied us. Tilak decided to go away tonight and did so by the midnight train. Babu Arobinda goes to Baroda tomorrow morning. I shall also leave for Berar tomorrow.

The Moderates' Version

The twenty-third Indian National Congress assembled yesterday [26 December] in the Pavilion erected for it by the Reception Committee at Surat at 2-30 p.m. Over sixteen hundred delegates were present. The proceedings began with an address from the Chairman of Reception Committee. After the reading of the address was over Diwan Bahadur Ambalal Sakerlal proposed that the Hon. Dr. Rash Behari Ghose having been nominated by the Reception Committee for the office of President under the rules adopted at the last session of the Congress, he should take the Presidential chair. As soon as the Diwan Bahadur uttered Dr. Ghose's name, some voices were heard in the body of the hall shouting "No, no" and the shouting was kept up for some time.

The proposer, however, somehow managed to struggle through his speech; and the Chairman then called upon Babu Surendranath Banerjee to second the proposition. As soon, however, as he began his speech — before he had finished even his first sentence — a small section of the delegates began an uproar from their seats with the object of preventing Mr. Banerjee from speaking. The Chairman repeatedly appealed for order, but no heed was paid. Every time Mr. Banerjee attempted to go on with his speech he was met by disorderly shouts. It was clear that rowdyism had been determined upon to bring the proceedings to a standstill, and the whole demonstrations seemed to have been pre-arranged. Finding it impossible to enforce order, the Chairman warned the House that unless the uproar subsided at once, he would be obliged to suspend the sitting of the Congress. The hostile demonstration, however, continued and the Chairman at last suspended the sitting for the day.

The Congress again met today [27 December] at 1 p.m., due notice of the meeting having been sent round. As the President-Elect was being escorted in procession through the Hall to the platform, an overwhelming majority of the delegates present greeted him with a most enthusiastic welcome, thereby showing how thoroughly they disapproved the organised disorder of yesterday. As this procession was entering the Pandal a small slip of paper written in pencil and bearing Mr. B.G. Tilak's signature was put by a volunteer into the hands of Mr. Malvi, the Chairman of the Reception Committee. It was a notice to the Chairman that after Mr. Banerjee's speech, seconding the proposition about the

President was concluded, Mr. Tilak wanted to move "an amendment for an adjournment of the Congress." The Chairman considered a notice of adjournment at that stage to be irregular and out of order. The proceedings were then resumed at the point at which they had been interrupted yesterday, and Mr. Surendranath Banerjee was called upon to conclude his speech. Mr. Banerjee having done this, the Chairman called upon Pandit Motilal Nehru of Allahabad to support the motion. The Pandit supported it in a brief speech and then the Chairman put the motion to the vote.

An overwhelming majority of the delegates signified their assent by crying "All, all" and a small minority shouted "No, no." The Chairman thereupon declared the motion carried and the Hon. Dr. Ghose was installed in the Presidential chair amidst loud and prolonged applause. While the applause was going on, and as Dr. Ghose rose to begin his address, Mr. Tilak came upon the platform and stood in front of the President. He urged that as he had given notice of an "amendment to the Presidential election," he should be permitted to move his amendment. Thereupon, it was pointed out to him by Mr. Malvi, the Chairman of the Reception Committee, that his notice was not for "an amendment to the Presidential election," but it was for "an adjournment of the Congress," which notice he had considered to be irregular and out of order at that stage; and that the President having been duly installed in the chair no amendment about his election could be then moved.

Mr. Tilak then turned to the President and began arguing with him. Dr. Ghose in his turn, stated how matters stood and ruled that this request to move an amendment about the election could not be entertained. Mr. Tilak thereupon said, "I will not submit to this. I will now appeal from the President to the delegates." In the meantime an uproar had already been commenced by some of his followers, and the President who tried to read his address could not be heard even by those who were seated next to him. Mr. Tilak with his back to the President, kept shouting that he insisted on moving his amendment and he would not allow the proceedings to go on. The President repeatedly appealed to him to be satisfied with his protest and to resume his seat. Mr. Tilak kept on shouting frantically, exclaiming that he would not go back to his seat unless he was "bodily removed." This persisted defiance to the authority of the chair provoked a hostile demonstration against Mr. Tilak himself and for some time, nothing but loud cries of "Shame, shame" could be heard in the Pandal. It had been noticed, that when Mr. Tilak was making his way to the platform some of his followers were also trying to force themselves through the volunteers to the platform with sticks in their hands.

All attempts on the President's part either to proceed with the reading of his address or to persuade Mr. Tilak to resume his seat having failed, and a general movement among Mr. Tilak's followers to rush the platform with sticks in their hands being noticed, the President, for the last time, called upon Mr. Tilak to withdraw and formally announced to the assembly that he had ruled and he still ruled Mr. Tilak out of order and he called upon him to resume his seat.

Mr. Tilak refused to obey and at this time a shoe hurled from the body of the Hall, struck both Sir Pherozeshah Mehta and Mr. Surendranath Banerjee who were sitting side by side. Chairs were also hurled towards the platform and it was seen that Mr. Tilak's followers who were brandishing their sticks wildly were trying to rush the platform which other delegates were endeavouring to prevent.

It should be stated here that some of the delegates were so exasperated by Mr. Tilak's conduct that they repeatedly asked for permission to eject him bodily from the hall; but this permission was steadily refused. The President, finding that the disorder went on growing and that he had no other course open to him, declared the session of the 23rd Indian National Congress suspended *sine die.* After the lady-delegates present on the platform had been escorted to the tents outside, the other delegates began with difficulty to disperse, but the disorder, having grown wilder, the Police eventually came in and ordered the Hall to be cleared.

An official statement issued on 28 December 1907 by Congress officials

The Convention

The 23rd Indian National Congress having been suspended *sine die* under painful circumstances, the undersigned have resolved with a view to the orderly conduct of future political work in the country to call a Convention of those delegates to the Congress who are agreed:–

(1) That the attainment by India of Self-Government similar to that enjoyed by the self-governing members of the British Empire and participation by her in the rights and responsibilities of the Empire on equal terms with those Members is the goal of our political aspirations.

(2) That the advance towards this goal is to be by strictly constitutional means by bringing about a steady reform of existing system of administration and by promoting *National Unity,* fostering public spirit, and improving the condition of the mass of the people.

(3) And that all meetings held for the promotion of the aims and objects above indicated have to be conducted in an orderly manner with due submission to the authority of those that are entrusted with the power to control their procedure.

The 23rd Indian National Congress, Surat an Account of the Proceedings

A Press Note containing an official narrative of the proceedings of the 23rd Indian National Congress at Surat has been published over the signatures of some of the Congress officials. As this note contains a number of one-sided and misleading statements it is thought desirable to publish the following account of the proceedings:–

Preliminary

Last year when the Congress was held at Calcutta, under the presidency of Mr. Dadabhai Naoroji, the Congress, consisting of Moderates and Nationalists, *unanimously* resolved to have for its goal Swaraj or Self-Government on the lines of self-governing Colonies, and passed certain resolutions on Swadeshi, Boycott and National Education. The Bombay Moderates, headed by Sir P.M. Mehta, did not at the time, raise any dissentient voice, but they seem to have felt that their position was somewhat compromised by these resolutions; and they had, since then, been looking forward to an opportunity when they might return to their old position regarding ideals and methods of political progress in India. In the Bombay Provincial Conference held at Surat in April last, Sir P.M. Mehta succeeded by his personal influence in excluding the propositions of Boycott and National Education from the programme of the Conference. And when it was decided to change the venue of the Congress from Nagpure to Surat, it afforded the Bombay Moderate leaders the desired-for opportunity to carry out their intentions in this respect. The Reception Committee at Surat was presumably composed largely of Sir Pherozeshah's followers, and it was cleverly arranged by the Hon. Mr. Gokhale to get the Committee nominate Dr. R.B. Ghosh, to the office of the President, brushing aside the proposal for the nomination of Lala Lajpatrai, then happily released, on the ground that "We cannot afford to flout the Government at this stage, the authorities would throttle our movement in no time." This was naturally regarded as an insult to the public feeling in the country, and Dr. Ghosh must have received at least a hundred telegrams from different parts of India requesting him to generously retire in Lala Lajpatrai's favour. But Dr. Ghosh unfortunately decided to ignore this strong expression of public opinion. Lala Lajpatrai, on the other hand, publicly declined the honour. But this did not satisfy the people who wished to disown the principles of selecting a Congress President on the above ground, believing, as they did, that the most effective protest against the repressive policy of Government would be to elect Lala Lajpatrai to the chair.

The Hon. Mr. Gokhale was entrusted by the Reception Committee, at its meeting held on 24th November 1907 for nominating the President, with the work of drafting the resolutions to be placed before the Congress. But neither Mr. Gokhale nor the Reception Committee supplied a copy of the draft resolutions to any delegate till 2.30 p.m. on Thursday the 26th December, that is to say, till the actual commencement of the Congress Session. The public were taken into confidence only thus far that a list of the headings of the subjects likely to be taken up for discussion by the Surat Congress was officially published a week or ten days before the date of the Congress Session. This list did not include the subjects of Self-Government, Boycott and National Education, on all of which *distinct* and *separate* resolutions were passed at Calcutta last year. This omission naturally strengthened the suspicion that the Bombay Moderates really intended to go back from the position taken up by the Calcutta Congress in these matters. The press strongly commented upon this omission, and Mr. Tilak, who reached Surat on the morning of the 23rd December, denounced such retrogression as suicidal in the interests of the country, more especially at the present juncture, at a large mass-meeting held that evening, and appealed to the Surat public to help the Nationalists in their endeavours to maintain at least the *status quo* in these matters. The next day, a Conference of about five hundred Nationalist Delegates was held at Surat under the chairmanship of Srijut Arabindo Ghose where it was decided that the Nationalists should prevent the attempted retrogression of the Congress by all constitutional means, even by opposing the election of the President if necessary; and a letter was written to the Congress Secretaries requesting them to make arrangements for dividing the house, if need be, on every contested proposition, including that of the election of the President.

In the meanwhile a press note signed by Mr. Gandhi, as Hon. Secretary, was issued to the effect that the statement, that certain resolutions adopted last year at Calcutta were omitted from the Congress programme prepared by the Surat Reception Committee, was wholly unfounded; but the draft resolutions themselves were still withheld from the public, though some of the members of the Reception Committee had already asked for them some days before. On the morning of 25th December, Mr. Tilak happened to get a copy of the draft of the proposed constitution of the Congress prepared by the Hon. Mr. Gokhale. In this draft the object of the Congress was thus stated; "The Indian National Congress has for its ultimate goal the attainment by India of Self-Government similar to that enjoyed by the other members of the British Empire" etc. Mr. Tilak addressed a meeting of the delegates the same morning at the Congress Camp at about 9 a.m. explaining the grounds on which he believed that the Bombay Moderate leaders were bent upon receding from the position taken up by the Calcutta Congress on Swaraj, Boycott and National Education. The proposed constitution, Mr. Tilak pointed out, was a direct attempt to tamper with the ideal of Self-Government on the lines of the *Self-Governing* colonies, as settled at Calcutta and to exclude the Nationalists from the Congress by making the acceptance of this new creed an indispensable condition of Congress membership. Mr. Tilak further stated in plain terms that if they were assured that no sliding back of the Congress would be attempted the opposition to the election of the President would be withdrawn. The delegates at the meeting were also asked to sign a letter of request to Dr. Ghosh, the President-Elect, requesting him to have the old propositions on Swaraj, Swadeshi, Boycott and National Education taken up for reaffirmation this year; and some of the delegates signed it on the spot. Mr. G. Subramania Iyer of Madras, Mr. Kharandikar of Satara and several others were present at this meeting and excepting a few all the rest admitted the reasonableness of Mr. Tilak's proposal.

Lala Lajpatrai, who arrived at Surat on the morning of that day, saw Messrs. Tilak and Khaparde in the afternoon and intimated to them his intention to arrange for a Committee of a few leading delegates from each side to settle the question in dispute. Messrs. Tilak and Khaparde having agreed, he went to Mr. Gokhale to arrange for the Committee if possible; and Messrs. Tilak and Khaparde returned to the Nationalist Conference which was held that evening (25th December). At this Conference a Nationalist Committee consisting of one Nationalist delegate from each province was appointed to carry on the negotiations with the leaders on the other side; and it was decided that if the Nationalist Committee failed to obtain any assurance from responsible Congress officials about the *status quo* being maintained, the Nationalists should begin their opposition from the election of the President. For the retrogression of the Congress was a serious step, not to be decided upon only by a bare accidental majority of any party either in the Subjects Committee or in the whole Congress (as at present constituted), simply because its session happens to be held in a particular place or province in a particular year; and the usual unanimous acceptance of the President would have, under such exceptional circumstances, greatly weakened the point and force of the opposition. No kind of intimation was received from Lala Lajpatrai this night or even the next morning, regarding the proposal of a joint Committee of reconciliation proposed by him, nor was a copy of the draft resolutions supplied to Mr. Tilak, Mr. Khaparde or any other delegate to judge if no sliding back from the old position was really intended.

On the morning of the 26th December, Messrs. Tilak, Khaparde, Arabindo Ghose and others went to Babu Surendranath Bannerji at his residence. They were accompanied by Babu Motilal Ghose of the *Amrit Bazar Patrika* who had arrived the previous night. Mr. Tilak then informed Babu Surendranath that the Nationalist opposition to the election of the President would be withdrawn, if (1) the Nationalist party were assured that the *status quo* would not be disturbed; and (2) if some graceful allusion was made, by any one of the speakers on the resolution about the election of the President, to the desire of the public to have Lala Lajpatrai in the chair. Mr. Bannerji agreed to the latter proposal as he said he was himself to second the resolution; while as regards the first, though he gave an assurance for himself and Bengal, he asked Mr. Tilak to see Mr. Gokhale or Mr. Malvi. A volunteer was accordingly sent in a carriage to invite Mr. Malvi, the Chairman of the Reception Committee, to Mr. Bannerji's residence, but the volunteer brought a reply that Mr. Malvi had no time to come as he was engaged in religious practices. Mr. Tilak then returned to his camp to take his meals as it was already about 11 a.m.; but on returning to the Congress pandal an hour later, he made persistent attempts to get access to Mr. Malvi but could not find him anywhere. A little before 2.30 p.m., a word was brought to Mr. Tilak that Mr. Malvi was in the President's tent, and Mr. Tilak sent a message to him from an adjoining tent, asking for a short interview to which Mr. Malvi replied that he could not see Mr. Tilak as the Presidential procession was being formed. The Nationalist delegates were waiting in the pandal to hear the result of the endeavours of their Committee to obtain an assurance about the maintenance of the *status quo* from some responsible Congress official, and Mr. V.S. Khare of Nasik now informed them of the failure of Mr. Tilak's attempt in the matter.

First Day

It has become necessary to state these facts in order that the position of the two parties, when the Congress commenced its proceedings on Thursday, the 26th December, at 2.30 p.m. may be clearly understood. The President-Elect and other persons had now taken their seats on the platform; and as no assurance from any responsible official of the Congress about the maintenance of the *status quo* was till then obtained, Mr. Tilak sent a slip to Babu Surendranath intimating that he should not make the proposed allusion to the controversy about the Presidential election in his speech. He also wrote to Mr. Malvi to supply him with a copy of the draft resolutions, if ready, and at about 3 p.m. while Mr. Malvi was reading his speech, Mr. Tilak got a copy of the draft resolutions which, he subsequently found, were published the very evening in the *Advocate of India* in Bombay, clearly showing that the reporter of the paper must have been supplied with a copy at least a day earlier. The withholding of a copy from Mr. Tilak till 3 p.m. that day cannot, therefore, be regarded as accidental.

There were about thirteen hundred and odd delegates at this time in the pandal of whom over 600 were Nationalists, and the Moderate majority was thus a bare majority. After the Chairman's address was over, Dewan Bahadur Ambalal Sakarlal proposed Dr. R.B. Ghosh to the chair in a speech which, though evoking occasional cries of dissent, was heard to the end. The declaration by Dewan Bahadur as well as by Mr. Malvi that the proposing and seconding of the resolution to elect the President was only a *formal* business, led many delegates to believe that it was not improbable that the usual procedure of taking votes on the proposition might be dispensed with; and when Babu Surendranath Bannerji, whose rising on the platform seems to have reminded some of the delegates of the Midnapur incident, commenced his speech, there was persistent shouting and he was asked to sit down. He made another attempt to speak but was not heard, and the session had, therefore, to be suspended for the day. The official press note suggests that this hostile demonstration was pre-arranged. But the suggestion is unfounded. For though the Nationalists did intend to oppose the election, they had at their Conference, held the previous day, expressly decided to do so only by solidly and silently voting against it in a constitutional manner.

In the evening the Nationalists again held their Conference and authorised their Committee, appointed on the previous day, to further carry on the negotiations for having the *status quo* maintained if possible, failing which it was decided to oppose the election of Dr. Ghosh by moving such amendment as the Committee might decide or by simply voting against his election. The Nationalists were further requested, and unanimously agreed, not only to abstain from joining in any such demonstration as led to the suspension of that day's proceedings, but to scrupulously avoid any, even the least, interruption of the speakers on the opposite side, so that both parties might get a patient hearing. At night (about 8 p.m.) Mr. Chunilal Saraya, Manager of the Indian Specie Bank and Vice-Chairman of the Surat Reception Committee, accompanied by two other gentlemen, went, in his unofficial capacity and on his own account, to Mr. Tilak and proposed that he intended to arrange for a meeting that night between Mr. Tilak and Mr. Gokhale at the residence of a leading congressman to settle the differences between the two parties. Mr. Tilak agreed and requested Mr. Chunilal, if an interview could be arranged, to fix the time in consultation with Mr. Gokhale, adding that he, Mr. Tilak, would be glad to be present at the place of the interview at *any* hour of the night. Thereon Mr. Chunilal left Mr. Tilak, but unhappily no word was received by the latter that night.

Second Day

On the morning of Friday the 27th (11 a.m.) Mr. Chunilal Saraya again saw Mr. Tilak and requested him to go in company with Mr. Khaparde to Prof. Gajjar's bungalow near the Congress pandal, where, by appointment, they were to meet Dr. Rutherford, who was trying for a reconciliation. Messrs. Tilak and Khaparde went to Prof. Gajjar's but Dr. Rutherford could not come then owing to his other engagements. Prof. Gajjar then asked Mr. Tilak what the latter intended to do; and Mr. Tilak stated that if no settlement was arrived at privately owing to every leading congressman being unwilling to take any responsibility in the matter upon himself, he (Mr. Tilak) would be obliged to bring an amendment to the proposition of electing the President after it had been seconded. The amendment would be to the effect that the business of election should be adjourned, and a committee, consisting of one leading Moderate and one leading Nationalist from each Congress Province, with Dr. Rutherford's name added, be appointed to consider and settle the differences between the two parties, both of which should accept the Committee's decision as final and then proceed to the *unanimous* election of the President. Mr. Tilak even supplied to Prof. Gajjar the names of the delegates, who, in his opinion, should form the Committee, but left a free hand to the Moderates to change the names of their representatives if they liked to do so. Prof. Gajjar and Mr. Chunilal undertook to convey the proposal to Sir P.M. Mehta or Dr. Rutherford in the Congress Camp and asked Messrs. Tilak and Khaparde to go to the pandal and there await reply. After half an hour Prof. Gajjar and Mr. Saraya returned and told Messrs. Tilak and Khaparde that nothing could be done in the matter, Mr. Saraya adding that if both parties proceeded constitutionally there would be no hitch.

This note, it is admitted, was put by a volunteer into the hands of Mr. Malvi, the Chairman, as he was entering the pandal with the President-Elect in procession.

The proceedings of the day commenced at 1 p.m., when Babu Surendranath Bannerji was called upon to resume his speech, seconding the election of the President. Mr. Tilak was expecting a reply to his note but not having received one up to this time asked Mr. N.C. Kelkar to send a reminder. Mr. Kelkar thereupon sent a chit to the Chairman to the effect that "Mr. Tilak requests a reply to his note." But no reply was received even after this reminder, and Mr. Tilak, who, though he was allotted a seat on the platform, was sitting in the front row of the delegate's seats near the platform-steps, rose to go up the platform *immediately* after Babu Surendranath, who was calmly heard by all, had finished his speech. But he was held back by a volunteer in the way. Mr. Tilak, however, asserted his right to go up and pushing aside the volunteer succeeded in getting to the platform just when Dr. Ghosh was moving to take the President's chair. The Official Note says that by the time Mr. Tilak came upon the platform and stood in front of the President, the motion of the election of Dr. Ghosh had been passed by an overwhelming majority; and Dr. Ghosh, being installed in the Presidential chair by loud and *prolonged* applause had risen to begin his address. All this, if it did take place, as alleged, could only have been done in a deliberately hurried manner with a set purpose to trick Mr. Tilak out of his right to address the delegates and move an amendment as previously notified. According to the usual procedure Mr. Malvi was bound to announce Mr. Tilak, or if he considered the amendment out of order, declare it so publicly, and to ask for a show of hands in favour of or against the motion. But nothing of the kind was done; nor was the interval of a few seconds sufficient for a prolonged applause as alleged. As Mr. Tilak stood up on the platform he was greeted with shouts of disapproval from the members of the Reception Committee on the platform, and the cry was taken up by other Moderates. Mr. Tilak repeatedly insisted upon his right of addressing the delegates, and told Dr. Ghosh, when he attempted to interfere, that he was not properly elected. Mr. Malvi said that he had ruled Mr. Tilak's amendment out of order, to which Mr. Tilak replied that the ruling, if any, was wrong and Mr. Tilak had a right to appeal to the delegates on the same. By this time there was a general uproar in the pandal, the Moderates shouting at Mr. Tilak and asking him to sit down and the Nationalists demanding that he should be heard. At this stage

Dr. Ghosh and Mr. Malvi said that Mr. Tilak should be removed from the platform; and a young gentleman, holding the important office of a Secretary to the Reception Committee, touched Mr. Tilak's person with a view to carry out the Chairman's order. Mr. Tilak pushed the gentleman aside and again asserted his right of being heard, declaring that he would not leave the platform unless bodily removed. Mr. Gokhale seems to have here asked the above-mentioned gentleman not to touch Mr. Tilak's person. But there were others who were seen threatening an assault on his person, though he was calmly standing on the platform facing the delegates with his arms folded over his chest.

It was during this confusion that a shoe hurled on to the platform hit Sir P.M. Mehta on the side of the face after touching Babu Surendranath Bannerji, both of whom were sitting within a yard of Mr. Tilak on the other side of the table. Chairs were now seen being lifted to be thrown at Mr. Tilak by persons on and below the platform, and some of the Nationalists, therefore, rushed on to the platform to his rescue. Dr. Ghosh in the meanwhile twice attempted to read his address, but was stopped by cries of "No, no," from all sides in the pandal, and the confusion became still worse. It must be stated that the Surat Reception Committee, composed of Moderates, had made arrangements the previous night to dismiss the Nationalist Volunteers and to hire *bohras* or Mahomedan goondas for the day.

These with lathis were stationed at various places in the pandal and their presence was detected and protested against by the Nationalist Delegates before the commencement of the Congress proceedings of the day. But though one or two were removed from the pandal, the rest who remained therein, now took part in the scuffle on behalf of their masters. It was found impossible to arrest the progress of disorder and proceedings were then suspended *sine die;* and the Congress officials retired in confusion to a tent behind the pandal. The police, who seem to have been long ready under a requisition, now entered into and eventually cleared the pandal; while the Nationalist delegates who had gone to the platform safely escorted Mr. Tilak to an adjoining tent. It remains to be mentioned that copies of an inflammatory leaflet in Gujarathi asking the Gujarathi people to rise against Mr. Tilak were largely distributed in the pandal before the commencement of the day's proceedings.

It would be seen from the above account that the statement in the official note to the effect that Dr. Ghosh was elected President amid loud and prolonged applause before Mr. Tilak appeared on the platform, and that Mr. Tilak wanted to move an adjournment of the whole Congress are entirely misleading and unfounded. What he demanded, by way of amendment, was an adjournment of the business of the election of the President in order to have the differences settled by a joint Conciliatory Committee of leading delegates from both sides. Whether this was in order or otherwise, Mr. Tilak had certainly a right to appeal to the delegates and it was this consciousness that led Mr. Malvi and his advisers to hastily wind up the election business without sending a reply to Mr. Tilak or calling upon him to address the delegates. It was a trick by which they intended to deprive Mr. Tilak of the right of moving an amendment and addressing the delegates thereon.

As for the beginning of the actual rowdyism on the day some of the members of the Reception Committee itself were responsible. The silent hearing given by the Nationalist to Mr. Surendranath, on the one hand, and the circulation of the inflammatory leaflet and the hiring of the goondas on the other, further prove that if there was any pre-arrangement anywhere for the purpose of creating a row in the pandal, it was on the part of the Moderates themselves. But for their rowdyism there was every likelihood of Mr. Tilak's amendment being carried by a large majority and the election of President afterwards taking place smoothly and unanimously. But neither Dr. Ghosh nor any other Congress officials seemed willing to tactfully manage the business as Mr. Dadabhai Naoroji did last year. Dr. Ghosh's speech though undelivered in the Congress pandal had been by this time published in the Calcutta papers, and telegrams from Calcutta received in the evening showed that he had made an offensive attack on the Nationalist Party therein. This added to the sensation in the Nationalist camp that evening, but the situation was not such as to preclude all hope of reconciliation. Srijut Motilal Ghose of the *Patrika,* Mr. A.C. Moitra of Rajshahi, Mr. B.C. Chatterji of Calcutta and Lala Harkishen Lal from Lahore, accordingly tried their best to bring about a compromise, and, if possible, to have the Congress session revived the next day. They went to Mr. Tilak on the night of 27th and the morning of 28th to ascertain the views of his party, and to each of them Mr. Tilak gave the following assurance in writing:–

Surat, 28th December, 1907

"Dear Sir, — With reference to our conversation, and principally in the best interests of the Congress, I and my party are prepared to waive our opposition to the election of Dr. Rash Behari Ghosh as President of 23rd Indian National Congress, and are prepared to act in the spirit of forget and forgive, provided, *firstly,* the last year's resolutions on Swaraj, Swadeshi, Boycott and National Education are adhered to and each expressly reaffirmed; and *secondly,* such passages, if any, in Dr. Ghosh's speech as may be offensive to the Nationalist Party are omitted."

Your etc., B.G. Tilak.

This letter was taken by the gentlemen to whom it was addressed to the Moderate leaders but no compromise was arrived at as the Moderates were all along bent upon the retrogression of the Congress at any cost. A Convention of the Moderates was, therefore, held in the pandal the next day where Nationalists were not allowed to go even when some of them were ready and offered to sign the declaration required. On the other hand, those who did not wish to go back from the position taken up at the Calcutta Congress and honestly desired to work further on the same lines met in a separate place the same evening to consider what steps might be taken to continue the work of the Congress in future.

At the Calcutta Congress, under the presidentship of Mr. Dadabhai Naoroji, it was resolved that the goal of Congress should be Swaraj on the lines of the Self-Governing British Colonies, and this goal was accepted by all, Moderates and Nationalists, without a single dissentient voice. The resolution on Self-Government passed there is as follows:–

"*Self-Government:*–This Congress is of the opinion that the system of Government obtaining in the Self-Governing British Colonies should be extended to India and that as steps leading to it, urges that the following reforms should be immediately carried out." (Here followed certain administrative reforms such as simultaneous examinations in England and India, reform of Executive and Legislative Council, and of Local and Municipal Boards.) The Congress Reception Committee at Surat did not publish the draft Resolution till the commencement of the Congress Sessions; but a draft Constitution of the Congress, prepared by the Hon'ble Mr. Gokhale, was published a day or two earlier. In this draft the goal of the Congress was defined as follows:–

"The Indian National Congress has for its ultimate goal the attainment by India of Self-Government similar to that enjoyed by other members of the British Empire and a participation by her in the privileges and responsibilities of the Empire on equal terms with the other members; and it seeks to advance towards this goal by strictly constitutional means, by bringing about a steady reform of the existing system of administration, and by promoting national unity, fostering public spirit and improving the condition of the mass of the people."

"Those who accept the foregoing creed of the Congress, shall be members of the Provincial Committee."

"All who accept the foregoing creed of the Congress ... shall be entitled to become members of a District Congress Committee."

"From the year 1908, delegates to the Congress shall be elected by Provincial and District Congress Committee only."

Remarks: It will at once be seen that the new Constitution intended to convert the Congress from a national into a sectional movement. The goal of Swaraj on the lines of self-government Colonies, as settled last year, was to be given up; and in its stead Self-Government similar to that enjoyed by other members (not necessarily self-governing) of the British Empire, was to be set up as the *ultimate* goal, evidently meaning, that it was to be considered as out of the pale of practical politics. The same view is expressed by Sir Pherozeshah Mehta in his interview with the correspondent of the *Times of India,* published in the issue of the *Times* dated 30th December 1907. The Hon. Mr. Gokhale must have taken his cue from the same source. The *reform* of the existing system of administration, and not its gradual replacement by a popular system, was to be the immediate object of the Congress according to this constitution; and further no one, who did not accept this new creed, was to be a member of Provincial or District Committees, or possibly even a delegate to the Congress after 1908. This was the chief feature of retrogression, which Sir P.M. Mehta and his party wanted to carry out this year at a safe place like Surat. It is true that the old resolution on Self-Government was subsequently included in the draft Resolutions, published only after the commencement of the Congress Session. But the draft Constitution was never withdrawn.

Bibliography

Adikaram, E. W.: *Early History of Buddhism in Ceylon,* D. S. Puswella, Migoda, 1946.

Agrawala, V. S.: *Shiva Mahadeva: The Great God,* Veda Academy, Varanasi, 1966.

Ahmad, Imtiaz: *State and Foreign Policy: India's Role in South Asia,* Vikas, New Delhi, 1993.

Ahmad, Jamil-ud-din: *Some Recent Speeches and Writings of Mr. Jinnah,* Lahore, Ashraf, 1952.

Aiyar, R. Krishnaswami: *Outlines of Vedaanta,* Chetana, Bombay, 1978.

Archer, W. G.: *The Kama Sutra,* Unwin Hyman, London, 1990.

Ashton, S.R. : *British Policy Towards the Indian States, 1905-1939,* London, Curzon, 1982.

Aurobindo, Sri: *Vyasa and Valmiki,* Acharya Press, Pondicherry, 1956.

Avalon, Arthur and Ellen: *Hymns to the Goddess,* Ganesh and Co., Madras, 1964.

Aziz, Ashraf: *Light of the Universe: Essays on Hindustani Film Music,* Three Essays Collective, New Delhi, 2003.

Bagchi, P. C.: *Studies in Dharmashastra,* University of Calcutta Press, Calcutta, 1939.

Bahadur, K.P.: *The Wisdom of Vedaanta,* Sterling Publishers Private Limited, New Delhi, 1996.

Banerjea, J. N.: *Pauranic and Vedanta Religion,* University of Calcutta, Calcutta, 1996.

Bankimchandra, C.: *Essentials of Dharma,* Sanskrit Book Depot, Calcutta 1979.

Basu, Manoranjan: *Dharmashastra: A General Study,* Shrimati Mira Basu, Calcutta, 1976.

Beaumont, Roger : *Sword of the Raj: The British Army in India, 1747-1947*, Indianapolis, Bobbs-Merrill, 1977.

Benjamin, Joseph : *Scheduled Castes in Indian Politics and Society*, New Delhi, Ess Ess Publications, 1989.

Bhattacharyya, B.: *Nispannayogavali of Mahapandita Abhyakara Gupta*, Oriental Institute, Baroda, 1949.

Borchert, Bruno: *Mysticism: Its History and Challenge*, Samuel Wiser, York Beach, 1994.

Bose, D. N.: *Dharmashastra: Their Philosophy and Occult Secrets*, Kali Press, Calcutta, 1965.

Bowle, John: *The Imperial Achievement: The Rise and Transformation of the British Empire*, Little, Brown, 1974.

Brockington, J. L.: *Righteous Rama: The Evolution of an Epic*, Oxford, London, 1984.

Bromley, D.: *Krishna Consciousness in the West*, Bucknell University Press, Lewisburg, 1989.

Brooks, E.: *The Original Analects: Sayings of Confucius and His Successors*. Columbia University Press, New York, 1988.

Bruhn, Klaus: *The Jina-Images of Deogarh*, MacMillan, Leiden, 1969.

Burke, Mary Louise: *Swami Vivekananda in America: New Discoveries*, Advaita Ashrama, Calcutta, 1966.

Chaudhary, M.: *Partition and the Curse of Rehabilitation*, Calcutta, Bengal Rehabilitation Organization, 1964.

Chaudhuri, Nirad: *Thy Hand, Great Anarch! India: 1921-1952*, London, Chatto & Windus, 1987.

Coomeraswamy, Ananda K.: *Buddha and the Gospel of Buddhism*, MacMillan, London, 1928.

Crawford, Cromwell S.: *Ram Mohan Roy: His Era and Ethics*, Acharya Press, New Delhi, 1984.

Dalton, Dennis : *Gandhi's Power : Nonviolence in Action*, New Delhi, OUP, 2001.

Danielou, Alain: *The Complete Kama Sutra*, Park Street Press, Rochester, 2000.

Dasgupta, Shahana: *Rani Lakshmibai: The Indian Heroine*, Rupa & Company, Calcutta, 2002.

Datta, V.N.: *Sati: Widow Burning in India*, Manohar, New Delhi, 1990.

David, M. D.: *John Wilson and his Institutions*, Mumbai, 1957.

De Bary: *Self and Society in Ming Thought*, Columbia University Press, New York, 1970.

De, Sushil Kumar: *Ancient Indian Erotics and Erotic Literature*, Firma K. L. Mukhopadhyay, Calcutta, 1959.

Deak, Istvan: *The Lawful Revolution: Louis Kossuth and the Hungarians 1848-1849*, Columbia University Press, 1979.

Dhar, Niranjan: *Vedanta and Bengal Renaissance*, Minerva Associates, Calcutta, 1977.

Dikshit, D.P. *Political History of the Chalukyas of Badami*. New Delhi: Abhinav, 1980.

Donat, K.: *Meditate the Tantric Yoga Way*, George Allen and Unwin, London, 1973.

Doniger, W.: *The Rig Veda: An Anthology*, Penguin, New York, 1981.

Duboi, Abbe: *Hindu Manners, Customs and Ceremonies*, Fifth Indian Impression, CUP, 1985.

Dwivedi, M.: *The Principal Upanishads*, Adyar Library, Madras, 1931.

Eaton, Richard M.: *Sufis of Bijapur, 1300-1700: Social Roles of Sufis in Medieval India*, Princeton University Press, Princeton, 1978.

Edwardes, Michael: *Battles of the Indian Mutiny*, London; B. T. Batsford Ltd., 1963.

Erickson, Erik H.: *Gandhi's Truth: On the Origins of Militant Nonviolence*, Norton, New York, 1970.

Farquhar, J.N.: *Modern Religious Movements in India*, Munshiram, New Delhi, 1967.

Fay, Peter Ward: *The Opium War, 1840-42*, University of North Carolina Press, 1975.

Fisher, Michael H.: *The Politics of British Annexation of India - 1757-1857*, Oxford, 1996.

Frauwallner, E..: *History of Indian Philosophy*, Motilal, Delhi, 1973.

Gambhirananda, S.: *Brahma Sutra Shamkar Bhasya*, Adavita Ashrama, Calcutta, 1977.

Gambhirananda, Swami: *Brahma Sutra Shamkar Bhasya*, Adavita Ashrama, Calcutta, 1977.

Gandhi, M. K.: *The Story of My Experiment With Trust*, Washington, Public Affairs Press, 1948.

Garbe, R.: *The Philosophy of Ancient India,* Chicago University Press, Chicago, 1899.

Goradia, Nayana: *Lord Curzon: The Last of the British Moghuls,* New Delhi, Oxford University Press, 1993.

Goudriaan, T.: *Ritual and Speculation in Early Tantrism,* State University of New York Press, New York, 1992.

Gough, A.E.: *The Philosophy of the Upanisads and Ancient Indian Metaphysics,* MacMillan, London, 1882.

Grant, G. P.: *Philosophy in the Mass Age,* Copp Clark, Toronto, 1959.

Grisenold, H.D.: *Insights into Modern Hinduism,* Oxford, New York, 1934.

Growse, F. S.: *The Ramayana of Tulasidasa,* Motilal Banarsidass, Delhi, 1995.

Gurumurthy, S. : *Hindu Heritage, Assimilative, Not Divisive,* Vigil, Madras 1993.

Haich, E.: *Sexual Energy and Yoga,* Aurora Press, New York, 1982.

Hasan, Murhirul: *Legacy of a Divided Nation: India's Muslims Since Independence,* New Delhi, Oxford, 1997.

Hasan, Mushirul: *India's Partition: Process, Strategy and Mobilization,* New Delhi, Oxford UP, 1993.

Heifetz, Hank: *The Origin of the Young God: Kalidasa's Kumara-sambhava,* University of California Press, Berkeley, 1985.

Heimann, Betty: *Facets of Indian Thought,* Geroge Allen & Unwin, London, 1964.

Heinsath, Charles: *Indian Nationalism and Hindu Social Reform,* Princeton University Press, Princeton, 1964.

Heschel, J.: *God in Search of Man: A Philosophy of Judaism,* Noonday Press, New York, 1997.

Hirschman, Edwin: *White Mutiny: The Ilbert Bill Crisis in India and the Genesis of the Indian National Congress,* New Delhi, Heritage, 1980.

Hixon, L.: *Mother of the Universe: Visions of the Goddess, Tantric Hymns of Enlightenment,* Quest Books, Wheaton, 1994.

Hopkins, J.: *Kalachakra Tantra Rite of Initiation,* Wisdom Publications, Boston, 1982.

Hopkirk, Peter: *The Great Game: The Struggle for Empire in Central Asia,* Kodansha, 1992.

Hume, R.E.: *The Thirteen Principle Upanishads*, Oxford University Press, London, 1971.

Hutchins, Francis: *Spontaneous Revolution: The Quit India Movement*, New Delhi, Manohar, 1971.

Irene, S.: *Vedic Heritage Teaching Program*. Arsha Vidya Gurukulam, Coimbatore, 1994.

Iyar, K.: *Vedanta: The Science of Reality*, Ganesh and Co., Mardas, 1930.

Iyengar, B.K.S.: *Light on the Yoga Sutras of Patanjali*, Aquarian Press, London 1993.

Jacob, K.: *Religion and Ethics in Advaita*, C.M.S. Press, Kottayam, 1982.

Jafar, Malik Muhammad: *Jinnah as a Parliamentarian*, Lahore, Afzar Publications, 1977.

Jain, Kailash Chand, *Lord Mahavira and His Times*, Saraswati Press, Delhi, 1974.

James, Lawrence: *The Rise and Fall of the British Empire*, St. Martin's, 1997.

James, Robert Rhodes: *The British Revolution, 1880-1939*, New York, Knopf, 1976.

Jean, M.: *Tantrik Yoga*, The Aquarian Press, Wellingborough, 1970.

John, B.: *Mantras: Sacred Words of Power*, George Allen and Unwin, London, 1977.

John, Elsner: *Pilgrimage: Past and Present in the World Religions*, Harvard University Press, Cambridge, 1995.

John, K.: *The Origin and Development of the State Cult of Confucius*, Paragon Book, New York, 1966.

Karmarkar, D.: *Sankara's Advaita*, Karnatak University, Dharwar, 1976.

Kaushik, Asha : *Globalization, Democracy and Culture : Situating Gandhian Alternatives*, Jaipur, Pointer, 2002.

Kaviraj, G.: *Aspects of Indian Thought*, University of Burdwan, Calcutta, 1966.

Kavlekar, K.K. : *Non-Brahmin Movement in Southern India, 1873-1949*, Kolhapur, Shivaji University, 19790

Keith, A.B. : *Rigveda Brahmanas*, Harvard University Press, Cambridge, 1920.

Keith, Arthur Berriedale: *The Religion and Philosophy of the Veda and Upanishads*, MacMillan, Delhi, 1925.

Kishwar, Madhu : *Religion at the Service of Nationalism, and Other Essays*, OUP, Delhi, 1998.

Klaus, K.: *A Survey of Hinduism*, State University of New York Press, Albany, 1989.

Knipe, M.: *Hinduism: Experiments in the Sacred*, Harper, San Francisco, 1991.

Knott, K.: *Hinduism, A Very Short Introduction*, Oxford University Press, New York, 1998.

Kosambi, D. D. : *The Culture and Civilisation of Ancient India in Historical Outline*, London, Routledge and Kegan Paul, 1956.

Kottackal, Jacob: *Religion and Ethics in Advaita*, C.M.S. Press, Kottayam, 1982.

Kuiper, F.B.J. : *Aryans in the Rigveda*, Rodopi, Amsterdam, 1991.

Kuppuswamy, Sastri S.: *Compromises in the History of Advaitic Thought*, Kalyani Press, Madras, 1940.

Louis, Fischer: *Essential Gandhi: An Anthology of His Writings*, Vintage, New York, 1983.

Low, D. A. and Brasted, Howard: *Freedom, Trauma, Continuities: Northern India and Independence*, New Delhi, Sage Publications, 1998.

Maheshwari, Shriram: *Rural Development in India: A Public Policy Approach*, New Delhi, Sage, 1995.

Makhan, L.: *The Ramayana of Valmiki*, Munshiram Manoharlal, New Delhi, 1978.

Mathew, Arnold: *Culture and Anarchy*, The University Press, Cambridge, 1935.

Mayer, A. : *Caste in an Indian Village: Change and Continuity 1954-1992*, Delhi, OUP, 1996.

Mazumder, Sukhendu : *Politico-Economic Ideas of Mahatma Gandhi: Their Relevance in the Present Day*, New Delhi, Concept Pub., 2004.

Mearns, David J.: *Shiva's Other Children: Religion and Social Identity amongst Overseas Indians*, Sage, Walnut Creek, 1995.

Mearns, J.: *Shiva's Other Children: Religion and Social Identity amongst Overseas Indians*, Sage, Walnut Creek, 1995.

Mehra, Parshotam: *A Dictionary of Modern Indian History, 1707-1947*, New Delhi, Oxford University Press, 1985.

Metcalf, Thomas R.: *The Aftermath of the Revolt: India, 1857-1870*, Princeton, Princeton University, 1964.

Mohan, K.: *The Mahabharata*, Munshiram Manoharlal, Delhi 1997.

Mookerjee, Ajit: *Kali The Feminine Force*, Thames and Hudson, London, 1988.

Mookerji, Satkari: *Modern Polity and Vedanta*, Sanskrit College, Calcutta, 1972.

Moon, Penderel: *The British Conquest and Dominion of India*, London, Duckworth, 1989.

Morris-Jones, W.H.: *The Government and Politics of India*, London, Hutchinson, 1971.

Nanda, B. R. : *Gandhi and His Critics*, Oxford University Press, Delhi, 1993.

Neale, Walter C.: *Economic Change in Rural India: Land Tenure and Reform in the United Provinces, 1800-1955*, New Haven, 1962.

Nevile, P.: *Lahore: A Sentimental Journey*, New Delhi, Penguin, 1993.

Oddie, G.A. : *Hindu and Christian in South-East India*, London, Curzon Press, 1991.

Pathak, Dr S.P.: *Jhansi during the British Rule*, Ramanand Vidya Bhawan, Delhi, 1987.

Preston, Diana: *The Boxer Rebellion*, Berkley Books, 2000.

Raimundo Panikkar: *The Vedic Experience: Mantramanjari*, Longman Todd, London, 1977.

Raja, C. Kunhan : *The Taittiriya Sarvanukramani of Yaska*, Madras, 1931.

Ramamurti, A.: *Advaitic Mysticism of Sankara*, Visvabharati, Santiniketan, 1974.

Ranajit Guha: *A Construction of Humanism in Colonial India*, CASA, Amsterdam, 1993.

Renou, Louis: *The Nature of Dharmashastra*, Walker and Co., New York, 1997.

Robson, Brian: *Sir Hugh Rose and the Central India Campaign*, Sutton Publishing Ltd for the Army Records Society, UK, 2000.

Satyapal Verma: *Role of Reason in Sankara Vedanta*, Parimal Publication, Delhi, 1992.

Savarkar, Vinayak Damodar : *The Indian War of Independence* 1857 Rajdhani Granthagar, Delhi, 1988.

Scheftelowitz, Isidor : *Die Kasmirische Rezension von Katyayanas Sarvanukramani,* Zeitschrift fur Indologie und Iranistik, 1922.

Shukla, D. N.: *Vastu-Shastra,* Motilal Banarsidass, Delhi, 1966.

Singh, Birendra Kumar: *Early Chalukyas of Vatapi, circa A.D. 500 to 757*, Delhi, Eastern Book Linkers, 1991.

Smith, Col. J. T. : *Silver and the India Exchanges,* Effingham Wilson, London, 1876.

Strauss, L.: *Political Philosophy,* The Bobbs Merrill Co., New York, 1975.

Swami Vishnu Tirtha: *Devatma Shakti,* Swami Shivom Tirth, Rishikesh, 1962.

Talageri, Shrikant : *Aryan Invasion Theory and Indian Nationalism,* Voice of India, Delhi, 1993.

Tejomayananda, Swami: *Hindu Culture: An Introduction,* Chinmaya Publications, Piercy, 1993.

Thapar, Romila : *Ashoka and the Decline of the Mauryas,* London, Oxford University Press, 1961.

Thompson, Edward: *The Making of the Indian Princes,* Oxford University Press, London, 1943.

Trautmann, Thomas R.: *Kautilya and the Arthasastra: A Statistical Study,* Leiden, Brill, 1971.

Trimingham, J.: *Sufi Orders in Islam,* Oxford University Press, New York, 1998.

Utpat, V.N.: *Riddles of Buddha and Ambedkar,* Itihas Patrika Prakashan, Thane 1988.

Vable, D.: *The Arya Samaj. Hindu without Hinduism.* Vikas Publ., Delhi, 1983.

Vedalankar, Pandit Nardev : *Basic Teachings of Hinduism,* Veda Niketan, Durban, 1978.

Visvantha, K.: *Essentials of Hinduism,* Narosa Pub. House, New Delhi, 1989.

Wendy Doniger: *Siva: The Erotic Ascetic,* Oxford University Press, Delhi, 1998.

Zaidi, A. Moin: *Evolution of Muslim Political Thought in India,* New Delhi: S. Chand, 1975.

Index

□□□